SCALE MODEL

RAILROADING

SCALE MODEL RAILROADING

by

Leslie Turner White

CASTLE BOOKS, NEW YORK

Grateful acknowledgment for permission to reproduce photographs is made to: Model Railroader Magazine, Linn Westcott, for pictures on pages 55 (bottom), 70, 73, 98, 111; Baltimore Society of Model Engineers, for pictures on pages 137, 140; Joe Dorazio, for pictures on pages 135, 136 (two at top); O. Winston Link, for picture on page 113; Douglas S. Smith, for picture on page 107; Gene Colborn, for picture on page 138; Pittman Electrical Developments, for pictures on page 61; Suydam Company, for pictures on page 142; Norfolk and Western Railway, for pictures on page 136 (two at bottom); William K. Walthers Inc., for chart on page 150.

This edition published by arrangement
with Thomas Nelson Inc.

Library of Congress Catalogue Card Number 64–24625

Printed in the United States of America

In gratitude

for what the hobby has meant to me,

this book is Dedicated to

the officers and the thirteen thousand

members of the National Model Railroad Association.

Foreword

This is meant to be a practical book, and I hope you find it so. It is intended to be read comfortably; to ease you into the hobby in logical progression, instead of hurling precepts at you out of context. Rather, I have adhered to the credo of my profession—that of a novelist—that a book must be interesting as well as informative.

However, it is intended as a guide, not as a code of irrevocable rules. The reason I have used the personal pronoun so extensively is because the subject is so highly individualized that another writer might take an entirely different tack and achieve the same result. My way may not be the best, but it has worked for me, hence I can only base my authority on experience and research.

If you hear or conceive of another way of accomplishing a result—try it; you may make an important contribution to the hobby. The suggestions and ideas herein were the best I could find and served me sufficiently to recommend them, but they are merely signposts, not laws, and all of them will be succeeded by better methods in the not-to-distant future. The joy of this hobby is in experimentation, not in following slavishly a set routine. But until you have gained some experience and are sure of yourself, it is wiser to follow in the accepted path, so that you do not lose your way in a labyrinth of detours.

There is no dearth of literature on model railroading. In fact, if all the information already in print was gathered together, it would take up more wordage and space than a full set of the *Encyclopaedia Britannica*. It is enough to appall the novice and make him wonder how and where to find a starting point. During my years in the hobby, I have waded through most of this plethora of information in search of facts I needed at the moment, and then attempted to catalog it for future reference. For when I'm interested in how to *age* a structure, for example, I don't want to concern myself with advanced cab control. Thus I discovered what I regard as a vacuum in the literature on the hobby; there is no single volume which serves as both a book of instruction *and* an impartial bibliography on other works which explore the multiple facets of model railroading in greater detail.

That premise is what makes this book unique. Of coure, it would be impossible to list all the excellent articles in the hobby magazines, but the books on specialized subjects which I have found helpful or invaluable will be listed at the end of each chapter dealing with that particular phase of the hobby. For example, I shall explain the basic details of electrical control sufficiently to help you get your train rolling, then if the electrical circuits intrigue you, as they did me, you will find listed at the end of that chapter at least two books which I deem indispensable —*How to Wire Your Model Railroad,* by Linn Westcott, and *Electrical Handbook for Model Railroaders,* by Paul Mallery. These two books go into the subject in depth and, as they are almost as large as this book, it is obvious I could not hope to compress their contents into the one chapter I can allocate to electrical control. In getting started, you may not feel such technical books necessary, but when you begin to grow into the hobby and discover the possibilities inherent in advanced control, you'll want the information only a specialized volume can supply.

Writing a general book about model railroading is something like writing a book about women; it is a subject of great diversity, with almost endless facets to explore. The fact that you have this book in hand indicates at least an interest in what some 250,000 Americans believe to be the greatest hobby of them all. Our aim and hope is to further your interest in it.

LTW

Contents

List of Illustrations

CHAPTER 1

What's It All About?

Scale model railroading is called the fastest growing hobby in America. Please note that I emphasize the word "scale," to differentiate it from the toy train set which fascinates children. It is primarily a man's hobby (the average age of all model railroaders is 34 years), although we have many women enthusiasts, some of whom rank with the best of the male craftsmen. It also has many teen-aged adherents who have grown into the hobby via the toy train route, and perhaps best of all, it can be—as it is with my family—a family enterprise. It can be as simple or as complex as you choose to make it. You can tack some ready-made snap-track on a piece of plywood and run your trains in a circle, or you can build yourself a real railroading empire, complete with scenery, signals, and cab control for the simultaneous running of many trains. In its advanced stages, especially if you delve into timetable operation with a clock altered to scale time, it can be as involved as tournament chess. The extent of your endeavors is up to you alone. It is at once the most diversified and individualistic of all hobbies. It requires no special talent to get started, but as you progress you will find yourself developing a whole gamut of skills of which you may not have realized you were capable of mastering—carpentry, electrical, artistic, mechanical, and the like.

These are some of the reasons why the hobby appeals to tired businessmen—why 37 per cent of scale model railroaders are business executives and professional men—doctors, dentists, lawyers, clergymen, *et al.*—men who not only want to relax but to feel the thrill of accomplishing something with their hands. It has a real therapeutic value, and the great Philadelphia Mental Hospital is finding it extremely helpful in their rehabilitation program.

But most important of all, scale model railroading is grand fun. It is creating a little world of your own in miniature. When Joyce Kilmer wrote the immortal line, "only God can make a tree!" he obviously had not seen the trees made by some of the master modelers of the hobby. This is not meant to be irreverent, but a mere statement of fact.

Compared to most hobbies, model railroading is relatively inexpensive; many happy, productive hours can be spent on a scratch-built structure—a bridge, for instance, will cost you less than fifty cents. At this writing, my son has just completed a small backwoods railroad station of balsa wood for a contest—a veritable gem in miniature—at a total investment of about two weeks in time and at a cost of less than twenty-five cents for materials.

All right, you ask, what is this scale business, and how does it differ from toy trains (which in the hobby we refer to as tin-plate)? Broadly speaking, *scale* denotes accuracy of measurement of all detail. Tin-plate, or toy trains, have to sacrifice accuracy of size and detail in favor of sturdiness. For example, the delicate piping on a well-made scale model locomotive wouldn't last ten minutes under the rough handling of a youngster, and the electrical control is, generally speaking, too involved for his comprehension.

In all model railroad literature, you'll find the terms "scale" and "gauge" in frequent use, sometimes interchangeably. Properly speaking, "scale" designates the proportionate size of the model to the prototype, whereas "gauge" indicates the distance between the rails. As a practical matter, the two words are considered synonomous. For example, in HO scale—by far the most popular size—3.5 mm equals one foot. Thus a prototype measurement of, say, ten feet is actually only 1.378 inches in HO scale.

Originally there used to be quite a number of different scales; now all but four are considered obsolete, although some OO gaugers will want to give me an argument on this score. But when you can no longer obtain parts or equipment in a scale it's as dead as the proverbial dodo.

The four surviving scales are O, S, HO, and TT. Each gauge has its staunch adherents.

Be that as it may, the choice of gauge or scale is essential to the beginner, for each scale has certain advantages and disadvantages which must be carefully considered by the individual modeler. The size of your models automatically affects the size of your overall railroad. Thus you may be able to make a circle of TT track on a coffee table, whereas you'd need a small room to make a similar circle in O gauge. It is this everlasting problem of space that has favored the smaller gauges. Let's take a brief look at each gauge separately, discussing their favorable points and their limitations.

For a long time, O gauge, the largest of the four, was by far the most popular. It scales out to ¼″ to the prototypical foot and is, therefore, large enough to put the utmost detail onto the models. Thus it boasted of being "the modelers' gauge," which at the time was true enough—when the hobby started, back in the early 1930s, few if any commercial parts were available and almost everything, even the wheels, had to be handmade. The drawback was, and still is, its space requirements. Figure 1-1 will show you the comparison in size of the four currently popular gauges.

It is obvious, therefore, that if a minimum main-line curve in O gauge requires 60″, you'll get a lot less trackage than in, say, HO gauge with its 24″ minimum, in any given space. Therefore, before you begin any actual layout planning, you must of necessity consider this factor and make your choice after careful deliberation.

There is a point I should mention, and that is that in O gauge, there are actually two gauges, and you'll come across diehards who insist that the proper scale of O gauge is *not* ¼″, but is properly 9⁄32″. It is a rather specious argument insomuch as we have adopted the easy-to-calculate ¼″ scale in this country and most, if not all, O gauge parts are made to this dimension. The mix-up occurred in this way: We imported the O gauge from England, where they used a scale of 7 mm to the foot, and for ease of measurement, we changed the *scale* to the easy-to-figure ¼″ to the foot, but at first we did not alter the *gauge*—the distance between the track—hence many old-timers still adhere to that gauge. So don't be misled by this quibbling; if you want to go into O gauge, do it the popular way so you won't run into difficulty with your equipment.

To summarize, unless you have plenty of space and plenty of money and are more interested in modeling than in operating a complete layout, O gauge is not for you.

S gauge is something of a compromise. It is large enough to allow for all the detail you'll care to put on it, yet takes up less space than its bigger sister gauge. Most of its adherents came in through the tin-plate route, as you can convert Amer-

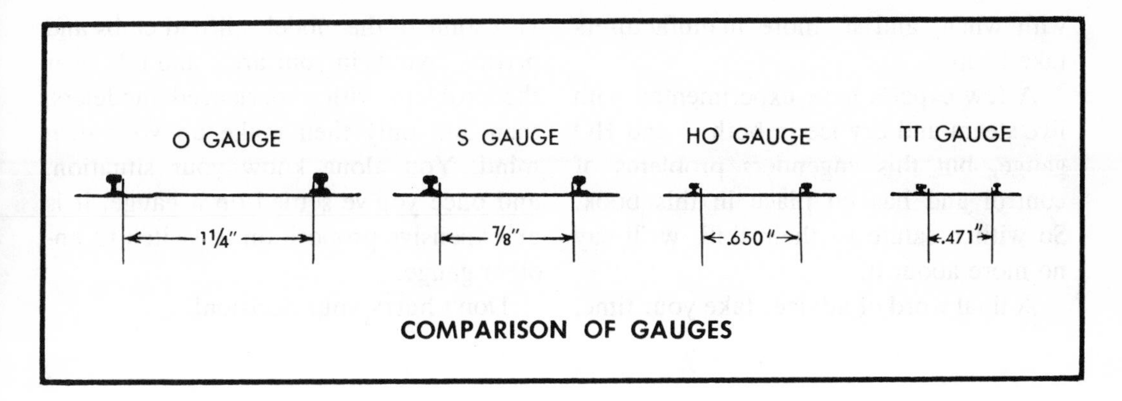

Fig. 1-1 Comparison of Gauges

ican Flyer tin-plate equipment to scale by replacing the original wheels with new ones which have smaller flanges for use on scale track. Unhappily for the S gaugers, there are fewer parts and kits available in this scale.

HO gauge was also an import originally. HO, which means half-O, is 3.5 mm to the foot, or about 1/87 of the prototype. This time the gauge was not tampered with, hence the distance between tracks is still 0.650″. This smaller scale permits far more trackage in a given space, as indicated in the comparative chart 1–1. In a survey of the hobby conducted in 1955 by *Model Railroader Magazine,* it discovered that 85.5 per cent of the model railroad fans preferred HO gauge. The average age of those who use this gauge is 32.4 years, as compared to the other gauges which is 7.5 per cent in O, with an average age of 40.6 years, S gauge showing 3.4 per cent, average age 33.2 years, and TT gauge, 1.7 per cent, average age 31.1 years.

All this gives HO a great advantage, for it means more suppliers are serving this gauge and that more equipment and parts are readily available. Because of its small size, some scoffers term HO the "jewellers' gauge" but a good craftsman can get nearly as much detail on a piece of HO equipment as anyone can put on O gauge, certainly all that is needed. I judged a model contest in New Jersey recently and saw a dining car with, incredibly enough, plates and silverware on the tables. So it *can* be done, if you're skillful enough.

I don't wish to show partiality in this battle of the gauges, but after looking over the situation carefully, I chose HO gauge for my empire. I can heartily recommend it to the beginner. Incidentally, HO gauge takes up about half the space of O gauge and the equipment costs less than half.

If smallness alone was the most desirable factor, TT gauge would seem the logical choice. It is our newest gauge, and while its size permits more trackage for the man troubled with space requirements, the newness is a disadvantage because of the limited source of supply. There are no TT scale lamp bulbs available, for example, which precludes the use of headlights unless, of course, you are craftsman enough to manufacture a system of lighting by reflection. However, its size may well make it a scale to reckon with when, and if, more manufacturers take it up.

A few experts have experimented with live steam and dry ice in both O and HO gauge, but this engenders problems of control and has no place in this book. So with a salute to their skill, we'll say no more about it.

A final word of advice: take your time, visit some of the model railroad clubs and private layouts in your area, and talk over the problem with experienced modelers, then and only then make up your *own* mind. You alone know your situation, and once you've settled on a gauge, it is an expensive proposition to switch to another gauge.

Don't hurry your decision!

CHAPTER 2

Before You Begin

Now I shall introduce you to a form of railroading more often practiced than talked about. It is a lot of fun, and may serve as a sort of aptitude test, as I'll demonstrate later. This particular phase of the hobby is known as "armchair railroading." Its virtues are that it requires no trains or track and no physical energy.

The preparatory steps are to collect a pile of model railroading and real railroading magazines. You can pick up back copies from either the publishers or dealers that specialize in old magazines—and in passing let me repeat Al Kalmbach's famous statement, "a magazine is never old until you've read it!"—and a few books on the Golden Age of Steam. (See suggested list at the end of this chapter.) Also arm yourself with a pad and a pencil for taking notes and making sketches.

Now pick the softest, easiest, and best-lighted chair in the house, ask the family to leave you alone, lay out your favorite pipes, make a highball or a pot of coffee for yourself, and place the books and magazines within easy reach; you don't want any unnecessary exertion. When I perform this ritual, which I do about once a month, I prop myself up in bed, with the literature piled around me like a dike, and settle down to make a night of it.

The idea is not to "read with a purpose," but to stimulate your imagination. Skim through the books and magazines, soaking up the atmosphere of railroading; look at the pictures, read the captions and any short pieces that intrigue you—and encourage your mind to wander. When you begin to hear train whistles (steam whistles, of course) outside your window, close your eyes and just dream.

Which way does your imagination roam? Do you see towering mountain passes, with little slim-gauge (narrow-gauge) kettles boiling up the gorge, hauling their precious cargoes to remote mines and little mountain towns, or do you dream of a busy terminal railroad shuffling a variegated collection of freight cars destined for a thousand different industries in a big city? Perhaps you imagine a long line of Pullmans or coaches ghosting through the velvet darkness rushing its human cargo to distant places? Are these gaudy little open-enders or are they sleek streamliners? What's at the head end—a thundering Pacific of the Golden Age, or a lithe diesel? In short, what sort of railroading comes naturally to your imagination? Do you see mountains or prairies, rivers or flatlands? A lot will depend on your background; my own imagination on these occasions turns to picturesque little peddler freights, ducking nervously into wayside sidings to avoid the roaring Limiteds that are thundering in the distances, as a rabbit hides to avoid the baying hounds. Don't try to guide your imaginings—let your mind run free and, as the old song says, "do what comes naturally."

Now let's analyze this pleasant excursion to nowhere. It won't take an expensive headshrinker to glean a few pertinent facts about your likes and dislikes. Perhaps you'll discover that you prefer steam to diesels, mountains to plains, and open-end coaches to modern streamliners. Put these facts down on paper so you'll remember them when you come to the important point of designing your own dream pike.

This daydreaming act is not absolutely

essential, though it helps, but at least study the magazines and books, especially a good volume on track planning, or layout designs, as they are properly termed. Always keep in mind that this is to be *your* pike, a reflection of what you like and want, and that you have complete and absolute control—unless, of course, the family shares your interest and is willing to share the fun of planning, as mine did. Possibly a brief resume of the way we approached the problem may give you some ideas.

Some forty-five years ago, I fired Moguls and Consolidateds (I'll tell you about the different types of locomotives in a later chapter) on the old Grand Trunk Railroad in Canada. I can't say I enjoyed heaving coal, though I scooped enough of the stuff to heat hell for about five years, but at least I got steam in my blood, and once you get it there, it doesn't wash out. So our first decision was to freeze time (remember, you are all-powerful when it comes to creating a world in miniature) in the 1920s; nothing, no model building, bridge, locomotive, or automobile goes on my pike if the original was built after 1925, preferably earlier. All the family shares my love of mountains and waterfronts, so we chose the tidewater area of Virginia as our imaginary locale. Our claim is that "we serve all Virginia from the mountains to the sea!" This type of thinking is essential to make your empire plausible. Someone called planning a model railroad "imagineering," a term so perfectly apt and descriptive it should go into the dictionary.

Some model rails prefer to reproduce a particular prototype railroad, and duplicate their equipment as closely as possible. That's all right, too, if you're in love with some special road, but we preferred to start from scratch. Having settled on a locale, we explored the traffic possibilities. The mountains of Virginia produce coal and timber; the valleys, cattle and grains. Now, as in a prototype road, we had to figure out what type of rolling stock we would need. That was easy. Plenty of hoppers for shipping coal, and logging cars for timber, cattle cars for cattle, and box cars for grain. Because of our mountainous terrain, we'd need some heavy motive power, and because of our time element, we settled on husky Mikados and an old-time articulated. Due to our steep grades and sharp curves, we decided on making the logging road a separate company which uses narrow-gauge trackage, picturesque little tea kettles, such as a Shay gear-drive locomotive, with an interchange having dual trackage, both standard and narrow gauge. (More about narrow gauge in later chapters.)

That done, we looked into the business of industries to use these products. Grain called for an elevator, timber for a logging pond and saw mill, cattle for processing plants and a cattle sale barn. We "dredged" out a small harbor which, offstage, opens onto the Chesapeake Bay, for shipping coal and other produce in barges and boats. The harbor offered a fine excuse for a boatyard, and a bascule bridge, and a swing bridge. People, even miniature people, require housing, shopping centers, and theaters, so we dreamed up a couple of small communities, complete with railroad stations and other facilities.

Parenthetically, I might say this offered a wonderful educational opportunity to the children, for we took them along on what we called prototypical junkets, photographing and measuring structures, bridges and the like, about the state. By the time we finished our grain elevator, for example, the kids had a thorough knowledge of what an elevator looked like and how and why it operated.

The point I want to make is how one thing leads to another in logical sequence. You can't plausibly place an Empire State Building in the middle of a cornfield. It is necessary to make your railroad equipment conform to the locale, although if a special type of equipment, such as chemical cars or tankers, appeals to you, you can always bring it in as if interchanging from another railroad off-stage. We have no oil wells on our pike, but our little people use oil, so the tank cars are brought in from "outside" and our road delivers them to the customers, as do the prototype roads.

Always bear in mind that the closer you adhere to prototype railroading practices, the more fun you'll get out of your pike. Keep your pike a scale model of the real railroad and try to operate it in the same manner as the prototype railroads do.

There are two other decisions you should make before going much further: the period and the type. In deciding the *period:* If, for instance, you are a Civil War buff, you may want to duplicate railroading as it was in the early 1860s. This can be very fascinating and colorful, with the open-ended coaches in gay colors and the snorting little diamond-stackers at the head end. In HO you can get some beautiful period pieces, many of them ready-to-run, or, at most, needing only a paint job. (More on that later.)

In the latter half of the nineteenth century, the railroads took great strides, both in operation and in equipment. It wouldn't take much researching to discover some appealing period to suit your individual tastes. Or, if you prefer the sleek streamliners with their stainless steel coaches, vista-cars, and panting diesels, you may want to create a modern setting. But remember—modern equipment is much larger than old-time rolling stock, and this in turn effects the overall size of your pike, regardless of what gauge you choose.

A word of caution: Don't be misled by some of the current advertising blurbs that claim their equipment will take 12- and 15-inch radius curves. True, some of the newer locomotives and cars will live up to this claim; they'll make the curve all right, but they'll not *look* right. A full-scale coach making a 15-inch curve hangs away out from the tracks, inviting troubles in coupling and cramping, and resembles a toy, not a train. The National Model Railroad Association recommends (and with good cause) a minimum radius of 24 inches for an HO curve, so keep well above the *minimum* if you hope to keep your cars on the track and enjoy good operation for large equipment. If you can't afford that much space, go into a smaller gauge.

The *type* of railroad is of similar importance. Do you prefer a short-line road with a single-track main line, with passing sidings for your peddler freights to dodge into out of the way of the passenger express? Or do you want a four-track main, with two tracks for eastbound traffic and the other two for westbound? Once again the problem of space raises its ugly head, but that isn't all there is to it. There is also the matter of operation.

I have a close friend who has a huge pike, with a four-track main and a tremendous passenger terminal. His chief interest is in his terminal, and the trackage simply gives him an opportunity to keep his trains on the move and out of the way of the terminal. It is essentially a one-man operation, and that's the way he likes it. He is currently building his dream pike, with a specially built railroad room 72 feet in length and he's using a smaller type of railroad.

As for me, I built, and shall always build, a single-track main because, to my way of thinking, it not only looks longer, but it offers more opportunity for prototypical operation. As Frank Ellison, the dean of model railroaders, so aptly phrased it, "Model railroading is primarily the art of condensing the essentials of real railroading so that they resemble the larger operations." And I well remember, when I was firing way freights on the old Grand Trunk, the thrill of bustling our drag into a siding and waiting for the highballing passenger trains to whoosh by and clear the main.

Another reason I recall it so vividly was a gag an old-timer pulled on me when the train crew was stretched out on the grass of a siding while waiting for the main to clear. I was only a green kid in my late teens at the time, and the men liked to tease me. An old shack (a brakeman) asked me if I knew what a highball signified. I told him that it meant the train was getting under way. Though that was correct enough, the others all laughed. My tormentor then said I was wrong. "A highball," he pronounced with great seriousness, "means, everybody sit down but the fireman!" I soon learned there was more truth than humor in that crack.

While a single-track main offers more chance of a cornfield meet (meaning "a collision") than a two- or four-track main, unless, of course, you have an automatic detection circuit with relays and signaling, it is more exciting and requires more operational skill. It is far more interesting to watch, and gives you a greater illusion of reality. So take your choice.

In summation, make your pike the way *you* want it—just be reasonably consistent. Create a story behind the scenes, give your road a purpose, so that it isn't just a matter of running trains in a circle. That's basically what differentiates tinplate toy trains from scale modeling and makes for reality. You'll get more fun out of your empire and visitors will enjoy it more.

BIBLIOGRAPHY

The Age of Steam, by Lucius Beebe and Charles Clegg. Pub. by Rinehart.
Steamcars to the Comstock, by Lucius Beebe and Charles Clegg. Pub. by Howell-North.
The Story of American Railroads, by Holbrook. Pub. by Crown.
Pioneer Railroads. Pub. by Fawcett Publications.
101 Track Plans, by Linn Westcott. Pub. by Kalmbach.

MAGAZINES:

Trains Magazine
Model Railroader
Model Trains
Railroad Magazine
Railroad Model Craftsman

CHAPTER 3

Getting Started

We'll assume that by this time you have settled on a gauge, a period that you like, and the type of railroad you want to build. Your next step is to secure a "right-of-way" in which to build your empire. This is strictly a personal problem, for you may have difficulty talking your wife or family out of an attic, a basement, or a spare room. Call me when you get this settled!

If you have a choice, consider these factors. Is the space well ventilated and dry at all times of the year? I know a model rail who built his first pike in a basement, but the dampness mildewed his structures and warped his track bases. He tore it all up and moved to his attic only to find it was too hot for occupancy in summer and too cold in winter. In milder climates, some model rails seize upon the garage, leaving the family car outside. Sometimes a spare room is available, properly heated and dry. My pike is in a workshop apart from the house, but in a humid summer I have trouble with the track swelling out of gauge. The only solution there is to install a dehumidifier. Others have solved their problem of space by rigging up ingenious methods of raising their pike to the ceiling on blocks to get it out of the way when not in use; some build a pike on a large piece of plywood and hinge it so that it can be folded against a wall. Others have built a pike on heavy plywood, then attached casters so they can slide the railroad under a bed. If you will peruse the model railroading magazines, you'll run into many clever ideas for circumventing this eternal problem of space.

While you're working on this, it might be a good time to find and make the acquaintance of a reliable hobby dealer. There are some phonies, but most of them are a special breed of man, different from any other type of shopkeeper. Take him into your confidence, tell him your situation, get his advice, *and follow it;* you'll save time, money, and heartbreak. He'll doubtless advise you to start small and not to attempt to build that dream pike until you've gained some practical experience. Take his word for it, and if not—take mine, for I learned the hard way.

On my first trip to the hobby shop, I bought a lot of kits and all the books and magazines I could find on the subject. From these, I picked out a layout design that seemed likely to serve my purpose and went back to the hobby shop to purchase the necessary track. When I showed my proposed plan to the dealer, he tried to talk me out of it. He advised starting off with a small circle to gain experience in tracklaying and assured me it would be time well spent as I could use this circle later for breaking in locomotives by continuous running and for use as a test track.

I gave in with bad grace, grumbling on the drive home, saying I would "slap" down the circle that evening, and start my real empire the following day.

Well, I *slapped* down the track, but when I tried to run a train on it, the locomotive turned over on its maiden trip. I decided there must have been a kink in the track—I was using flexible track in those days for the snap-together track had not yet been invented—so I ripped it up and laid another circle. I also laid another egg!

I wasn't discouraged, but I was intrigued. Plainly, there was more to this stuff than I had anticipated! Next time I was extremely careful, following each step of procedure meticulously. And the train ran without a hitch!

That circle didn't look so small and simple then, believe me! It seemed very complete and very wonderful. And when I started on my big pike, I had a new appreciation of the work involved and built it with the same care.

For your first pike, I would definitely recommend that you get a good book on layout design, and there's not a better one than *101 Track Plans* by Linn Westcott. In it are plans for every imaginable type of space, all tested, all *gapped* (see Chapter 5) and showing where to make your wiring connections. Proper layout design is a highly technical art, and you'll avoid a lot of headaches by using a reliably published track plan in the beginning. In any event, such a book is chock full of ideas when, and if, you are determined to design your own. I still enjoy *101 Track Plans* when I want to take a session of armchair railroading, for it stimulates the imagination. You can get a copy from your hobby shop.

Perhaps it is only fair to say, however, that someday you'll *want* to draw up your own plan, or at least redesign one of the published ones, for when the day comes that you *know* exactly what you want, no one can do it except you. That is one of the many paradoxes of the hobby.

Another splendid book to help you design your own plans is *Model Railroad Track and Layout* by A. C. Kalmbach. Unfortunately it is now out of print, but perhaps you can borrow a copy from a friend or from a library.

This is as good a time as any to suggest that you join the National Model Railroad Association, (NMRA), which offers you fellowship with over thirteen thousand other model railroaders in the United States, Canada, and over thirty-five other countries of the world. The NMRA is broken up into Regions, covering all parts of the country, and most of these Regions put out a periodical monthly or bimonthly, telling you about model contests, fan trips, and local conventions. The monthly NMRA Bulletin and the data and standard sheets of the association are worth more than the small cost of joining, which, at this writing, is three dollars a year, with a small additional charge—a dollar or, in some instances, fifty cents—for your local Region.

You'll be well advised to subscribe to one or more of the hobby magazines, such as *Model Railroader, Model Trains,* and *Railroad Model Craftsman*. These magazines are crammed with excellent articles on how-to-do-it—how to build a layout, put together kits, freelance, scratch-building, and hosts of other ideas. See your hobby dealer; he usually keeps all three in stock.

Very well, if you have taken our counsel up to this point, you know your gauge, your period, the type of railroad you want to build, and, presumably, you have chosen a track plan that suits your purpose. Since you cannot practically run scale trains on the floor, your next step is to build a table of sorts.

Such tables fall into two categories: flattops and grid construction. The first is doubtless the most common type in use, but the second is by far the best, especially for a fairly large pike. The flattops are usually a piece of 4′ x 8′ plywood, preferably ¾″ thick, although a piece 5′ x 9′ would be better, allowing for

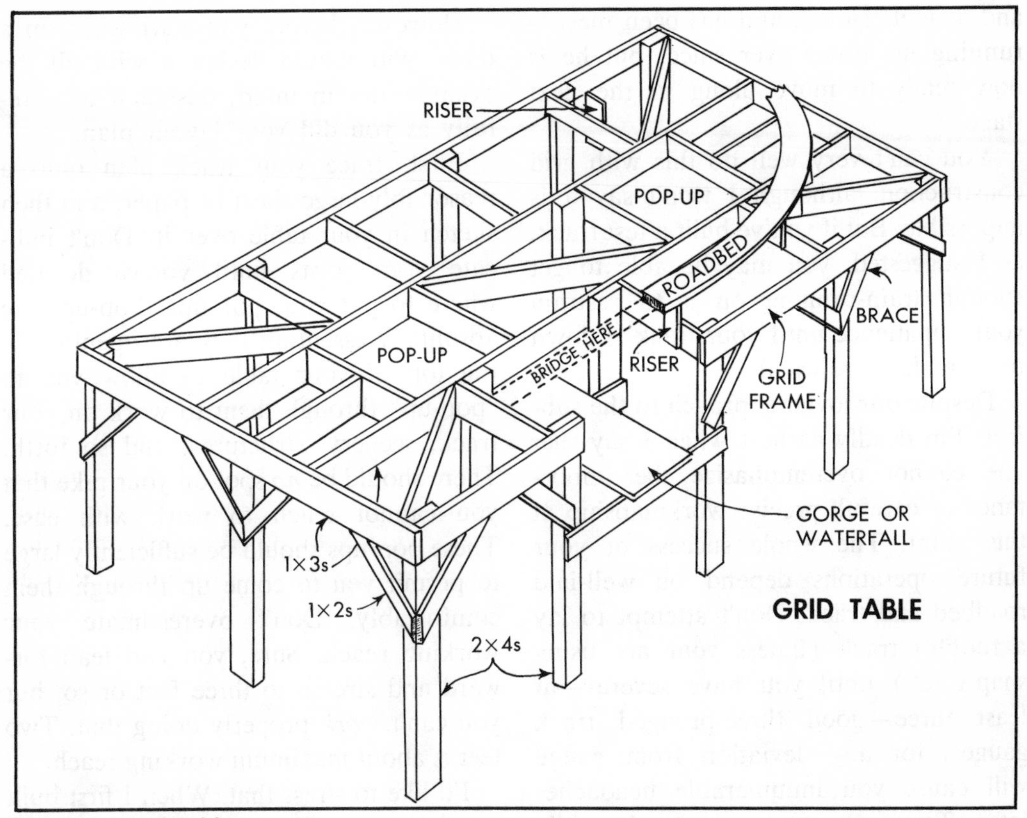

Fig. 3-1 Grid Table

generous 24-inch radius curves, if you are in HO, with room to spare. The grid construction consists of an open-framework table called a grid. (See Fig. 3-1.) It may take a bit longer to construct, but is not more expensive than plywood, and has infinitely more advantages in helping you get a more realistic effect, especially if you like rivers and bridges and multilevel track, not to mention mountains. Nearly all large pikes are of grid construction.

My son, now ten—actually too young to attempt a scale pike of his own—has worked with me for over five years on our large family pike, but recently announced that he wanted to build his own railroad empire. Realizing how many of the steps were beyond his experience, I bought him a copy of Linn Westcott's excellent book, *The HO Railroad That Grows.* This is a step-by-step description of how to build a 4′ x 8′ flattop, with a drop-leaf "yard," in eight easy stages. In Westcott's foreword he says of the book: "Traditionally a model railroad is built by completing all the framework, then track and wiring, and finally, all the scenery. We break with tradition here to do a little of each several times over. After each stage of construction, the railroad is in good working order and looks completed."

This unique approach is ideal for the beginner who is overanxious to get his trains running. Only too well aware of my son's impatient nature, I deemed this plan made-to-order for him. It was a good guess, for he stopped at the completion of stage 1, with a circle of track and a single siding, and has been merrily running his trains ever since, but he is now ready to move along to the next stage.

You can't very well do this with grid construction, although I won't say it is impossible. But if you've built a test track, as I suggested, you may be able to get enough train-running on it to restrain your impatience until your track is down on your large railroad.

Despite our jovial approach to the subject, I'm deadly earnest when I say that one cannot overemphasize the importance of careful, precise workmanship at this point. The whole success of your future operations depend on well-laid roadbed and track. Don't attempt to lay a foot of track (unless your are using snap-track) until you have several—at least three—good three-pronged track gauges, for any deviation from gauge will cause you innumerable headaches later. Test your gauge constantly while laying track, and after each stretch, run a car back and forth along it to see that you have no kinks or bumps.

Figure 3-1 shows the general idea of a grid table. The framework *can* be nailed together, but you would be well advised to use screws for the sake of solidity. I used screw *and* glue at every joint of my table and, after about seven years of hard use it doesn't have a quiver.

If you live in a rented house, or expect to move, you may want to consider a portable table. If your layout plan is not too large, you may be able to carry a small table out *in toto;* if too large, it might be a good idea to make the grid table in sections, bolted or otherwise fastened together, so that later, by cutting through your scenery, you can move your pike in sections.

However, before you start work on a table, you should design it with all the eventualities in mind; design it as carefully as you did your layout plan.

First, trace your track plan onto a reasonably large sheet of paper, and then sketch in your table over it. Don't indicate your joists until you've decided where to put your pop-ups. Pop-ups are absolutely essential; they are openings in the top of your table to allow you to "pop-up" through them to work on your track, scenery, structures, and so forth. There should be *no* spot on your pike that you cannot reach to work with ease. These pop-ups should be sufficiently large to permit you to come up through them comfortably. Don't overestimate your working reach. Sure, you can lean forward and stretch to three feet or so, but you can't *work* properly doing that. Two feet is about maximum working reach.

I'd like to stress that. When I first built my dream empire, I thought if I did the original work properly I'd have no need to reach every part of the pike. That was a sad blunder, and later I had to cut through the joists and scenery in three separate places to allow for more pop-ups —a messy chore that should have been done right in the first place. If you feel that this may spoil the appearance of your pike, be reassured; you can disguise them with scenery if you object to their original appearance, or cover them over. Several of my pop-ups are invisible from the front of the table.

Well, back to the drawing: *After* you have allowed for pop-ups, decide where and if you want a turntable—and who doesn't? This should have a firm base supported by joists. Then if you plan to have a low gorge or river below tabletop level, indicate this on your drawing.

When all such deviations are sketched in, then draw in your joists, to either support such riverbeds or keep clear of the pop-ups. See Fig. 3-1. Try to keep your joists running at right angles to your track for better support.

Your next decision, and a major one, is the height of your table. This holds true for either flat-top or grid construction. There are two factors to reckon with: (1) Trains appear more realistic at nearly eye level, and (2) your wiring, and possibly your switch machines (see later chapters on these points), will have to be *worked* from underneath your table. However, there are practical limits to extreme height; if too high, you won't be able to see anything except what passes right in front of your eyes.

While I was in the planning stage, I visited a pike that had a tabletop height of about 24 inches above the floor. During my visit, a turn out (a railroad switch is called a *turn out* in model railroading to keep from confusing it with an electrical switch, which is known in the hobby as a toggle) jammed and my host had to crawl under the table to fix it. His curses turned the air blue, for he had to push himself in under the pike on his back, in the fashion of an overturned worm.

Impressed, I decided to make my tabletop height the maximum and built it about five feet above the ground. But there was one thing I had not taken into consideration—that the tabletop *per se* is *not* the track level. The roadbed, or what you might call normal ground level, is set up above the tabletop by the *risers,* wood supports which are fastened to the joists to allow for grades and variations in track height. Hence when I got my roadbed laid, I had to stand on a cinderblock to see the other side of my pike. Believe me, it was a herculean task to lower that whole mess without taking it apart! (See Fig. 3-1 for risers.)

So while the usually recommended height for a grid tabletop is about 37″, I personally have found 45″ preferable. That brings your average track level to about 51″, which is about right for adult viewing. With flattop construction, you would get somewhat the same effect by making your tabletop about 50″ above the floor. For youngsters, make it correspondingly lower.

A flattop can be made of ½″ plywood if you brace it strongly underneath, but we preferred ¾″, one side clear, and carefully supported by joists. This is sturdy and solid, and permits moving without danger of buckling or sagging. You can set it up on legs of either wood or pipe or, as we did for my boy's pike, you can set it up on wooden sawhorses, which makes it wobble-free, permits ease of handling and allows for raising or lowering as the situation may later require.

For grid construction, 1″ x 4″ or even 1″ x 3″ boards, if well made, will suffice. Don't use green lumber that is liable to warp or shrink for then you're begging trouble for yourself; use only properly seasoned lumber. You can use the same lumber for the legs if you brace them stoutly, but as I was making a permanent installation, I chose 2 x 4's for the legs, glued and fastened with carriage-bolts. Beware of any weakness from knots or the like. This doesn't need to be the best or most expensive lumber, but it must be good and it certainly must be strong.

Two points to keep in mind when you're constructing your table. First, keep your leg braces as short as consistent with strength because you'll spend a lot of time later moving around under your pike and you want a minimum of obstructions. Later, I'll tell you how to make a special chair with casters on it for wheeling yourself around under the table when you're wiring and the like. The second suggestion is to keep your legs back from the front of the table (that is, from the viewing side) as far as practicable, say a minimum of six or eight inches—more if possible. Anchor the back of the pike against a wall, if you can, for stability. Leaving this overhang in front will make it easier to run wiring and other under-pike necessities.

With the table completed, we'll move along to the problem of a roadbed. Here there are many theories and differences of opinion, some modelers insist on solid wood running from riser to riser; others prefer what might be termed a "sandwich" construction. I selected the latter for the reasons that it seemed quieter, easier to get smooth rounding curves, and if a trifle more work, was actually simpler to construct.

My own procedure may serve as a model for the tyro. I decided to make a sandwich-type roadbed, consisting of Homosote on top, then light plywood, ¼″ or ⅜″, with a bottom of a fiber board known as Celotex. I bought a huge sheet of Homosote, about 9′ x 12′, laid it out in the backyard and drew the track plan on it with heavy pencil. Then I roughed this out with a power saw, cut it into suitable lengths for ease of handling, and finished it neatly on a band saw. Then I numbered each piece, and indicated the same number on the smaller track plan. After that, I traced each piece on a sheet of plywood and cut and trimmed it in the same manner, cutting its length either four or five inches longer or shorter to permit a kind of dovetail joint where the different lengths would connect. See Fig. 3-2 for details.

I did the same with the Celotex, after which I sandwiched the various layers together with a casein-type glue, such as Weldwood, tacking the layers together with ⅝″ brads. The reason for not using longer brads was to avoid any possibility of transmitting noise by the nails. Perhaps this was being overcautious, but I didn't want to run the risk. Then I laid these pieces on the grid-top and marked on the joists where I figured the risers should go. When you're investing that much time and effort into a construction, it pays to be overcautious.

Your risers are very important, and

Fig. 3-2 Joining Sandwich-type Roadbed

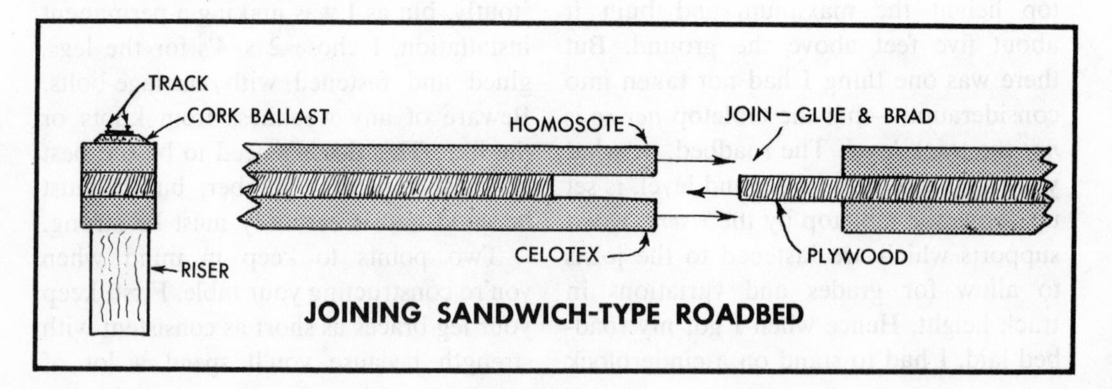

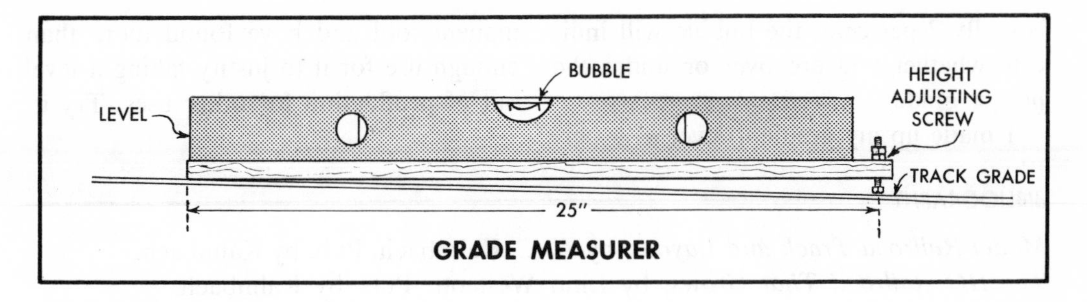

Fig. 3-3 Grade Measurer

while scrap lumber may be used it should be well cured, preferably kiln-dried, and about 1″ x 3″ or wider in HO for double-track or passing sidings, and of whatever height necessary to raise your roadbed to the desired level.

Don't glue or nail your risers to the joists because you may want to adjust them later. The best method is to hold them in place with C-clamps until you're satisfied you have a smooth, even road-bed, then secure them semipermanently with screws. It's surprising how often you will have to adjust your riser height later.

So far, I have avoided mentioning the subject of *grade*. This can become very complex, and if you have used a reputable and proven track plan, the grade will be indicated on it. In general, avoid grades on curves if possible, and on main lines keep the grade down to a maximum of about 2 per cent. The steeper the grade, the shorter your trains have to be for, roughly speaking, a 1 per cent grade will cut a train length in half, depending on the power of your locomotive. However, you *can* make them steeper if you don't object to the limitations. I held my grades down to not over 2 per cent on main-line traffic but went hog-wild and put in a 7 per cent grade on my narrow-gauge mountain timber line. I did it deliberately, despite the curtailment in the number of logging cars I can haul, because I wanted the spectacular effect of my old Shay straining up such a grade.

One of the handiest gadgets you can have for checking and planning your gradients is an adjustable level you can make for yourself. All you need is a two-foot wooden level, a straight, flat piece of seasoned wood about ⅜″ or ½″ in thickness and about 1½″ wide (these dimensions are not critical) and exactly 26″ in length, and a ⅜″ bolt about three inches long with two nuts to suit. Now one inch in from one end of the board drill a snug hole to take the bolt, with one nut on either side of the wood. This is your adjusting screw. Now attach the wood to the bottom of the level, with glue, screws, or brads, with the bolt projecting one inch over the end of the level.

Now if you have followed the plan (see Fig. 3-3) the distance from one end of the level to the screw is exactly 25 inches. Inasmuch as a 2 per cent grade simply means a rise of two inches in 100 inches, it follows that the grade will rise one half inch in 25 inches—the length of your homemade grade-tester. So adjust your bolt so that it will project exactly ½″ below the bottom of the board. Thus when you read your glass, if your grade is really 2 per cent, the bubble will indicate whether you are over or under the proper grade.

I made up my gradient level as a permanent tool and have found more than enough use for it to justify taking a level out of production for other uses. Try it.

BIBLIOGRAPHY

Model Railroad Track and Layout, by A. C. Kalmbach. Pub. by Kalmbach.
The HO Railroad That Grows, by Linn Westcott. Pub. by Kalmbach.
Frank Ellison on Model Railroads, by Frank Ellison. Pub. by Fawcett.

CHAPTER 4

Trackwork

Those of you old enough to remember when the air of America was perfumed with the steam and smoke from great locomotives instead of the stench of diesels, to have been lulled by the happy song of clacking wheels on rail or the thunderous roar of trains passing, and to have been charmed by the lonely call of a train whistle in the night, know that a railroad is a living thing. It is more. Tracks are the arteries of the world for they carry the lifeblood of commerce and produce into the remotest regions; they spawned towns and cities and even states; they brought civilization to the wilderness. It is indeed a backward country which is not crisscrossed with the shining steel ribbons of rail.

As I mentioned elsewhere in this book, one half of good operation depends on good track, the other half on good wheels. Thus wheels and track must be as compatible as salt and pepper or as Romeo and Juliet. What makes this romance possible is the tiny flange on all railroad wheels; without that little almost unnoticed rim railroading as we know it would be impossible.

In the dawn of railroading, some observant individual noticed how difficult it was to force the wheels of a buggy out of the deep ruts in a road, so it seemed logical that railroad tracks should be designed as a sort of metal rut, with the flanges on the track, as in a piece of channel iron. This was successful—up to a point—and for a time was the method used on the earliest railroads. Then some unsung and forgotten genius had the startling notion that the difficulties and dangers of a grooved track might be overcome if the flanges were built onto the *wheels* instead of the track. Few ideas in history have had such a profound effect upon civilization.

When you pause to consider it, a railroad wheel is a remarkable little thing. I use the word "little" advisedly, because compared to the vast bulk towering above them, they are scarcely noticeable, yet they carry the bulk of the world's commerce on their shoulders. These tiny shoulders are the flanges.

Hence, since we are attempting to reproduce a miniature of the real thing, it behooves us to further this romantic conjunction of track and wheel with loving care. The surest way is by careful tracklaying and the use of easements, or transitional curves.

A few months ago I had a group of cattlemen at my home for a committee meeting at the conclusion of which one of the men asked to see my pike. The others went along as a matter of course.

But they were not interested. One caustically remarked that he had "given up playing with trains when he was fifteen." I as caustically told him that if he had sense enough even to turn on the controls and run a train around the tracks, I would give him the pike. After one glance at the control panel, he didn't accept the challenge.

However, as they were leaving, one man—a civil engineer by profession—chanced to glance along the tangent (the straight track) and noticed the curve at the far end. He stopped short in amazement.

"Say!" he said in surprise. "Do you use easements on this pike?"

"Of course!" I told him.

He turned and walked down to get a

better look at the curve. "How in the world did you figure that out?" he asked. "That's one of the most difficult mathematical problems in engineering!"

"I've been trying to tell you chaps that this isn't child's play," I reiterated. "If you want good trackwork, you have to construct it as the railroads do, difficult or not."

As the NMRA says: "It is an unfortunate truth that too many model railroads suffer from carelessly engineered and hastily constructed right-of-way and track. The finest model equipment built can perform only as well as the track on which it runs will permit." And again quoting: "The ideal condition for passage of flanged wheels along the track is the level straightaway—any departure from this ideal carries a penalty in performance. The minute a curve is introduced flange friction commences and adds to the axle friction the locomotive must overcome to move its train. . . . To keep this problem to a minimum, change curvature gradually, easing from one into the other by degrees rather than all at once."

In other words, use easements!

Well, what is an easement? Have you ever watched a toy train blunder into a curve with a lurch that would throw passengers onto the floor—if it had any passengers? This whiplash is caused not so much by the tightness of the curve itself, but chiefly by the lack of a gradual approach, or easement, into the curve—a series of everlessening radii, or what the real railroads term a transitional curve. Such easements not only greatly improve the beauty of your track's appearance, but cause fewer derailments, permit higher speeds on curves, and make for better coupling connections because they do away with the sudden jerk between cars.

Now as my cattleman friend observed, the way the real railroads work out a transitional curve is quite a mathematical problem, but don't let that deter you because I'll show you a simple method of making transitional curves freehand, unless, of course, you prefer to do it the hard way.

This is illustrated in Fig. 4-1. Drawing "A" shows a curve with no easement. You can easily imagine that if a train comes down the tangent it will lurch badly when it hits the beginning of the curve. Drawing "B" indicates the method of putting in an easement. I have deliberately left out any dimensions because these will depend on the space you have and the gauge you are using. The dimensions are not critical; for myself, I figure them by eye.

Fig. 4-1 Easements

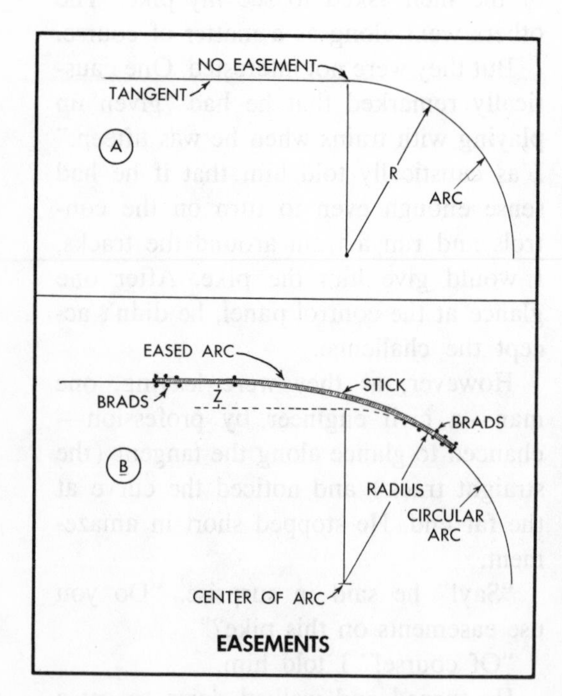

The steps are as follows: first draw your curve and tangent as in "A." Then draw in a tentative tangent line outside the first one. The distance between these is indicated by the letter "Z." The wider the distance (within reason) between these lines, the smoother your curve. As a rough estimate, I'd try about 2 to 2½ inches for HO gauge—for Z. Then find a thin, flexible stick to draw your line, but make sure it bends perfectly. I use a yardstick for this chore. Next, put in some small finishing nails, or brads, as shown, to hold one end of the stick to the curve you have drawn and then bend it carefully until it joins your tangent line in a graceful arc. Then put in more brads to hold it in place until you draw in your easement.

Remember that despite all the complicated mathematics and calculations worked out by the engineering departments of real railroads, the actual tracklaying is done by eye. The boss gandy dancer (tracklayer) gets down on his hands and knees and sights along every piece of track put down to see that it is smooth and well connected. This is a good practice for a model railroader as well. Your eye can pick up a crook or a hump in the track better than any instrument yet made.

Keep in mind that track is model, too! Most modelers forget that, but there are a few who specialize in beautiful track work. Granted it takes a lot of skill to manufacture your own turnouts, but it can be done and is well worth the effort. Visit your nearest railroad and study the details of their trackwork; see how gracefully crossovers and turnouts flow into each other with flawless precision.

Figure 4-2 affords a glimpse of the approach tracks to the Norfolk and Western station at Roanoke, Virginia, taken from a bridge. With the light glinting on the polished rails, it was a thing of sheer beauty.

Fig. 4-2 Roanoke Trackage

Unfortunately, as I've said before, model railroading is a compromise and the limitations of space preclude the flowing sweep of the prototype trackage. Turnouts on a model have to be sharper than on the real railroads. But the model rail should use turnouts as large as possible within the limitations of space.

When I was designing my big layout, I settled on #6 turnouts, even in the yards, where most modelers use #3's. But at one point, where I had plenty of space, I put in a #8 turnout. Of course it took up more room, but the improvement in appearance was amazing. If I build another large pike, I'll settle on #8's or even #10's—perhaps larger, if I can get them in.

Another point worth mentioning: If you plan to run your trains in one direction most of the time, you should arrange, wherever possible, for trailing turnouts, as the real railroads do. The difference between a "facing" turnout and a "trailing" turnout is important. A "facing" turnout is when the points of the turnout "face" toward the oncoming train, and, conversely, a "trailing" turnout is when the frog is nearest the approaching train. Far more accidents and derailments are caused by "facing" turnouts because the flanges of the wheels often catch on the points, whereas they will usually ride through a "trailing" turnout without difficulty.

Obviously on a single-track road, this is an impossible ideal, but at least you should make certain the points of your turnouts fit snugly against your main line. This is a problem not only of installation, but of maintenance as well.

There are three types of track used on model pikes: brass, which is most common; steel, which is used rarely; and nickel silver, which is relatively new. I have all three on my pike, but any future track will be exclusively of nickel silver. The principal disadvantage of brass is that it oxidizes so rapidly and requires constant attention to keep it clean—and it doesn't resemble the prototype. Steel rail has the most realistic appearance, but in humid weather will rust. Nickel silver avoids both these hazards and looks good. Some modelers paint the outer edges of their rail either black or Tuscan red, which improves the appearance somewhat. But do not get any paint on the contacting surfaces or you'll have trouble.

While most model rails spike their track down, I prefer glue. For the so-called flexible track—which I use everywhere except on the narrow-gauge line—I use Weldwood glue, putting just enough spikes down to hold it firmly to the roadbed. It is advisable to shove the spikes in with a pair of long-nosed pliers. I have seen some men set the spikes with a hammer and a small nail-set, which is all right if you are experienced and have very good control. But, if you drive a spike in a mite too hard, you run the risk of kinking your track, so it's hardly worth the risk.

My method of putting down the track is to mix up the Weldwood powdered glue to a rather watery consistency, then spread it on the roadbed just as far as one length of track. Then I put the track down on the glue, spike it lightly until I have squinted along the track to make sure it is even, after which I set the spikes to hold it firmly until the glue dries, taking another sight along the track to make certain it hasn't shifted out of true line during the process.

While the glue for that particular length of track is still wet, I pour my ballast in between the ties and along the sides. You can purchase realistically colored ballast—small gravel or stones—at your hobby shop, or you can use canary gravel, which is cheaper and obtainable at any pet shop or supermarket. Tamp this ballast down and when the glue has dried sweep off the surplus. But make sure you get off *all* the surplus because it will cause a derailment if you don't!

A word of caution is in order here: Don't smear much glue around a turnout, especially near the points. A tiny piece of gravel or, I should say, "ballast" may adhere to the points of your turnout and keep them from closing properly or, worse, the glue may "freeze" your throwbar and not permit the turnout to operate at all. The safest method is to use no glue at all under the turnouts, but trust to spikes alone.

If you are very ambitious and decide to lay individual ties, as the real railroads and the best modelers do, you can use much the same procedure in putting down your ties—with Weldwood glue and ballast—but be careful none of the ballast sticks to the top surface of your ties or you'll have difficulty getting a smooth track.

When you have your ties down properly and have at least three or four good three-pronged track gauges handy, you are ready for the job of putting down rail. As there is no standard method and as every experienced model rail does it his own individual way, I can only tell you how I do it and hope you succeed.

For adhering the rail to the ties, I use Pliobond glue, finding it holds the rail firmly to the ties. You have to work fairly rapidly on this job to get your rail down before the glue dries. I find it easier to lay all the inside or the outside rail one day, and the opposite rail the next day so that the first rail has time to set perfectly. With a fine-pointed stick, such as a wooden match or a toothpick, I put a spot of Pliobond on each tie at what I judge to be the proper place. Then I carefully lay the rail and sight along it to make sure it is straight or, in the case of a curve, properly curved. This sighting business goes on constantly because a slight move in the rail may spoil the whole job. When I am satisfied the rail is in good shape, I go back and spike it every four or five inches, just enough to keep it in contact with tie and glue.

The opposite rail is the tough one to lay, although the procedure is much the same. But when laying this second rail be sure to use your track gauges. When you have it spiked down, and feel sure you are in gauge, take a pair of trucks and run them up and down the track as a double check against·the gauge. Be sure to put in sufficient spikes at the ends of each length of rail where they butt. Later, when the glue has properly set, you can withdraw any spikes you think unnecessary.

Don't feel overwhelmed if, when your track has set, you find it has moved slightly out of gauge. It's not hard to fix. Simply touch the tip of a hot soldering iron to the rail that is out of line. This will temporarily melt the glue and permit you to shove the rail over to where it ought to be. Then spike it again and the glue will harden as before.

I cannot overemphasize the importance of keeping your track *clean!* This is vital to good operation. Accumulated dust on your track will adhere to the wheels of locos and cars, oxidization will keep locos from getting power, and, in general, dirt will ruin performance.

All this is aptly summed up in a directive issued to members of the Baltimore Society of Model Engineers, by their president Clyde Gerald, regarding preparations for their annual show. Says Clyde: "How's your equipment? Wheels built up 6 scale inches with accumulated gook; couplers low or high by NMRA standards, or pinned on so that a little operation will alter their alignment; equipment in need of lubrication; cars falling apart; locos that run jerkily; truck king-pins off center so that the car goes down the track sideways; or equipment with inferior fittings such as out-of-gauge wheels or couplers that won't couple?"

If experienced and veteran model rails need such a reminder, it is evident that the tyro shoud be equally alert to these failings. So if your operation when you think you've finished your job is disappointing, look to these troubles. They may well be yours.

CHAPTER 5

Electrical Control

The term "model railroading" is not a hyphenated word. It is not only two distinct words, but actually describes two distinct hobbies or, perhaps more accurately, two phases of the same hobby. *Modeling,* per se, is one thing, *railroading* quite another. The connecting link between the two is electrical control. With the exceptions noted before—i.e. steam and dry ice, etc.—scale model trains are operated by electricity.

One of the most frequently asked questions by a beginner is: "Can I use a toy train transformer to run scale model trains?" The answer is *No*—and a qualified *Yes.* The No is because toy transformers give out alternating current, known as a.c., which will quickly burn out the miniature motors used in scale model equipment, which require direct current, or d.c. as it is termed. The reason I use the "qualified Yes" is because if you connect a toy transformer to a component known as a rectifier, you will thus obtain direct current, which is what you need to operate scale locomotives. We'll go into that more thoroughly in a little while.

The standard source of power for two-rail model trains is called a "power pack." These can be purchased at your hobby shop and come in various sizes at varying prices, depending on your needs. All you have to do is plug the input wire into your house outlet and attach the output wires to your track, and presto, they will give you the proper 12 volt d.c. voltage to operate your equipment. It is as simple as that—in the beginning.

However, all power packs are not the same nor are they all of equal quality. While for your first venture into electrical control it is advisable to purchase a complete unit rather than to attempt to make up one of your own (unless, of course, you have had considerable skill in constructing such equipment), it would be well to ask, and take, your dealer's advice on the right pack for your purpose, after you decide what you need. Needs vary with the individual; and as there are a number of points to consider before you buy a pack, I'll try to clear these up so as to help you with your selection.

In Fig. 5-1, I have diagrammed the components of a typical power pack. In reality it is two drawings of the same thing; the upper portion is a pictorial representation to help the novice recognize the various components, while the sketch below is a schematic diagram of the same thing. If you intend to go into the hobby thoroughly, it is well to learn to read schematic drawings because many books and articles on the subject use this style of illustrative shorthand to make their points. Most experienced craftsmen prefer this simplified outline.

Now to examine the diagram in detail: at the far left you will find the plug that goes into the house current. Above it is a simple on-and-off switch to cut off the current when not in use. When you turn this switch *on,* the house current goes into the transformer, which *transforms* or reduces the house voltage down to approximately 16 volts a.c. At this point it is advisable to have, or to insert, a *circuit breaker,* which is similar to a fuse, so that if anything goes wrong with the transformer a sudden surge of power will not burn out the rest of your components. It is convenient, also, to have an indica-

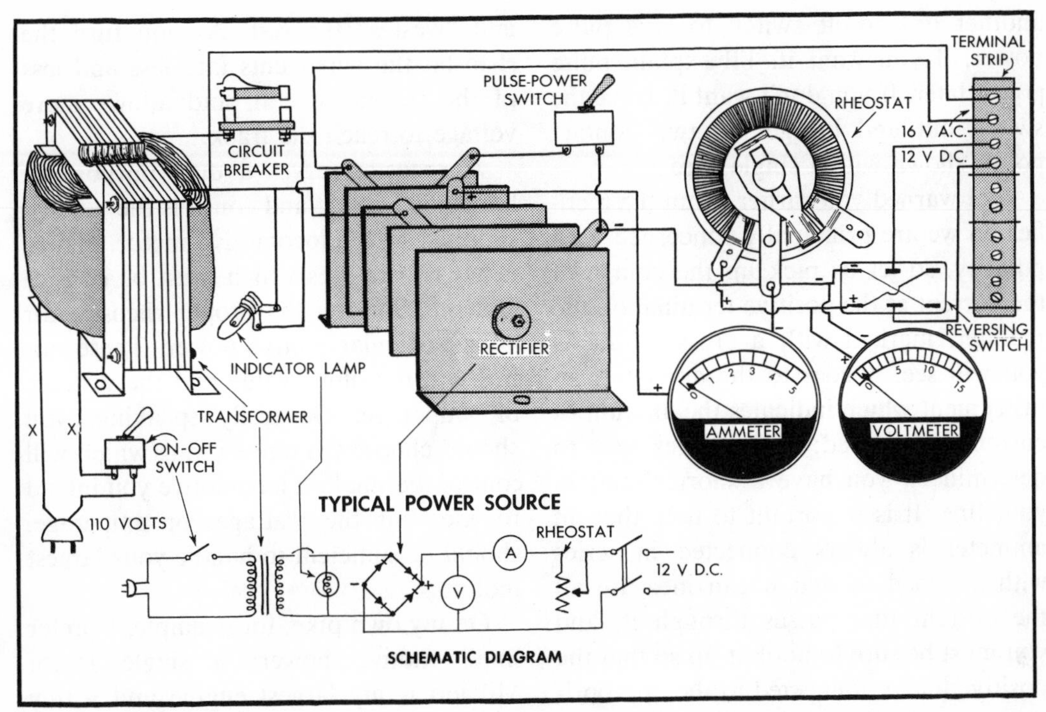

Fig. 5-1 Power Pack

tion light hooked in here to let you know at a glance whether the power is on or off. From there, the 16 volts a.c. goes into the *rectifier* which changes the current from a.c. to d.c. This device can be compared to a wye in a highway which separates the traffic from two-way to two lanes of one-way traffic. This is a critical point because from the rectifier on we are concerned with the *direction* of our two-way electrical current or, properly, its *polarity,* which is indicated by the *positive* (+) and *negative* (−) symbols, usually referred to as "plus" and "minus," as in the storage battery of your automobile.

While in the limited space of this single chapter I cannot go too deeply into a technical discussion of electricity, let us pause briefly to clarify this business of a.c. and d.c., for it is essential to understand the difference between the two. Alternating current, as the name implies, flows first one way and then the other in cycles, usually 60 times a second. Thus the average house current is listed as 110 volt, 60 cycles a.c. Direct current, on the other hand, always flows in one direction; leaving its power source as *positive,* doing its job, and returning as *negative.* The little d.c. motors used in scale model trains are governed by this polarity; for example, if the positive wire is hooked to one terminal, they will turn in one direction, but if hooked to the other, they will operate in the opposite direction. This is the basis of control.

For a more complete explanation of this phenomena, I refer you to the two technical books listed at the end of this chapter.

Now let's get back to our examination of the power pack in Fig. 5-1. Above and to the right of the rectifier I have shown another on-and-off switch to give pulse power, if you want it. I'll explain pulse power later. If you don't want it, leave the switch out and bridge the two contact points shown with a single wire.

As I warned you earlier, from the rectifier on we are principally concerned with polarity, so let us pick up the course of the current at the positive terminal on the rectifier, marked with a cross (+). As you will see, it goes to the ammeter, an instrument which indicates the amount of current being used; it is a quick way to determine if you have a short circuit in your line. It is important to note that an ammeter is always connected in series with the load so that it can measure all the current that passes through it, and you must be sure to hook it up so that the positive line is connected to the appropriate terminal on the back of the ammeter. From the negative terminal of the ammeter the wire leads to the lower stationary input lug on the rheostat.

The rheostat is the actual regulator of your trains; it is comparable to the throttle on a prototypical locomotive or the accelerator pedal on your automobile; it starts, runs, and stops your trains. When you look at the drawing, you see the backside of the rheostat; the reverse side has a knob for turning the wiper around the coiled resistance wire. The purpose of the rheostat is to "waste" voltage. That means that while, for example, 12 volts is put into the rheostat, it permits you, by turning the knob, to give out a fraction of that amount of voltage so that your trains start slowly. Without the rheostat, or some other controlling device, your trains would take off like a rocket if the full 12 volts were thrown into the motor at once. The rheostat doles out what voltage you actually need, whether one, two, or three volts, and "wastes" the rest. As you turn the rheostat the wiper cuts into less and less of the resistance coil, and allows more voltage to reach the track.

A rheostat serves a dual purpose; it limits the current and controls the voltage supplied to the locomotive motor. Hence it has two ratings which must be considered in choosing the proper rheostat for your particular motive power. These ratings are the ohms value and the wattage or amperage. Generally speaking, you should choose the ohms rating which will control the smallest locomotive you intend to use, but the wattage, or amperage, should be sufficient to handle your largest motor.

On my own pike, for example, I prefer small motive power; a single motor Mikado is my largest engine and a tiny four-wheel switcher is my smallest. Hence a 50 ohm-50 watt rheostat gives me adequate speed control. If you are in doubt about your own equipment, ask the advice of your hobby dealer. It is his business to know these things. If he doesn't know, you'd be well advised to seek a dealer that does know.

Most rheostats used in model railroading are of the circular, knob-controlled type shown in our illustration but, as turning a plastic knob for driving a locomotive is obviously not a prototypical operation, many model rails have experimented with a handle-type controller that more aptly resembles the prototype throttle in a locomotive cab. The making of one of these throttles is a mechanical feat beyond the capacity of the average modeler, but now you can purchase such a "throttle rheostat" made especially for model railroad use. Such a rheostat is shown in Fig. 5-2. It is known as a Marn-O-Stat and manufactured by Arvid L. Anderson,

Box 392, Frederic, Wisconsin, and a little beauty it truly is. It gives much better control than a conventional rheostat and pulling the big comfortable handle helps the illusion of a real throttle. It comes in a wide variety of ratings which permits its use on any pike from a large, O gauge layout to the smallest TT pike. It is a good investment.

Now back to our drawing. When our load line leaves the lug on the lower left-hand side of the rheostat it goes to the directional control switch, commonly called a "reversing switch" which governs the polarity of the tracks, thus controlling the direction of the trains. But before we go into the business of directional control, please note that we have cut in another meter—the voltmeter. As the name implies, the voltmeter indicates how much voltage is getting to your track, much as a speedometer on a car indicates your speed.

Some model railroaders dispense with meters, regarding them as a luxury, but I wouldn't operate without them. Fuses and circuit breakers may protect your power pack, but they won't protect your locomotives—and a new motor for one locomotive costs more than a voltmeter or ammeter. Thus, in addition to the service for which they are made, namely indicating voltage and amperage, they are cheap insurance for your locomotives.

It is important to note that the voltmeter is connected across both leads from the power source, which is necessary to measure the voltage passing between these leads. But don't make a mistake and connect the ammeter in this manner as the extra current will probably burn out the delicate meter.

In the diagram you are shown the bottom side of a double-pole, double-throw,

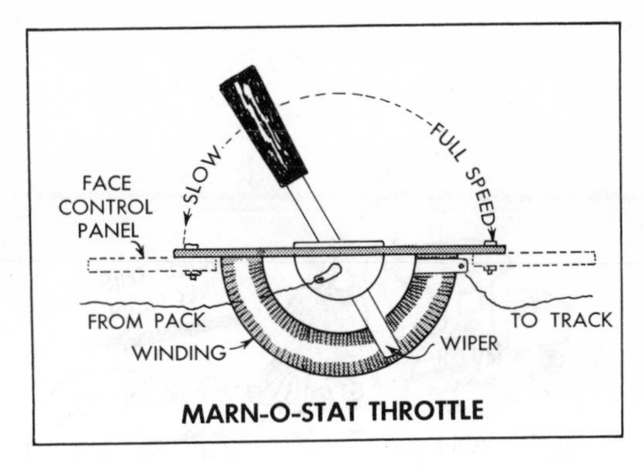

Fig. 5-2 Marn-O-Stat Throttle

center-off toggle switch, known usually as a dp.dt. toggle. I'll get back to it in a moment, but first, let's follow our wiring, for this directional-control switch is going to require a bit of explaining.

Going back to the negative terminal of the rectifier, you will see that the negative, or minus, line runs directly to the upper left-hand lug of the reversing switch. From the center terminals of this switch—which are not marked because the polarity, as we shall soon see, is controlled by the way in which the toggle is thrown—the two leads go to a terminal strip usually on the outside of your power pack, or, if you make your own pack, the terminal strip will probably be on the inside of your control panel.

These should be marked 12 volt d.c. because about 4 volts are used up between the rectifier and the rheostat. Now if you will again refer to the drawing, you will discover two more leads which take off from the transformer wires *before* they enter the rectifier (they run across the upper portion of the drawing). Since they have bypassed the rectifier, they are obviously carrying alternating current, and as they also bypassed the rheostat they are not subject to its control. These two leads should have a place on your terminal strip

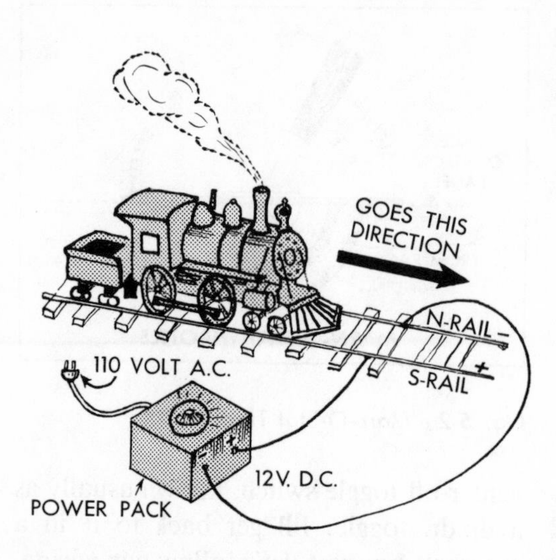

Fig. 5-3A Loco and Power Pack

and be marked 16 volt a.c. as they are useful for the various accessories you may have, such as supplying lights in structures, operating signals, and the like—all of which can utilize a.c. current without complications.

Now for this business of directional control. Whether you have a single oval track on a piece of 4′ x 8′ plywood or a

Fig. 5-3B Loco and Power Pack, Wires Reversed

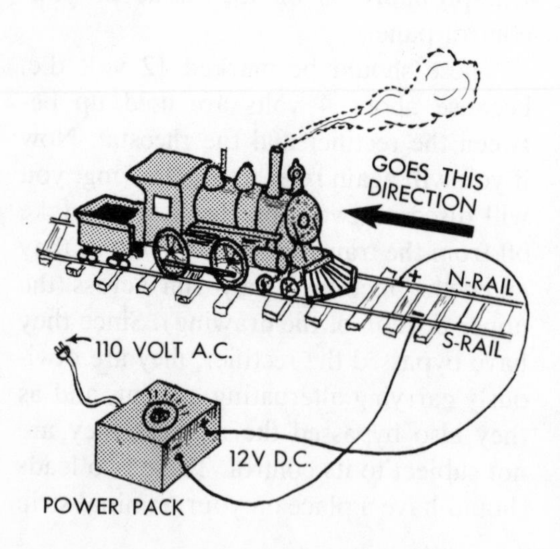

70-foot layout with multiple track spreading in all directions, it is advisable to utilize the convention of "traffic direction" used by the majority of real railroads, the concept of "eastbound" or "westbound," no matter which way your track points. On an oval-type track, assume arbitrarily that all trains going in a clockwise direction are westbound and those going in a counterclockwise direction are eastbound. This not only simplifies operation, it simplifies the wiring of your track.

Accepting this convention of traffic direction, you then adopt another—you designate the outside rail of your two-rail track the south rail or, for convenience, the S rail, and the inside rail the north, or N, rail. On a single oval track, this is simple because the inside rail is always the N rail and the outside the S rail. However, when you begin to twist your track into loops so that it resembles a plate of spaghetti, you will have to trace it out carefully so as to distinguish the N and the S rails.

Now if you were going to be satisfied to run only one train around a single oval of track, with no sidings or turnouts, and always in the same direction, you would have no need for a direction controller. As illustrated in Fig. 5-3A, all you would have to do is connect a wire from the plus terminal of your power pack to the S rail of your track and a wire from the minus terminal to the N rail, set your locomotive on the track, and feed your power. Your locomotive will proceed in an easterly, or counterclockwise, direction and you're in business. It wouldn't make any difference which way you headed the loco on the track; if you aimed it west, and had the plus wire to the S rail, it will back up in a counterclockwise direction.

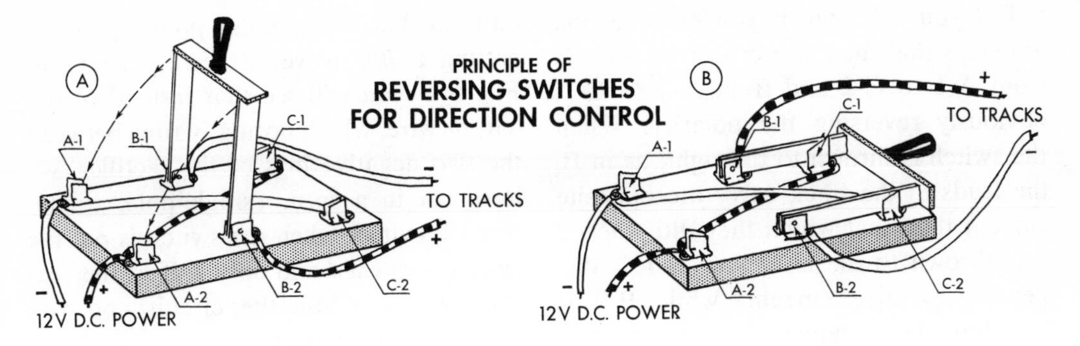

Fig. 5-4 Knife-switch Reversing

This is caused by the polarity of your track because the current flows from the power source to the rail, passes through the motor, and then back through the other rail to the power pack. If there is any break in this ring-around-the-rosy chain, the motor will not operate.

As only a very small child is likely to be satisfied with such a limited one-way setup as we have described, it becomes necessary to understand how to control the direction of our locomotive—which brings us back to our "reversing switch" or "directional controller."

If you look at Fig. 5-3B, you will see that if we want to make the locomotive shown in Fig. 5-3A back up, or reverse its direction, we simply disconnect the wiring at the track and attach the plus wire where the minus was before, and the minus where the plus was. But as this would be a very tedious operation, inasmuch as the feed wires should be soldered to the track, we solve our problem by cutting the wires at some convenient spot between the power pack and the track and insert a reversing switch for direction control.

Although most of the commercial power packs have a built-in direction controller, many do not, and in any event when you get into turning tracks and reverse loops you will need to have a thorough knowledge of the principles of reversing polarity to your tracks. And while the principle itself is very simple, I have discovered that many model railroaders do not understand it, even when they examine a properly wired reversing switch because they do not understand precisely how a switch operates inside.

To make this clear, I have in Fig. 5-4, chosen an old-fashioned knife switch to illustrate the principle because all the parts are in the open. Naturally you will not want to use one of these old relics, but the principle is the same, no matter whether you use a dp.dt. toggle, a rotary switch, or a telephone key.

Study drawing A of Fig. 5-4. The checkered wire designates the course of the positive current; the plain white wire the course of the negative. They come from the power pack to the reversing switch at terminals A-1 and A-2. In the left-hand sketch the switch is in the *off* position. Now when the switch is thrown to the left the blades contact the A-1 and A-2 terminals. The positive current passes from A-2, through the near blade to B-2, thence to one rail of your track, where it goes through your motor and returns to B-1, along the blade to A-1, and back to the power pack, completing the chain.

But you will note if you examine the drawings that there are crisscrossed leads from A-1 to C-2 and from A-2 to C-1, obviously reversing the polarity. When the switch is thrown to the right, as in B, the leads to the track carry the opposite current than that which they did when it was thrown to the left. Now B-1 is dispensing positive current, while B-2 is handling the negative. Thus by putting jumpers across the poles of practically any two-pole double-throw switch, you can make a direction controller.

PULSE POWER

Model railroaders, or model rails, as they call themselves, are always seeking new ways to improve the control and operation of their miniature trains. One of the basic problems is inertia. Real trains start very slowly and take a long time to come to a stop; but most model trains start like frightened jackrabbits and stop as suddenly as if they had hit a stone wall. A lot of methods have been investigated in the hope of finding an answer to smooth operation at the low speeds needed for starting and switching in the yards.

When some genius discovered pulse power, it hit the model railroad hobbyists in epidemic proportions; it seemed to be the final answer. The principle behind it is rather complex, but the general idea is to alter the electrical impulses, or waves, so that instead of flowing smoothly to the motor, they come in longer beats, like the human pulse, in such a fashion that the armature of the motor tends to vibrate somewhat; this "jerkiness," or vibration, breaks the inertia and gets the locomotive started sooner than it normally would. This lengthened beat, or pulse, is accomplished by cutting a full-wave rectifier in half, so that under pulse power you are getting a *half*-wave. Referring again to Fig. 5-1, you will see that instead of the bar, or wire, which normally runs between the two negative lugs of the rectifier, we have cut in a sp.st. (single-pole, single-throw) switch; when the switch is *on,* the circuit is *opened* and only half of the rectifier works. Close the circuit and you have full-wave power.

This, in essense, is pulse power, yet in practice it isn't all "beer and skittles" as some would have you think. The *vibration* makes the locomotive unpleasantly noisy, and even more important, the heat of the motor is almost doubled when using pulse power. Under certain conditions, this can cause serious trouble. When pulse power first became the rage, I cut it into all my power packs but, after using it a while, I banished it in favor of a method I personally feel is vastly superior—the use of variable transformers. Take your choice; I won't argue the point, and if you like pulse power, I suggest that you read the two technical books mentioned before.

VARIABLE TRANSFORMERS

The best method I have found to date for improved control is the use of a variable transformer. I emphasize "to date" because at this writing the experts in the hobby are working on a new transistor control that seems to promise miracles, although it is not yet on the market, still being in the experimental stage. If you read the model railroading magazines, you can keep abreast of developments in this investigation.

Essentially, a variable transformer is a continuously tapped autotransformer, marketed under the trade names of Variac and Powerstat, purchasable at any radio-supply house. In appearance, it resembles a large rheostat, but though it takes the place of a rheostat, it is not a rheostat and the hookup is entirely different, as you will see.

The variable transformer, or v.t. as it is commonly called, delivers from 0 to 115 volts, and is hooked into the circuit *ahead* of the power pack. In Fig. 5-1 you will find two X's just above and to the left of the on-and-off switch leading to the transformer. This is where the v.t. should be cut in.

A word of caution is appropriate here. The v.t.'s are not encased and you are dealing with 110 volts both at the input and the output ends. This can give you a bad jolt if you inadvertently touch it with your bare hands, an easy thing to do when the rest of your circuit is only 12 to 16 volts. I cover my v.t. contacts with small plastic cases so as to avoid this momentary unpleasantness.

In using the v.t. you can either turn your rheostats full on and forget them or, as I did, remove them altogether, as you control your trains by turning the dial of the v.t. While a Powerstat or a Variac is slightly more expensive than the average rheostat, the control is so much smoother and superior to that of a rheostat that you will be pleasantly surprised and consider it well worth the difference.

If you add headlights to your locomotive, you will find that you get a smoother start, with or without a v.t. The current drawn by the lights gives you a higher voltage to your motor, which tends to eliminate the so-called jackrabbit starts.

Another point worth mentioning here is that if you use a v.t., you cannot use the 16-volt accessory terminals of your power pack because the v.t. varies the voltage in the whole pack. This is relatively unimportant for you can utilize an old toy transformer or the power transformer of an old radio for the accessories, but you should know this before you get involved with trying to light your structures from the accessory terminals we mentioned earlier.

Model rails are great experimenters and they have evolved many interesting methods for smoother control of trains. Some have used potentiometers instead of rheostats, claiming better regulation at slow speeds. Others have made and inserted tiny flywheels into their locomotives to maintain the coasting effect of the momentum, so that the locomotive comes to a gradual stop even after the power is turned off. Still others have rigged up complicated devices with larger flywheels on separate electric motors which, in turn, control the rheostats so that the power is cut down much more gradually than can be accomplished by hand. They insert a "panic button," or "brake," in the line so that if the train coasts too long, the power can be cut off entirely before a wreck occurs.

But the new transistor method of control holds great promise. I have been told by some of the experts that a train will coast as much as ten minutes after the power has been cut off. Inasmuch as a real locomotive takes about two full miles to stop, this should greatly increase the realism, but will require considerable skill to operate. I repeat, you can keep abreast of these developments if you read the model railroad magazines, for this is not a static hobby; it is constantly developing.

To cover all the interesting facets of electrical control in one chapter is impossible; to explore the subject in depth would require a volume larger than this whole book. That is why, for the hobbyist who wants more technical data, I sug-

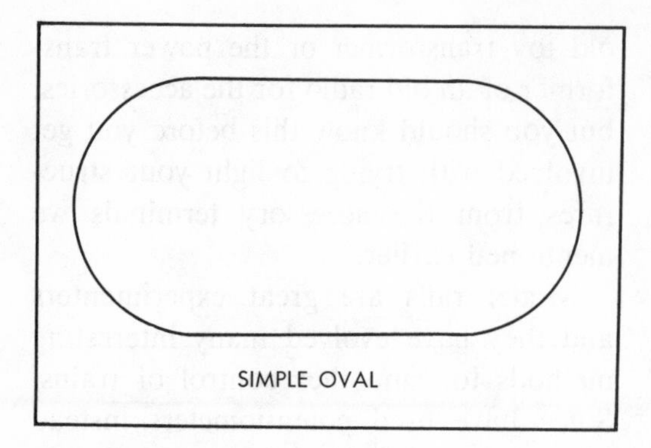

Fig. 5-5 Simple Oval

gest that you read Mallery and/or Westcott.

TURNOUTS AND REVERSE LOOPS

So long as you use a single oval track, as in Fig. 5-5, with no sidings, spurs, or return loops, you have relatively few electrical problems—and very little operational fun. As the slogan is "Model Railroading Is Fun," we'll assume you want to expand your empire. But the moment you insert your first turnout, or track switch as it is sometimes called, the complications begin.

When I started in the hobby, long before the advent of so-called "snap-track"

Fig. 5-6 Turnouts

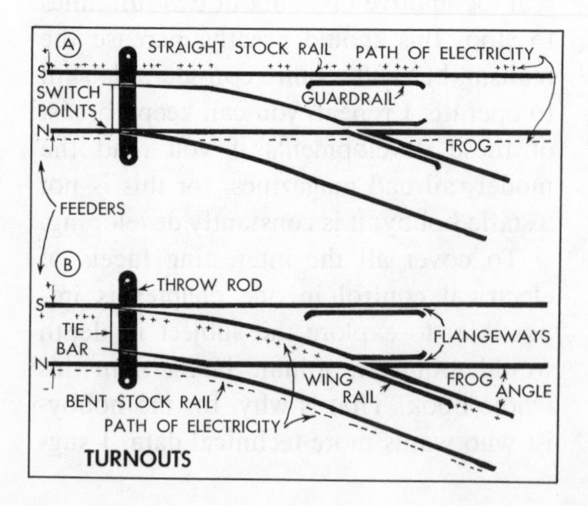

and the ready-to-use plastic turnouts now so popular, it was even more complicated; but at least the complications were consistent and the rules could be stated definitively. Now we have different rules for the different types of turnouts. This difference comes in the way the turnouts are built. Most ready-to-use turnouts are wired to send power down both branches at the same time, whereas the homemade and kit-built turnouts are built to power only one branch at a time.

It is obvious that you cannot leave a train standing on a siding while another passes on the main line if both branches are powered because both trains will be in operation at the same time. However, when you want the advantages of selective control, you can easily convert the ready-to-use turnouts by putting in gaps and extra toggles to cut off the power on the branch you wish to remain "dead." Westcott goes into this phase of wiring in depth. Meanwhile, I'll proceed on the assumption that you prefer the selective-control type of turnout.

An ordinary selective-control turnout which draws its power from its points is illustrated in Fig. 5-6 A and B. Thus either branch is powered depending on how the turnout is thrown but only one branch at a time. This is truly "selective" control.

But if you trace out the course of the power in the sketch, you will readily see that where the rails meet at the "frog," where the N rail crosses the S rail, we will have a short circuit if we don't do something to prevent it. This something is the insertion of a *gap* in the rails behind the frog.

As the name implies, a *gap* is a break in the rail to prevent electricity from passing through it. See A-C in Fig. 5-7. If your track is already laid you can cut a gap with a power tool or a Zona saw, but if you have designed your track plan carefully in advance, so that you know where gaps have to be inserted (and there will be need for many of them in a fair-sized pike), you can use a plastic rail joiner (purchasable at your hobby shop) to keep the rails isolated as in Fig. 5-8 B. What I did was to lay my track first, then cutting in my gaps as required when it was time to electrify the layout. One problem you may encounter is that sometimes the rails creep, or heat will make them expand, closing the gap and causing a short circuit. Some model rails solve this by squirting a little glue in the gaps to prevent the gap from closing, as in C of Fig. 5-8, but I preferred to insert the flat end of a toothpick (D in Fig. 5-8) or a piece of cardboard or thin insulating material between the rails, trimming the material and filing it smooth with the rail. In this way, it is impossible for the gap to close.

Since the frog is the fly in the electrical ointment of the selective-control turnout, it makes obvious the reason for one of the prime rules in wiring—*always attach your feed wires ahead of the points!* See Fig. 5-7 E.

However, there are exceptions, or at least modifications, to every rule, as shown in Fig. 5-7 D. Here we have a passing siding where we obviously have no choice but to put our feeder wires behind the frog

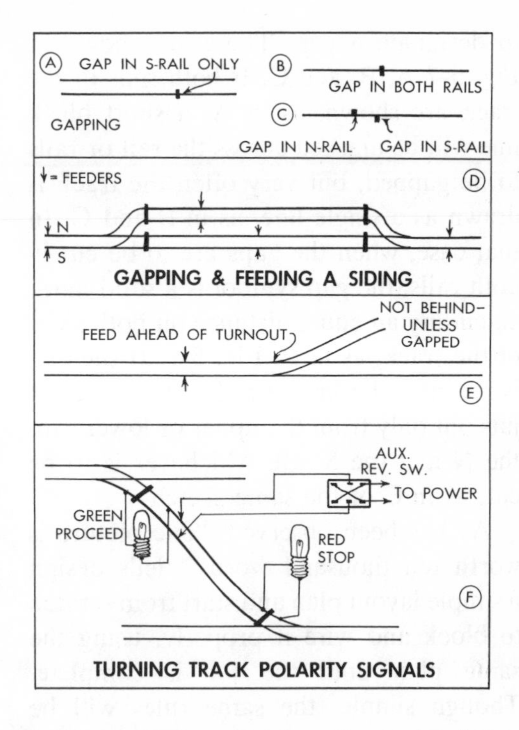

Fig. 5-7 Gapping; Feeding; Turning-track Polarity Signals

in order to move our trains. But we avoid a short circuit at the frogs by gapping all four rails, as shown, to prevent the branch and main-line feeders from leaking power to the frogs. This makes both the siding and this portion of the main line isolated blocks, each controlled at the control panel by a separate electrical switch.

Incidentally, in designing your electrical circuit or in studying published plans, you should know the symbol used

Fig. 5-8 Track Techniques

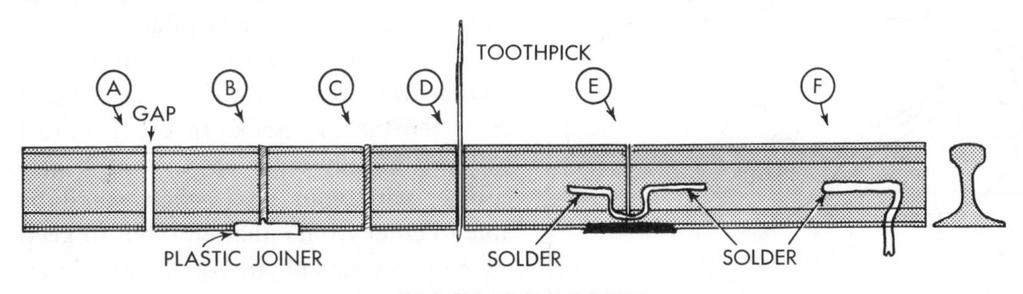

to designate a gap. These are shown in Fig. 5-7 A, B, and C. If both rails of the track are shown, as in A, a short black line will be marked across the rail or rails to be gapped, but very often the track is drawn as a single line, as in B and C. In that case, when the gaps are to be cut in both rails, the gap symbol is a solid mark extending an equal distance on both sides of the track, as in B, Fig. 5-7. If the gap is meant to be in one rail or the other, it juts out only from the upper or lower rail, the N and the S rail, whichever is to be cut, as in C of the same sketch.

As has been observed, "one picture is worth ten thousand words," let's design a simple layout plan and start from scratch to block and wire it properly, using the same plan until the job is complete. Though simple, the same rules will be applicable to a larger or smaller plan. See Fig. 5-9.

In this plan you will see that at the left end there is a loop by which a westbound train can cut diagonally across the center of the oval and head in an eastbound direction. In other words, it changes direction. This is called a "return loop" or "turning track," which requires very special wiring.

Here's why: Let us imagine a train moving in a clockwise direction, as indicated by the arrow, and after a few turns

Fig. 5-9 Oval with Turning Track

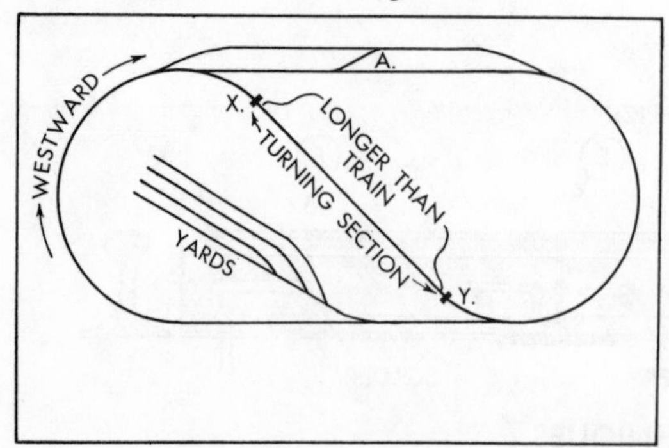

of the oval, the engineer decides to leave the main line at X and cut across the diagonal toward Y. He is boiling along happily with his right-hand wheels riding the N rail but when he returns to the main line at Y, his right-hand drivers now find themselves on the S rail instead. He has run into a dead short circuit! And either the circuit breaker will pop or something else will give way. Gapping alone will not get him out of his difficulty for the contigency is physical as well as electrical. In actual fact, the N rail runs into the S rail. What to do?

There is only one thing to do and that is declare the track between X and Y a "turning section," and isolate it from the rest of the trackage as you would a smallpox victim, and feed to it a special type of wiring.

There are certain points to consider here. The turning section must be longer than the longest train you will run through it. Next, you cut gaps in both rails at both ends of the turning section, at X and Y in Fig. 5-9, to isolate it electrically from the rest of your track, which also removes it from the control of your main reversing switch. Then you cut into your power line ahead of the main reversing switch and insert another reversing switch, known as the "aux" (auxiliary) reversing switch and attach the feeders from the center terminals of this switch to the turning section. This gives you independent control of the turning section without regard to the main line.

At this point, you must decide the direction from which you will customarily enter the turning track. In other words, will you usually enter at X or at Y? Of course, with your aux switch you'll be able to enter from either end, but to keep your operation smooth you should designate one end the *normal* entrance and the other the *reverse* entrance. It's much like deciding whether you will usually go into your house by the front door or the back door. The reason for this designation is so that you'll know how to line up the polarity of your turning track with the main line at the point where you enter.

Let us assume, for purposes of illustration, that you decide on X as the normal entry. Then make it clear, to yourself at least, whether you have the S track of your main line lined up with the S track of your turning section. You can do this, perhaps, by the way the handles of your reversing switches are thrown, or, if you want to be fancy and doubly certain, you can put in a couple of indication lamps at X and Y, as I have in Fig. 5-7 F. Use 12- or 18-volt lamps and connect them to the track as shown. If your polarity is lined up properly to receive your train, the yellow, for caution, or green, for go ahead, will light. If the red light goes on instead, throw your aux direction controller the other way, so that the green or yellow light will burn. At the other end of the turning track (at Y) your red light should be on.

Now take your train for a journey around the loop. It will pass point X without a ripple if your polarity is right. When the last car has passed from the main line into the turning section, quickly throw the main-line reversing switch, *not the aux switch,* and your go-ahead light at point Y will come on, indicating that the polarity at the main line at Y is ready to receive your train. Then you continue merrily on your way. To enter the turning track at Y, the reverse entrance, you merely line up your turning-track polarity with the main line at Y, instead of at X, and proceed in the same fashion.

Of course, if you forget to throw your main-line direction controller (reversing switch) when the train is in the turning section, you'll run into a dead short circuit when you attempt to go back on the main line, so don't let some nonrailroading visitor fool with your controls until you are sure he understands the operation of turning tracks. Short circuits are hard on the nerves, not to mention the equipment.

A turning track on a loop such as we have sketched is easy enough to find, but on some involved track plans they are not so obvious. A handy trick to make sure you have no hidden turning tracks is to sketch out your track plan with red and blue pencils. Draw in both rails, using red for the S rail and blue for the N. If you find a red rail runs into a blue rail, you have discovered a hidden turning section, and you must then isolate it. But be sure to make it longer than your longest train, or you'll be inviting trouble.

Westcott in his book on *How to Wire Your Model Railroad,* covers this problem in great detail, whereas I have only space to indicate the principle.

Before we can intelligently approach the problems of track wiring there are some decisions the newcomer to the hobby must make, and some of these may be a bit difficult for the beginner because he hasn't had enough experience to know precisely what he does want or intends to do. One of these decisions is—are you satisfied with running just one train, or do you want to run several at the same time? Parenthetically, I might remark that model railroading, for most of us, is an utterly incurable disease; it won't kill you, of course, but you'll very likely be afflicted with it the rest of your life. And it grows on you—once you get the bug you will probably dream of larger and larger pikes, with a multiplicity of trains weaving back and forth across your empire.

The reason you have to solve the size problem in the beginning is to save useless work and money, for the power source and wiring are relatively simple for one-train operation but grow complex if you hope to acquire more trains. Since we have pretty well covered the subject of one-train operation, let's move along to the control systems for two or more trains.

First, there is the question of power supply. There are three systems in use, known as *Single Power Supply, Twin Power Supply,* and *Multiple Power Supply*.

Taking them in order: the single power supply system was the original system. In using it, you purchase one big power pack with sufficient amperage to cover all the trains you expect to use. This may be the cheapest of the three systems, but it has disadvantages. First, there is the large investment in the beginning for a quality pack, rated well above what you will actually use because, if it isn't top quality, you will have difficulty getting one train to run slowly while another goes at normal speed. Another drawback is that you cannot use common-rail wiring (which I will come to shortly) for two or more trains if you use a single power pack. Common-rail wiring is a distinct advantage due to its simplicity.

Twin power supply is something of a compromise. This method is hooked up so that all eastbound trains operate from one pack, and all westbound trains from the other. You have the same disadvantages as in the single power supply system of running two or more trains from one pack at a time, with the resulting poor regulation, but at least you can use common rail and save on your wiring and switches.

Multiple power supply is the modern system and, if you elect to use it in the future as your pike grows larger, you can save money on your first pack. The basis of this system is that you use one pack for each train on your pike. That may sound formidable at first but, as you are not likely to buy several locomotives at the same time when you begin model railroading, you do not have to buy all your packs at the same time. Just plan to add one small pack for every locomotive you intend to use at a time.

The packs used in multiple power supply do not need to be as large or of as good quality as those used in the other two systems and, while in the long run they will probably cost you more than one big powerful pack, you'll be, in effect, purchasing your power on the installment plan, as you do your locomotives. Since most HO locomotives do not draw more than one amp a one-and-a-half- to two-amp pack will give you all the power you need for this gauge. Inasmuch as each train will operate from its own pack you will have better control and better regulation without the irritating slowing down of one train when another starts up. If you are in S gauge or O gauge you will require a more powerful pack even for multiple power supply. And, of course with multiple power supply, you have the decided advantage of common rail, if you choose to utilize it.

COMMON RAIL

The advantages of common rail are many, such as being able to use sp.st. switches on your control panel instead of the more expensive dp.dt. switches. This is possible because with common rail only the plus power goes through the switch; the minus, or negative, line goes directly to your terminal panel or to your power pack. The difference between no common rail and common rail is illustrated in Fig. 5-10. In A, all the N feeders from each block pass through the necessary dp.dt. switches, while in the common rail, B, it returns directly to your pack. You will also notice that in the lower sketch, B, in Fig. 5-10, there are no gaps shown in the N rail. While it is true, especially in theory, that fewer gaps are necessary with common rail than without it, there are times when you will want gaps in your N rail for operating convenience, if not as an electrical necessity. In any event, please remember what I said before in discussing turning tracks: A turning section must have both its rails, the plus as well as the negative, powered through an aux dp.dt. switch because this stretch of track is electrically isolated from the rest of the trackage.

I employ a sort of compromise method of using common rail. I gap all the trackage as if I wasn't using common rail at all and I attach N feeders to all N rails. But instead of bringing each N feeder back to the control panel and through a dp.dt. switch, I attach them to a special common-rail bus. This bus consists of a stout length of 14-gauge solid copper wire, one end of which is attached to the N lug on my terminal strip behind the control panel, while the rest of this heavy wire is stapled to the underside of my work bench in a circle that goes around the underside of the whole pike. This can be bare wire, if you like, but I prefer to use insulated wire. To this bus I attach all the N feeders so that the current can flow back to the terminal and thence to the power pack. All the S feeders, of course, lead back to the control switches in the main control panel.

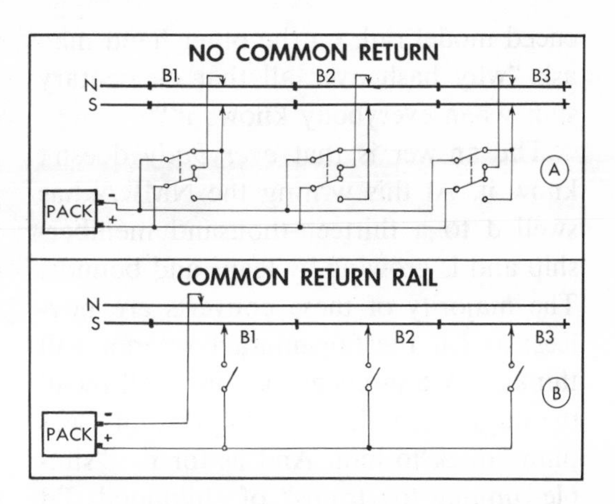

Fig. 5-10 Common Return Rail and No Common Return Rail

This system gives me the advantage of having a good electrical contact on the N rail of each block and doesn't depend on track joiners to carry the power through the whole N rail trackage. It also makes for easier troubleshooting in the not unlikely event of a short circuit somewhere in the line, for I can easily disconnect the N wiring anywhere along the bus. I may have a few more gaps than absolutely essential, but since each block has an N feeder attached as well as an S feeder, it makes no difference in practice. The common-rail system saves on wiring and on trouble, and permits the use of less expensive switches; but it cannot be used on turning sections or on single power supply systems for multitrain operation.

As I reread what I have written so far, I realize I am likely to get two reactions from two different types of readers. The beginner may think that I am making a great to-do about the simple business of running trains around a piece of track, and that when the reader was nine or ten years old he had an electric train set that was easy to work and he didn't have to know an amp from an apple. The experienced model rail, on the other hand may ask "why hash over all that elementary stuff when everybody knows it?"

The answer is that *everybody* doesn't know it. At this writing the NMRA has swelled to a thirteen-thousand membership and is growing by leaps and bounds. The majority of these converts are novices; and if the fair-minded veteran will think back a moment, he may well recall the days when all this "simple stuff" was pure Greek to him. And as for the "simple-running toy trains" of childhood, I'd like to reemphasize that scale model railroading is not "playing with toy trains"; it is an adult hobby for men who like to solve problems and "operate" trains in prototypical fashion.

Since our miniature locomotives are not propelled by steam, and do not have living engineers with years of seniority in the cabs, we have to control these tiny replicas by electricity from a control point outside the cab. Prototypical operation necessitates the ability to run trains to any point on the track where they are needed to do a job, such as spotting a freight car on a siding, a hopper under a coal tipple, or sending a passenger train around the track on schedule. A real railroad keeps many trains going at the same time, in different directions, and at varying speeds. This is when the operation of a pike gets to be real fun.

To accomplish this minor miracle on a model railroad, we must divide our track into "control blocks." Keep in mind that our "control" is electrical, hence to dominate the movements of two or more trains each train must be separated, electrically speaking, from every other train. This is accomplished by blocks.

Fig. 5-11 Elaborating on Simple Layout

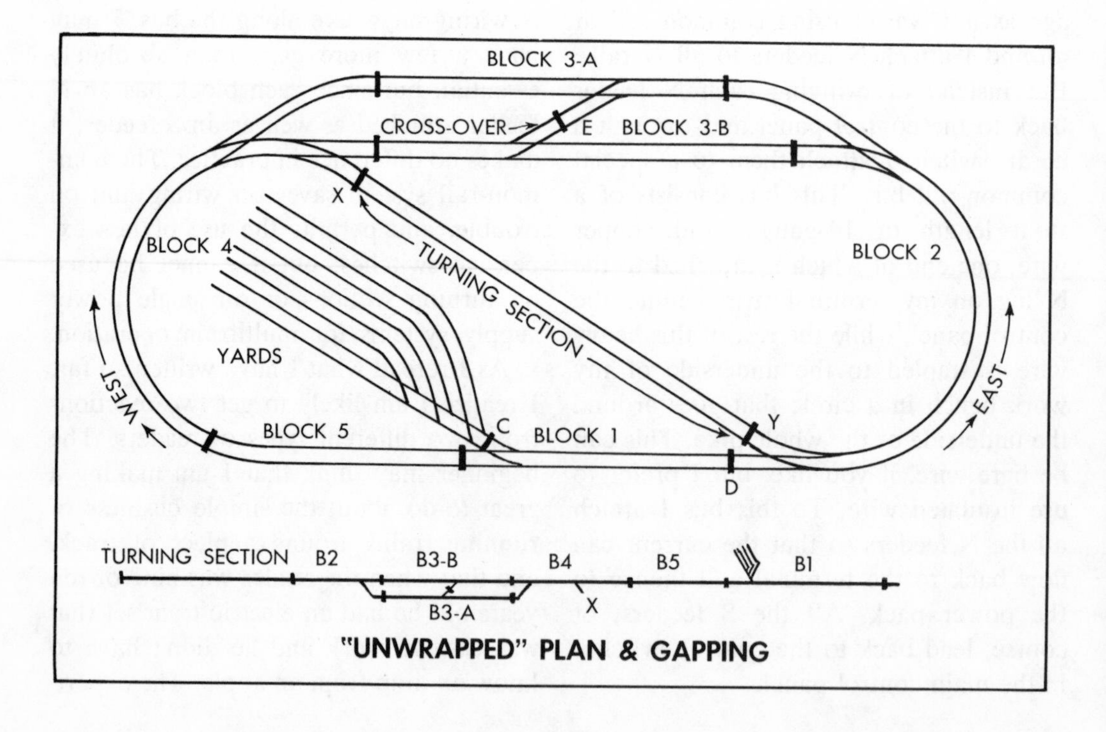

A *block* is simply a segment of track completely isolated, by gaps or insulated track joiners, from every other segment. I showed you a greatly condensed version of blockage in Fig. 5-10A when we were discussing common rail. Of course, in practice, you will want the blocks much longer than indicated in that illustration.

Normally, a block should be longer than a train, although there are exceptions to that generalization in some large layouts where you may need a few very short blocks to facilitate operation.

Let us stick to the simple track plan shown in Fig. 5-9 and block it properly as in Fig. 5-11. Imagine that our train has been made up in the yards, and moves out to Block 1. We cut gaps at C to isolate the yards so that our switcher can make up or break up trains in the yards while other trains operate on the main line. Let me say that, parenthetically, I treated my own yards something in the fashion of a turning section; that is, I gave it a reversing switch of its own, so that one man can operate the yards, while another works the main line. While this is not absolutely necessary, it is a convenience for multitrain operation.

Another set of gaps is made as at D in the sketch, so that the train can stand in Block 1 until the main line is cleared sufficiently for it to move out into Block 2, and start its eastbound journey around the layout. Now it has a choice of two routes; it can either continue on the main line into Block 3B or it can take the branch line and go into the passing siding of Block 3A. Incidentally, by convention the main line of a passing siding is usually designated as B, whereas the siding is termed A. Sometimes, where there are multiple sidings stacked up, the others are designated C, D, etc.

Now if our train takes the A branch, it again has a choice of cutting back onto the main line over the crossover, marked E, or continuing along the siding and joining the main line at point F. In such a short siding, this crossover would be superfluous, but I put it in to illustrate that a crossover must be gapped as at E to keep the current from flowing between the main line and the branch, thus causing a short circuit. Once our train is in Block 4 it can continue around the oval or, if the "engineer" elects, it can back through the turning track to the main line at Block 2, and thus change its direction from eastbound to westbound by throwing the switch in Block 1 so as to continue west into Block 5, Block 4, etc. Thus the "turning section" derives its name.

I trust this illustrates the principle of block control.

The number of blocks on your pike is irrelevant; it depends on the size of your layout and the complexity of your operational plans. My own pike is divided into twenty blocks, while a friend of mine is building a large pike with a hundred and twenty-odd blocks. But the principle is the same whether you have five blocks or two hundred.

Before I attempt to describe the actual wiring for the pike under discussion, let us pause to examine the different accepted methods of electrical control. There are four standard systems in use: plain control, block control (which we have been discussing), section control, and cab control with its various subdivisions.

For lack of space, we'll touch on these just enough to help you decide which one you prefer; if you want more detail, refer to the books at the end of this chapter.

Plain control uses just one controller, as we explained earlier, with just enough gaps behind turnouts, etc. to prevent short circuits. It is not suitable for multitrain operation for the reasons covered earlier.

Block control is the basis of multitrain operation; all other systems are predicated upon it. In it, you gap for operational convenience as well as for electrical necessity, for reasons already explained. It allows you to run several trains at the same time in any direction you choose and at any speed.

Section control is one of the earliest methods of multitrain operation, and is still used by many old-timers in the hobby, though it has been largely superseded by the more modern system of cab control. In using section control, you divide your pike into sections, each having its own separate electrical control, such as a rheostat. A section is not a block; it may include one block or many. Each section is, electrically speaking, a separate railroad. When the train runs from one section to another, it passes on to the control of another rheostat. And herein lies its greatest disadvantage. When the train moves from one controller to the next, a jerk is inevitable, even if the rheostats are set for the same amount of power. But at least this system permitted multitrain operation, which elevated the hobby of model railroading out of the toy train category. Then some genius evolved the system of cab control and this difficulty of jerkiness was negated.

Cab control might be termed the opposite of section control. In section control the operator controls all the trains in his section and then passes them along to the operator in the next section. Cab control permits any operator of a cab to control his train anywhere on the layout that is not being used by another operator at the same moment.

In cab control the operator becomes, in effect, the engineer. As in a real railroad, he can run his train anywhere the dispatcher permits or where the signals are not set against him. Hence, the name "cab" control; theoretically, the operator of a train is "in the cab." Depending on the size and complexity of your railroad, you can have as many cabs as you have trains, each with its own "engineer."

This flexibility of operation is obtained by the manner in which you wire your layout. Before we go into the wiring, let me briefly mention the several subdivisions of cab control.

First, there is the two-cab system, or dual control, which is the the most popular, especially for the main control panel, because it permits two operators to work from the same panel. It has been called the "father-and-son" control because it allows a novice to operate trains if the other operator understands the controls. It is made possible by the use of dp.dt. center-off switches on the control panel, as I shall describe later. Thus by throwing the switch to the left, for example, the left-hand operator powers the block; throwing it the other way gives the power to the right-hand operator.

There are two other types of cab control which deserve mention, although they are both beyond the scope of this book. These two are route cab control and progressive cab control. When I started in the hobby route cab control was just coming into being and because, in theory at least, it is such an improvement over the older systems, I decided to use it on my large pike.

Here is the general idea: Before a train is started you preselect the route it is to take around your trackage. This is done by arranging for route-selector switches which prepare, or line up, the path of the power to the blocks you select. The power is then sent to the proper blocks by a block selector—either a specially contrived rotary switch or a series of push buttons—which you turn or punch as the train passes from block to block. You know when to "step" your power from a series of signal lamps on your control panel which, in turn, is controlled by relays.

Inasmuch as punching push buttons or turning rotary switches is not a true prototypical function, someone carried the idea one step further and devised a method of stepping the power to the blocks by turning a rotary switch with an electric motor. This requires, in addition, a "pilot box" having several relays and a "detection circuit" which watches for trains or other obstructions on the tracks in the blocks ahead of your train.

But these methods require a knowledge and skill beyond the capacity of the average model rail and, hence, have no place in this book even though many such systems are in use around the country, especially by the larger model railroad clubs. I have heard of at least one man who has an electric-eye set across the doorway of his railroad room so that when he enters the room his trains begin to run automatically. But I fail to see the fun in this; it's more of a stunt than an operating convenience.

I mentioned earlier that I had installed route cab control in my own pike. It is an excellent system, especially for a large club, and is almost identical to the one used in the well-known York Model Railroad Club in York, Pennsylvania. However, these larger clubs invariably have several electrical wizards among their members, who are sufficiently skilled to troubleshoot any difficulty which may occur—and believe me, there are many problems that arise in the maintenance of such a system. So at this time I am planning to change back to the less complex dual cab method of control. With two dual cabs, my family of four can operate simultaneously—two operators at each cab. This may seem to be regression, but it will permit my young son and daughter to take part in the operation under the guidance of my wife and myself, without chance of fouling up the whole system.

CONTROL PANELS

Now any of these methods of control require one or more control panels, or "cabs." Building control panels is fun, and there is a great deal of satisfaction in constructing one that is neat looking and efficient. They can be simple or they can be complex; that is for you to decide. A general idea of a control panel is given in Fig. 5-12. It is a recent photograph of my own main panel, propped up vertically so that you can see the arrangements of the controls; normally, it lays at an angle of about 45 degrees from the horizontal.

The only unique feature of this control center is the panel itself. It is made of asbestos Flex-Board, a product of the Johns Mansville Company. Sanded by hand and painted with dull varnish, it has a marbleized appearance that is attractive and, though only an eighth of an inch thick, it is strong and rigid and fully insulated by the material of which it is made; it drills and cuts easily with ordinary tools. I have never known anyone else to utilize this material for a panel.

To explain the controls: If you study the photograph, you will see that the panel is divided by thin lengths of strip

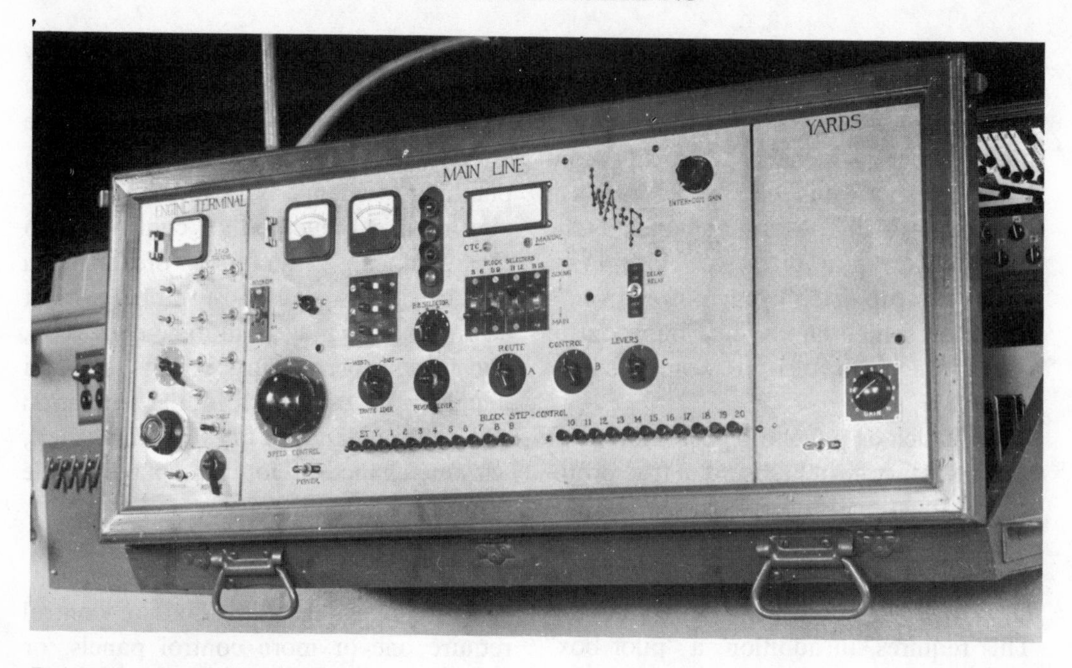

Fig. 5-12 My Own Front Panel

wood into three areas. The division at the far left is for control of the engine terminal, which has its own power pack (not shown) and its own rheostat. At the top of this section is the ammeter with the circuit breaker to the left of it. Below the circuit breaker are two toggles: the uppermost toggle, if thrown to the left, gives control of the engine terminal to its own controller; thrown to the right, it passes the control to the central panel. The lower toggle selects which of the two main tracks of the terminal receive the power; the incoming track or the outgoing track.

To the right of the division are shown eight more toggles arranged in two rows of four each. These control the small blocks of the two tracks. I have divided my terminal tracks into very small blocks, each the length of my largest locomotive. See Fig. 5-13. Thus if I have a locomotive standing on the inspection pit, for example, I can move another locomotive close up behind it without disturbing it.

To the left of the third toggle in Fig. 5-12, you will see an eleven-throw rotary switch. This is to select which of the roundhouse stalls or waiting track an engine on the turntable can take. Under it and to the left is a red indication light (shown as a black dot in the photograph) which tells me whether the power pack is on or off. Below it is the rheostat, or throttle, as we usually term it, for setting the locomotives into motion. To the right of the throttle is a double-throw, spring-return switch which rotates the turntable. I use a spring-return switch for this job so that I can line up the tracks easily by sight. Below the rheostat is an on-and-off toggle which cuts off or turns on the power pack; also at the same time it controls the indication light. The rotary switch to the right of this toggle is the cab-reversing switch, which controls the direction of the locomotives in the terminal.

As I remarked earlier, a layout is never

finished, and this panel is no exception, hence the subdivision to the far right is blank, except for its throttle. Eventually it will have toggles and other switches for control of the yards.

Breaking down the central portion of the panel, from left to right across the top, we have the circuit breaker, the ammeter, the voltmeter, and the indication lights of the detection circuit, for this is a route-control system, as I said before. To the right of the voltmeter is a blank "instruction" card, intended originally to assist new operators in the use of the panel. Next to it you will see the initials WA&P (for White Anchors & Potomac, the official name of my pike). These initials are drilled with many fine holes and serve to camouflage the radio speaker behind it, for I have an intercom system installed between my two main cabs so that I do not have to bellow at the operator controlling the second cab. The mouthpiece of this intercom system is shown at the end of the curved pipe which arcs above the panel and is separate from it. The dial for controlling the volume of the speaker is shown to the right of the initials.

In the second row of controls in this division, starting again at the left, the white-handled key turns the intercom on or off. The rotary switch next to it is an extra double-throw rotary I put in for future use; it serves no purpose at the moment. To the right are three aux (or auxilliary) telephone-type switch keys for controlling my three turning tracks. Directly below the indicating lamps is a four-pole block selector for switching power to whichever of the four siding tracks of Block 2 I may choose. To its right are four switch keys for the other four sidings on the main line; they are double-throw, center-off telephone-type

Fig. 5-13 My Engine Terminal Wiring Diagram

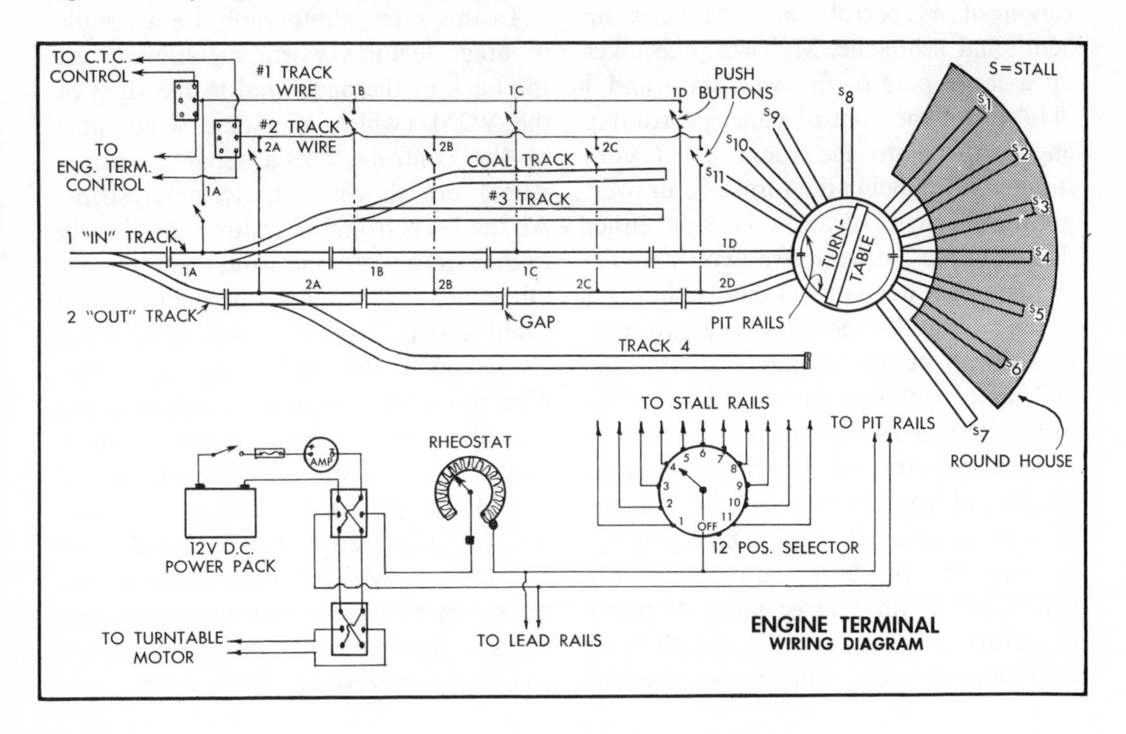

switch keys. The remaining toggle in this row controls the delay relay which I use for double-heading locomotives on the steeper grades.

The large knob to the left in the third row is the main-line throttle, a variable transformer known as a Powerstat; this is my main throttle. To the right of it is a double-throw rotary switch, known as the traffic lever, which controls the direction of traffic on the whole pike. The next is a reversing lever for controlling the direction in the particular block I am operating in. The remaining three rotaries are route-control levers for prechoosing what route I will take around the pike.

Below the main throttle is the on-off power switch, while the twenty buttons beyond it are the push buttons for stepping the power from block to block.

So much for the controls. One of the problems of any model railroad is that of space. Usually, a model rail fills all available space with the pike itself, so that location of a control panel becomes an additional headache. My own pike takes up a large part of my workshop and I didn't want the control panel protruding any further into the room. So I constructed my panel in the form of a drawer, putting a length of angle iron on either side that slides between two two-by-four's, so that when not in use I can push it out of the way under the pike. The two handles shown below the panel are for the purpose of pulling it out when I am ready to use it. This is a great convenience.

As to size, this will depend entirely on the size of your layout and the number of controls you will need. Once you figure this out, the best method is to lay your controls on a large piece of paper or cardboard and make a template of your panel before you begin construction. It might be wise to make it a trifle larger than you think you'll actually need because you may later decide on some refinements which will necessitate additional switches.

My panel is on the large side. It measures 42″ x 17″ on the face, and protrudes into the room about 15″. It hinges at the bottom so that it can be opened readily, permitting work to be done on the inside. This is illustrated in Fig. 5-14. I made a stand out of a piece of two-by-six, notched to carry the weight of the panel, which is considerable, and padded to protect the finish. Shown are my ten-year-old son and myself testing a circuit with a VOM (volt/ohm meter) a handy gadget to have around a pike. Parenthetically, it is amazing how much information a child of this age can pick up if you let him assist you in the intricacies of your electrical circuits. My boy picked up enough to wire his own 4′ x 8′ pike which he is building in his room.

In this same photograph are a couple of other features worth mentioning. At the back of the panel and to the right of the VOM (which of course is not part of the controls, but a separate instrument) are shown eight terminal strips. All the leads from the controls go directly to these terminals, and from them to eight other identical terminals permanently located under the pike, which in turn are connected to the track. The reason behind this double terminal business is the ease of tracing troubles. I grant that most model railroads use only the one set of terminal strips, but I prefer to have two sets, for in the event that I should want to move the whole control panel to the work bench, I can easily disconnect the wires at the first bank of terminal strips, and as easily reconnect them later.

Fig. 5-14 Two Figures at Open Panel

Directly above the control panel is another dual-purpose panel. See Fig. 5-15. The upper half of this second panel contains my track diagram, showing sidings, yards (to the far right), and engine-terminal tracks. Each of the turnouts in this board bears a number, as do each of the twenty-odd blocks of the main line. This makes for greater ease in operating —with so many turnouts it is easy to for-

Fig. 5-15 Diagram Panel and Air Valves

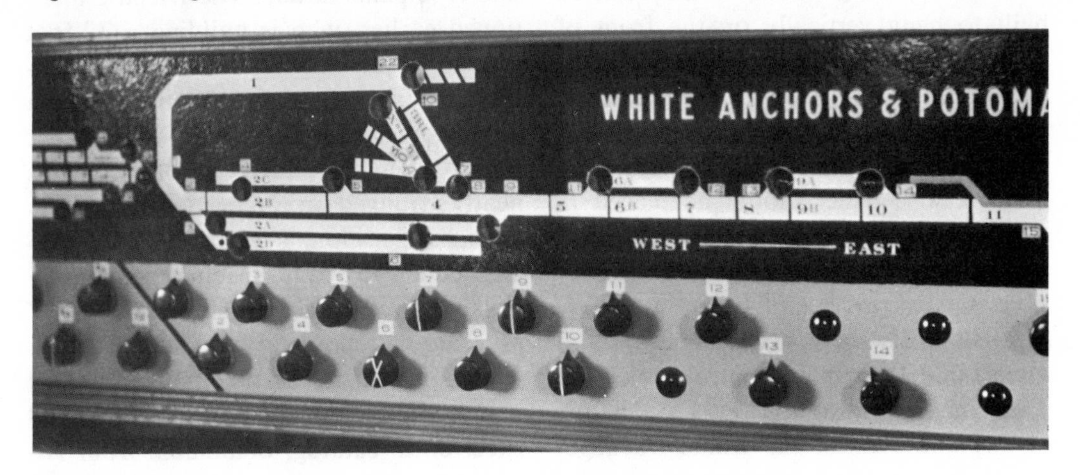

get their numbers unless you run the trains constantly. The double row of controls shown below the diagram board are the air valves for controlling the turnouts. Most model rails use electrical switch machines for operating their turnouts, but I prefer switch machines operated by compressed air. We'll go into the question of operating turnouts later in the book.

Now back to control panels in general. Inasmuch as your control panel is the nerve center of your pike, the time spent on its construction and arrangement is worthwhile. There are no standardized rules, save those of logic, simplicity, and ease of operation. To my knowledge, there are no commercial control panels available, except the simplest possible which sometimes are built into the face of a power pack; a practical control panel has to be tailored to suit your individual pike.

They can be built vertically, horizontally, or at any angle between the two extremes. I have found a 45-degree angle to be to my liking, although my small trolley panel, and my projected narrow gauge panel, will both be vertical for practical reasons of space. They can be built in the style of a drawer, as I have done on my main panel, or they can be built to hang vertically on the front of your pike, or they can be horizontal.

Without being actual rules, there are a few practical suggestions which should be considered. One is the location. The main control panel should be placed in such a position as to give you a good overall view of the whole layout, if possible. Club layouts and other large layouts with lots of space and headroom often build their main control panels on a balcony, affording the operators a sort of airplane view of the whole trackage. Small specialized panels, such as those controlling terminals and yard, or complicated switching sidings, are best placed as near as possible to the point of operation, so that if any handling of the equipment is necessary (and it often is) the operator can reach the car or locomotive without leaving his panel.

Another consideration is one of height. If you plan to sit down at your control panel, you must build it with enough clearance to slide your legs underneath when you sit on a bench or chair. If you prefer to stand up to operate, as I do, tailor the height of your panel so that your hands reach the controls comfortably. This will depend upon your own height. About 32″ from the floor to the lowest portion of a panel is about right for me, but I'm a trifle on the stocky side. Just make sure that the top of your panel doesn't block your view of the track.

Some model rails build a recess into the front of their pike to house the main control panel so as not to block the aisles in front. Others build their panels on a table, with casters to slide it under the pike when not in use. For a very large pike with a multiplicity of controls a console-type panel is fine. The friend I mentioned earlier, who is building a 72-foot layout, is planning a console-type control unit shaped in a half-circle, like a large concert organ, which will permit him to sit in the middle with his controls neatly arranged on three sides of him. As a final suggestion, I repeat: Fit the control panel to your specific needs. An organ-type console panel on a 4′ x 8′ plywood flattop would be ridiculous.

A great aid to the planning of control panels and electrical circuits is the Allied Electronics catalog, obtainable from Allied Radio, 100 N. Western Avenue, Chicago 80, Illinois. It is a mine of information for studying the plan of panels; although they do not have any model railroad panels, they illustrate other types of control equipment which may give you many ideas. They also show an infinite number of electrical components, such as various types of switches, relays and meters, which they offer at very reasonable prices. It's a wonderful "wish book" to thumb through.

As for the materials best suited to a panel, wood is preferred for the box or frame. It is the easiest material to work and maintain. For the face of the panel, you have a wider choice. Plywood is cheap, but hard to smooth to a fine surface. Many modelers use tempered Masonite, in either 1/8″ or 3/16″ thickness. Masonite does not splinter as does plywood and gives a smooth finish. If you want to be very fancy, hard rubber makes a beautiful surface but is more costly. I prefer the asbestos Flex-Board because of its sturdiness and light color, which makes it easier to see the controls at a glance.

Many model rails put the diagram of their trackage on the main control panel and put the switches on the exact place they control. This is great for beginners or operators strange to the particular layout, but once you get used to the control system the straight-line method of lining up your controls is to be preferred. You can then set a diagram board above your panel, as I have done, or you can build a larger one and hang it on the wall nearby for easy reference.

The easiest way to make a diagram board, whether on your panel or elsewhere, is to draw it out in detail on a full-sized sheet of paper and use this as a template to transfer it to the face of your panel. Before you transfer this to your panel, paint or spray the entire panel the color you want the diagram. Yellow is beautiful, but use any color you prefer. When this color dries, transfer the design of your template onto the panel. Then take strips of masking tape of a width you prefer—I used 1/4″ for the main-line trackage and 1/8″ for sidings—arrange this as neatly as you can and, if you want to distinguish your blocks easily, take a razor blade or modeling knife and cut out a 1/16″ space where you have your block gaps on your actual trackage. Do not attempt to make your diagram to scale. It is only a schematic representation, not a working plan. Your blocks need be only long enough to take the necessary control toggles, if you choose to insert them in the diagram. I use my diagram for reference only.

When you are satisfied with the taped layout, press the tape tight at the ends and edges so paint cannot flow under it, then spray or paint the whole panel, tape and all, with whatever background color you have decided upon. Dull black is excellent, or a dark green or blue. When the paint is dry, carefully remove the masking tape and you will have your track diagram clearly outlined. Now drill the holes for your toggles or indication lights, and you are in business.

WIRING YOUR PIKE

Because of the exigencies of space, a track plan is usually a circle, an oval, or a series of ovals, loops, and tangents. For reasons of clarity, it is often advisable to "unwrap" your plan and stretch it into a comparatively straight line, especially in a wiring diagram. Let us first unwrap the layout shown in Fig. 5-11. We will cut it at point D and again at point X, at the north end of the turning section, unfolding it in a clockwise direction until it stretches into a flat line, at bottom of Fig. 5-11. Now we can visualize clearly where our feeder lines will run. You may prefer to arrange your diagram board in this fashion, as I did in the one shown in Fig. 5-15, although I left my return loops in their original shape to save space. There is no standard way of unwrapping—do it to suit yourself.

Let us assume you have decided to use common-rail wiring and a dual cab type of control for two trains, which necessitates two power packs. You can use sp. st. center-off switches if you prefer, but I'd recommend dp.dt. center-off switches so that later, when you want to "pretty up" your panel, you can insert indication lights to show you whether the blocks are powered or not. A double-pole switch, as you know, is one that handles two separate circuits, and the same physical motion on your part turns on the indication lights from your accessory circuit at the same time as it powers your block.

In Fig. 5-16 I elected to draw a pictorial, rather than a schematic, plan because I felt it would be more comprehensible to the novice, who has not yet learned to read the symbols used in schematic diagrams, which, to the veteran model rail, are actually much simpler because they do not have the "rat's nest" tangle of wires, as we have here.

When it comes to the actual running of the wires, the man with experience will doubtless elect to do his wiring in bunches, that is, he will probably run all his leads from the track to the terminal strip and then hook up all his switches at the same time. The novice can do this, too, if he is very careful, but the safest

Fig. 5-16 Dual Wiring Diagram

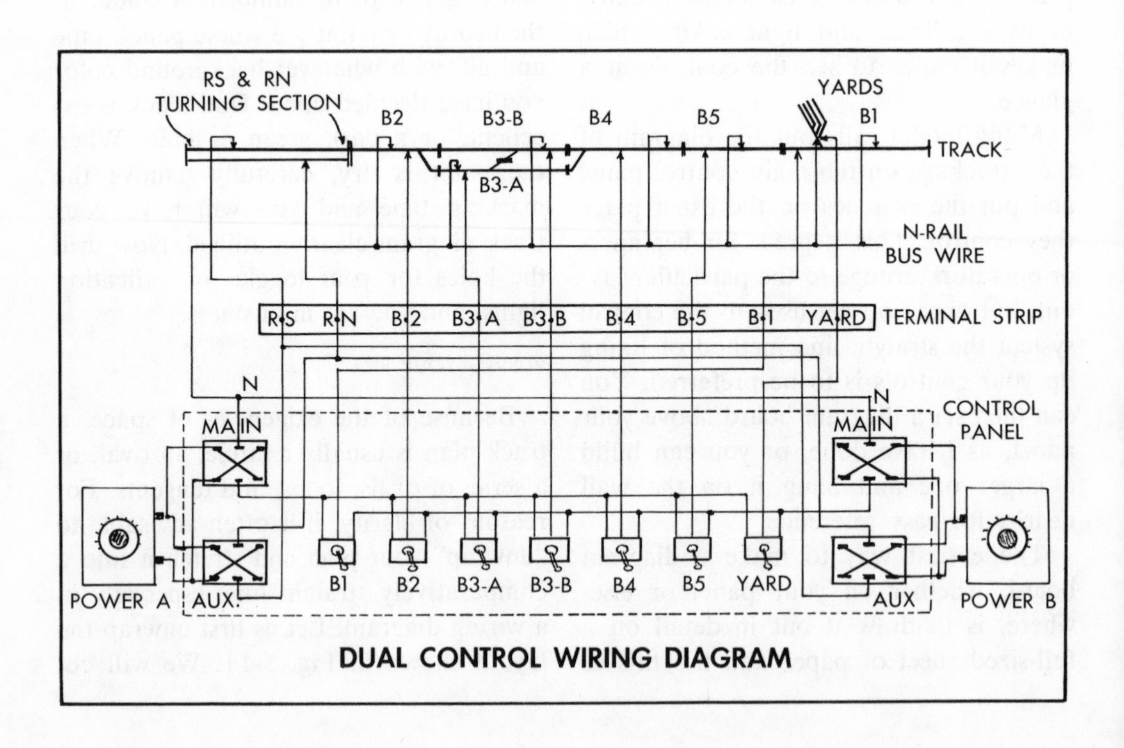

course for the beginner is to link up one block at a time.

If you do not have a VOM handy, it might be well at this point to pause and make yourself a test light, as shown in Fig. 5-17. A Christmas-tree lamp is ideal, for most of them have 12-volt bulbs. Be sure it is 12 volts or it will not work. Put alligator clips on the wire leads and snap them onto both rails, as illustrated. Then as you wire each block and toggle, turn the power on, and if your wiring is correct, the bulb will light. You will also have plenty of use for this little gadget later in your maintenance.

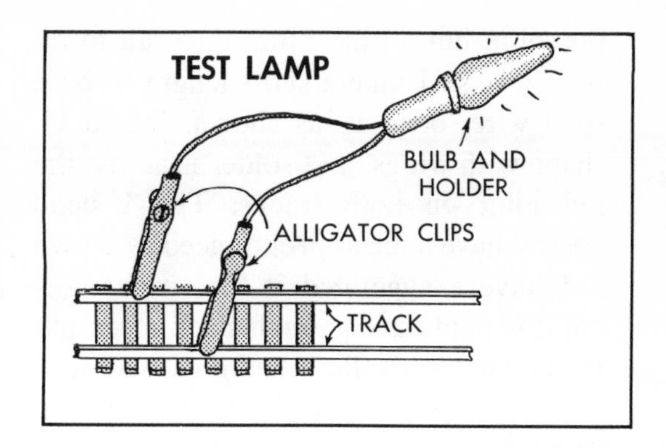

Fig. 5-17 Homemade Test Lamp

Stranded 18-gauge hookup wire is about right for pike wiring. It is more flexible than solid wire and easier to cable into bundles for neatness. Some modelers prefer a lighter gauge, say 22, but 18 gauge is safer and about standard for pike work. Plastic-covered wire is preferable because it is easier to strip when making connections, such as at terminal strips, switches, and at the track. Bare it for about three quarters of an inch when making connections; if that proves too much, you can always clip off the surplus wire. Hookup wire can be obtained at your hobby shop or at a radio-supply house, and comes in a great variety of colors for coding. You can use a different color for each lead, if you like; it makes it easier to keep your wiring straight. I use a dark wire for the S lead and a white or other light-colored wire for my N leads. Another good suggestion is to tie small price tags, such as are used in stores, to the wires under your pike so that if you have any troubleshooting to do later, you can tell at a glance which wire is which, such as Block 4 or R N, etc. This suggestion may save you a lot of trouble later.

In connecting your leads to the track it is best to solder them firmly. Do not be afraid of soldering; you will need to know how to solder for many things you will want to build later on. We will discuss simple soldering further along in this book, so for the moment we'll get along with our wiring. However, if you are determined you do not want to solder, you can obtain commercial clips for joining your leads to the rails at your hobby shop.

If you will turn back to Fig. 5-8, part F will show you how to bend the bared end of your wire into an inverted L-shape and attach it to your track with solder. Many modelers, including myself, prefer to use a piece of solid wire at this juncture. Cut the solid wire about 8″ long (the length is not critical) bare both ends, and attach one end to your rail, then lead it through a small hole in your pike to the underside. Wrap it securely around a screw or a nail, then solder the other end to the stranded wire leading back to your terminal strip. This makes a firm connection. Wrap this latter joint with a piece of insulating tape so you don't have a short circuit if another wire should inadvertently cross it at this point.

Item E in this same drawing illustrates a good way of insuring contact between nongapped rail joints. Patent rail joiners are supposed to carry the current through the joint, but all too often they fail to do their job, so I take a short length of bare solid wire, bend it, as shown, into a U-shape with wings, and solder it across the rail joint on both tracks. The U-bend doesn't have to be as pronounced as shown —I have exaggerated it for emphasis— but it should have enough slack to permit the inevitable swelling and contraction of the rails which are usually caused by heat or cold.

As most toggles and other switches have soldering lugs on them, if you won't solder, you'll have to obtain special switches with wrap-around screw terminals. Don't forget this when you go to purchase your switches.

Let us work from left to right on our pike plan in Fig. 5-16. Attach your terminal strip in some convenient location, preferably on the back of your control panel, and then drill holes and install your main and auxiliary switches. Secure your RS lead to one rail of your turning section, it doesn't make too much difference which one, except as to which direction you want the handle to point, because as I said before, there is no definite south or north rail on a turning section. Run these leads to your direction-controller switches via the terminal strip. Attach your "trouble light" to both the turning section rails, and turn on your power pack. If the lamp lights you have done a perfect job, so proceed to wire up your block switches in the same manner, tracing out the wires in the illustration carefully so that you get the right lead to the proper rail. Check each block for power with the trouble light and you can't very well go wrong.

When all is complete, make sure that when you throw your switches toward the left, the left-hand pack is dispensing the power, and when you throw them to the right, that the power comes from the right-hand pack. If your hookup works the opposite way, reverse the leads at the switches so that they work properly. Do not be discouraged if you make such a mistake; wiring a pike is largely a matter of trial and error, and the most experienced modelers often make the most obvious errors in their wiring. Patience is the cardinal virtue in this hobby.

For the sake of neatness and ease in troubleshooting, it is wise to leave enough slack in your track leads so that you can run a number of them side by side and wrap them with string, or tape, into neat "cables" as experts do—then you won't have a tangle of individual wires running helter-skelter under your pike like the proverbial rat's nest. You can secure these cables to the joists of your framing with hooks or insulated staples. It usually takes a beginner some time before he learns the value of such neatness.

If you do not care for dual control, or indication lights, but prefer to operate just one train at a time for your own amusement, you can substitute st.sp. switches for the dt.dp. switches I have indicated. In such a case, just leave out the second set of main and aux reversing switches and ignore all the wiring presently shown leading from the second power pack. As the st.sp. switches will have only two contacts instead of three, you won't have any difficulty. Otherwise your wiring remains the same. By the same token, if you have more blocks than we have shown in Fig. 5-11, simply add as many additional switches as you have extra blocks. The principle remains the same.

Some readers may wonder why I have used only one toggle to handle all the tracks in the yard. The explanation is that, if you use selective control turnouts for the stub tracks of the yard—which require no gapping—the points of the turnouts will automatically power the branch you chose by throwing your turnout.

ELECTRIC MOTORS

The tiny electric motors used in your scale model locomotives put the "go" into your trains: they are the guts and the muscles of your locomotives. And they are a special breed of cat, being a permanent magnet type which, unlike most household motors, run on direct current and not alternating current. They not only have to be very powerful, but also very small to fit into the confined space allotted them in a miniature locomotive. As the best-known brand of these is manufactured by the Pittman Electrical Developments Company I asked my friend Charles Pittman for photographs of his most popular motors. They are shown in Figs. 5-18 and 5-19. The former is the famous DC 60, for small HO locomotives and trolleys, etc., which develops .0019 horsepower and is only 1⅞″ long, ¾″ wide, and ⅞″ high. Shown in Fig. 5-20 is the DC 71B, a heavy duty HO motor for larger locomotives. It develops .004 horsepower and measures 2⅛″ x 11⁄16″ x 1 1⁄16″.

The technical data Mr. Pittman supplied in his accompanying letter is so concise and to the point that I am quoting him verbatim:

"Direct current, permanent magnet-field motors have been used for HO locomotives ever since the infancy of the hobby in this country during the early 1930s. Motors like those used in England were designed for optimum output at 6 volts, d.c., until the Second World War. After the war, the NMRA standardized 12 volts, d.c., and all motors produced in this country have been so designed in

Fig. 5-18 D.C. 60 Motor

recent years. The British, in general, operate HO locomotives at 12 volts, although many European modelers use motors designed for 20 volts.

"The advantages of permanent magnet-field motors are less heating, higher efficiency, simplicity of reversal (by reversing armature current polarity), and frequently smaller or more convenient size for the same output by comparison with a.c.-d.c. universal motors. Polarity reversal of permanent magnet-field motors makes possible realistic directional control of locomotives operating on the two-rail track so popular everywhere today.

"Motors for model railroad use range from a size suitable for TT gauge all the way up to a motor capable of powering the largest O gauge locomotive."

Fig. 5-19 D.C. 71B Motor

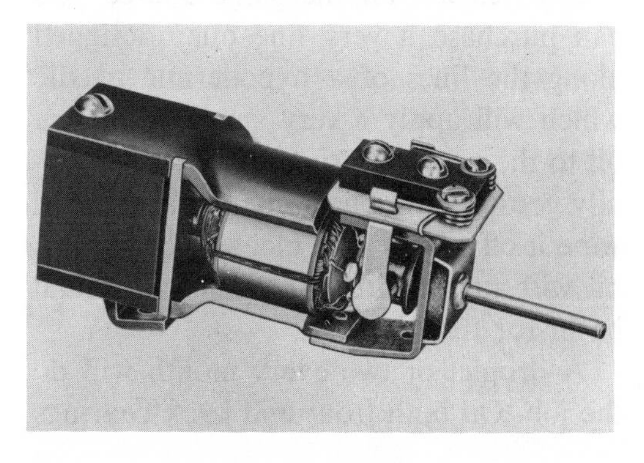

As these tiny electric motors are about as close to perfection as any man-made piece of machinery can be, the problems of maintenance and repair are, relatively speaking, negligible. The principle job is to keep them clean and properly oiled.

Dust and dirt are the nemesis of all scale model railroad motive and rolling stock, and have to be combated everlastingly. The combination will gum up your track, the treads of your rolling-stock wheels, and get into your motors. Among your arsensal of weapons in this war should be a bottle of good cleaning fluid. Carbon tetrachloride is an old favorite but lately science has discovered that under certain circumstances "carbon tet" can be a deadly killer, so I would not recommend it for the novice. But your hobby shops have special (and safe) liquids compounded especially for model use.

Ordinary pipe cleaners are a great boon for cleaning rolling stock and locomotives because the fine stems will reach into out-of-the-way places impossible to get to with a piece of rag.

Oil can do more harm than good if you use it too lavishly. A good rule of thumb is that if you can see where you have already oiled, you have used too much. Do not use the ordinary dime-store "household" oil; use only a good grade of clock oil, usually sold at your hobby dealers. At the same source you can purchase a very fine oiler designed along the lines of a hypodermic needle which will apply a very small droplet of oil to the necessary spot. If you accidentally get more oil on the part than needed wipe it off with a pipe cleaner for surplus oil will attract dirt and grime and you'll be in for trouble.

A droplet or two every month will do the job. Oil both front and back bearings of your motor; get them *both* because if one bearing goes, your motor will be as bad off as if both bearings go—and that means a return to the factory, or at worst, a new motor. But whatever you do, *do not* get any oil on the *other* parts of the motor!

During these periodical cleaning sessions, examine the motor's permanent magnet for any fragments of metal that it may have picked up during its journeys around your track.

Permanent magnets have an annoying habit of picking up loose spikes and other debris which can ruin your commutator, the small drumlike part that revolves. This commutator is made up of small copper segments against which the motor brushes contact and must always be kept clean and shiny for good conductivity. You can brighten this commutator with a thin piece of very fine sandpaper (never use emery cloth). If more serious trouble develops, return your motor to the manufacturer for repair, or replace it. Never attempt to take it apart or to remove the armature from its field; you may destroy the power of the magnet. Some experts can accomplish this by putting a *keeper,* an iron slug, across the magnet, but the amateur had better not try this.

So to sum up: Keep the motor bearings oiled, keep the armature clean, and brushes in good contact, and the motor may well last the life of your locomotive. The same remarks go for trolleys and diesels or any other equipment you may have that uses permanent magnet motors.

ENGINE TERMINALS AND FREIGHT YARDS

Engine terminals and freight yards present what might be termed opposing problems, electrically speaking. In the former, practically every piece of equipment is motive power, and unless special wiring is installed, when you put power to the tracks, all your equipment will move simultaneously. On the contrary, since your frieght yards are for storing cars (without motors in them) you can turn the power on full blast and nothing will move, unless you have a switcher in the yards.

A track plan and a wiring diagram of my own engine terminal are shown in Fig. 5-13. Study it carefully, so that you get the general idea of how it functions. Track #1 is the "in" track and incoming locomotives enter the terminal from a turnout on the main line to the left of the drawing. On the "in" track they are inspected and fueled and either put in the roundhouse or turned on the table and headed out on the #2 track, ready to take the road again.

Now, inasmuch as we do not want to limit these busy and important tracks to just one locomotive at a time, I have divided—by gapping—these two tracks into four small blocks each. Each block is the length of my largest locomotive. Thus a locomotive can stand quietly on, say, Block C of the #1 track while a second locomotive can roll up over the inspection pit (not shown) in Block 1-B, and so on. The toggles to control each block are shown at the top of the drawing in the track-wire circuit. These toggles will, of course, be on your control panel, not in the terminal itself. Because a visitor once flipped the wrong toggle and plunged a Mikado into the turntable pit, I took out the toggles operating blocks 1-D and 2-D and installed push buttons instead. Thus, to move a locomotive on these two blocks, the operator has to hold down the push-button. We haven't had an accident since these were installed.

In the upper left-hand corner of the sketch you will see two dp.dt. switches, marked "To C.T.C. Control" and "To Eng. Term. Control." This is a convenience for one-man operation. If I am alone, or without an operator for the engine terminal, I flip the toggles so that the power comes from the central control panel, and run the road engines into the terminal. On the other hand, if I have a "hostler" on the job to handle the engine terminal, I flip the toggles over to the engine terminal control cab and he's in charge.

The other three tracks draw their power through the turnouts leading off both #1 and #2 tracks. The coal track leads to the terminal powerhouse and is used exclusively for delivering coal hoppers to the power plant. Track #3 is where the "big hook," the heavy crane, is stored, ready for instant use. Track #4 is for storing work cars, snowplows, and other emergency equipment.

The "S" or "stall" tracks are self-evident. From numbers 7 to 11 are storage tracks for equipment that has been worked on or is to be worked on when its turn comes to enter one of the roundhouse stalls.

The wiring diagram on the lower half of the sketch indicates the routing of power to these stalls. Obviously, to have separate control of the engine terminal it must have its own power pack or source. Below the ammeter you will see two reversing switches. The upper one is the main reversing switch for the whole trackage; the lower one is for reversing the turntable only. Since my turntable is not automatic—that is, it doesn't automatically line up the turntable and the tracks—I have to do the lining up by eye. This proved impractical with an ordinary toggle, so I installed a type of switch known as a "spring return"; that is, you have to hold the handle of the toggle the way you throw it, like a push button. By this means I get a very sensitive control and can stop the table instantly be releasing the handle.

The clocklike switch to the right of center is merely a 12-position rotary selector switch. You "select" in advance the stall track you desire, then turn the switch to the "S" number you want and the power is guided by the switch to that particular stall, leaving all the others "dead."

At first it may appear like a complicated setup, but if you follow the wires through, you see that it is actually quite simple, and a great convenience in operation.

A plan of the WA&P freight yards is shown in Fig. 5-20. Track #1 is where a train is "made up"; i.e. the freight cars are shifted to this track in the order designated by the yardmaster and, when ready, a road engine is backed up to the string and the train goes off about its business. Tracks #2 and 3 are for through freights, that is, trains going off-stage, ostensibly to other cities or other lines. Tracks #4 and 5 are for the local way freights, whether eastbound or westbound. Track #6 is for storing the cabooses, the "offices" of the trains. The caboose track is usually close to the yardmaster's office for the convenience of the conductors and the crews.

As not all industries in a community have private sidings, railroads have what are known as "team tracks" where a consignee can pick up his freight with a truck or whatever means he has available. The crossover shown between tracks #6 and 7 is for the convenience of the yard shifter or yard locomotive.

The simplest—though not necessarily the best—method of powering all these tracks is through the turnouts. The power-feeder connections are shown in the upper right-hand corner of the drawing. Instead of having a complexity of toggles, the turnouts pick up the power from the lead tracks, and inasmuch as each track is a spur, that is, it doesn't connect with any other track at the end away from the turnouts, you will not have a short circuit.

However, you will have to keep the points of your turnouts clean in order to conduct electricity, hence many model rails prefer to cut a gap behind each turnout and install a separate toggle switch for each track. You can achieve an even

Fig. 5-20 WA&P Freight Yards

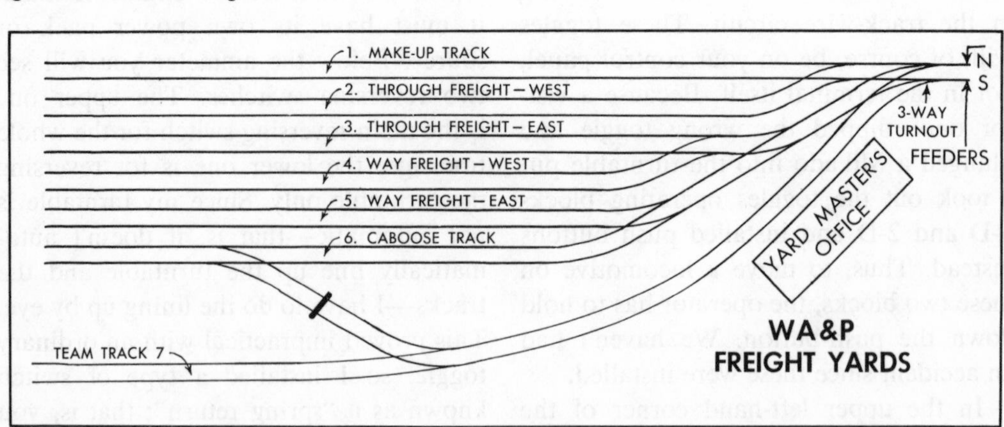

better conductivity by putting in electric power routing by special contacts operated by the throw bar of your turnouts.

CONTROL OF TURNOUTS

While some model rails control their turnouts by automobile choke wires and/or fishline, the great majority use electrical switch machines, which operate like a solenoid. A few others, including myself, use switch machines operated by compressed air.

There are a considerable number of electrical switch machines on the market, and if you have found a reliable and experienced hobby dealer, I'd recommend that you take his advice on the best machine for your purpose. In selecting the best machine, try to obtain one having a lot of extra electrical contacts built into it, so that you can control indication lights on your panel—to indicate which way the turnout is thrown—and for routing power to the track you select without having to depend entirely on the turnout points to do the job.

You must also decide at this point whether you want to install the machine on top of your pike or below it. A great many modelers do put their machines out of sight below the pike and control and the throw of the runout by means of spring wire. Whichever switch machine you select will have complete instructions for installation and as there are so many different systems in use we cannot hope to cover them in this book.

After your dealer has shown you a switch machine which seems to fit your purpose, buy *one,* and try it out before you invest in all you may need. Test it on your own pike, and when you are completely satisfied, then get the others. It might be a good idea to buy two or three different machines and test them. Any standard switch machine will work, but some may work better than others.

Since switch machines draw a lot of amperage to do their job, they would soon burn out if a regular toggle switch was used for control, so the usual method of safeguarding against this expensive mishap is to use a momentary switch, such as a doorbell-type push button or a spring-return toggle. The Walthers Company makes a special key-type switch for this purpose. Ask your dealer to show you the various types of switches he stocks for this purpose.

Air-switch machines are now manufactured by Carnel Products Co., 311 Cindy Lane, Wheeling, Illinois. They are easy to install on the tabletop, give a good, positive action, and require little maintenance. These machines require either an air compressor or a tank of carbon dioxide or its equivalent. They have much more power than an electric switch machine of comparable size, but inasmuch as they are nonelectrical, you have to use contacts operated by the throwbar of your turnout to work indication lights and other electrical devices. If you are interested you can write to the Carnel Company for literature on these machines. I am very pleased with mine.

Before leaving the subject of turnouts, let me warn you that if you expect your turnout points to carry the electric circuit, you have to keep the points clean and the contacts perfect. A few pipe cleaners and a bottle of track cleaner will simplify this job.

BIBLIOGRAPHY

How to Wire Your Model Railroad, by Linn Westcott. Pub. by Kalmbach.

Electrical Handbook for Model Railroaders, by Paul Mallery, Pub. by Simmon-Boardman.

CHAPTER 6

Scenery

A pike without scenery is comparable to the skeleton of a woman without flesh. While a professional anatomist might find such a skeleton interesting, most of us prefer our women with a little meat on their bones. Not too much, mind you, but enough to fill in the curves and lend beauty and reality to the structure.

Because scenery is not a standardized product that you can buy *in toto,* it is surprising the number of model rails who shy away from it. I have seen huge layouts, filling an entire basement, that consisted of nothing but bare track and raw roadbed. These modelers claim that creating scenery is an art, and that they are not artists.

Well, scenicking a pike *is* an art, but not a difficult one; it is far simpler than, for instance, superdetailing a locomotive. It is one of the most interesting facets of the hobby; it is truly scale modeling at its best. It is the one thing that lends absolute individuality to your layout; the one aspect that makes your pike different from any other in the country. For even if two modelers work from the same general design, the workmanship will be different and so will the result.

And perhaps best of all, it is the cheapest phase of the hobby, because most of the material used in scenicking can come from your scrap pile and no special tools are required. Some old window screening or hardware cloth, some odds and ends of lumber, and a little cement or plaster, plus some ingenuity, are about all you need.

The one essential is wrapped up in a single word—*consistency*. To develop consistency, you must first consider the imaginary locale your pike is presumed to represent. An eastern railroad doesn't pass through a desert nor does the Santa Fe run into Grand Central Station in New York City. This may sound obvious and facetious, but many modelers make such unrealistic boners.

In the preparatory stage, one of the best methods is to collect a lot of good clear photographs, preferably in color, of the terrain you hope to duplicate. You do not have to copy these, but they will help to keep you consistent; they'll serve as a guide. Remember your main objective is to create a world in miniature, but don't make the mistake of trying to include the *whole* world.

Remember, too, that scenery is an illusion; it doesn't have to *be* real, it must *look* real, like the background in a well-designed play. Scenery has the effect of making your layout seem much larger than it actually is. A tiny train disappearing into a miniature tunnel seems to be gone a long, long time. Of course, we all know that a mountain chain often runs for hundreds of miles, so you cannot create a mountain to actual scale, but a model mountain towering, say, three feet about your imaginary "set level" will give the illusion of immensity, and a rolling terrain on your pike will add greatly to its apparent dimensions.

Another trick to this scenery business is diversity. Break it up! Have mountains if they fit into your locale, but also have roads and villages and rivers. Rivers call for bridges (which we will discuss in another chapter) and bridges add color and interest to any layout. Don't forget that with relatively rare exceptions, there are few perfectly flat spaces in nature. Railroad yards and engine terminals may be flat, but we can safely assume that they were bulldozed to that condition before they were built.

A word of caution: In real life the ravines and mountains and rivers were created long before the railroads came into being. Tunnels had to be burrowed through those mountains at the most logical places, and when cuts were made both sides of the cut were usually left standing. As it is not feasible to put in your scenery before you have a good, well-tested roadbed secured, you have to reverse this process of nature and build your scenery after the track is down. Nevertheless, it is essential, in the finished product, to make it *look* as if the mountains and river were there first. If you are blessed with the type of mind that can plan details in advance, it would be wise to give some thought to the scenic possibilities when you design your layout in the first place.

There are no absolute rules for creating scenery—save only that of consistency. Study nature, note the textures and colors, the placement of trees and rocks and geological formations; make your transitions from mountains to valleys logical and lifelike. And always keep scale and proportion in the forefront of your mind. And while you can use certain real weeds and foliage and some small pieces of rock in your scenery, don't make the mistake of assuming that because it is real it will *look* real. All things in nature do not scale down in appearance. Take water, for instance. While it is true that some modelers use real water in the rivers and ponds of their pikes, it seldom appears authentic, except, perhaps, in extremely large layouts, and even then it is a perpetual headache. Real water goes stale and the effect of the dampness usually causes much more trouble than the effect is worth. Worst of all, it seldom looks real. You can get a much more realistic effect by the use of a special plastic, which I'll describe later.

Over the years, I have noticed that most non-model-railroading visitors have shown more enthusiasm for the scenic setting than for the operation of the trains. And while we are not building our pike for the sole edification of visitors, it does indicate that the setting is important to the creation of this miniature world we are striving for.

Well, then, how to begin? How do you create mountains and gorges and rivers and rolling countryside? What is the method used? The difficulty of a pat answer is that there are literally scores of methods used, all aimed at the same target—*realism*. Some modelers get involved in the use of *papier-mâché,* a mixture of paper pulp, sizing, and rosin; others soak brown wrapping paper, or feed bags in plaster and drape it over frames to harden in the desired shape. But these are messy procedures, and after a deal of experimenting with various methods, I have settled for the good old reliable screen-and-plaster technique.

Since this method has proven highly successful on my own pike, I'll explain how I do it; and then if you choose to do your own experimenting with other techniques, that's all right too. You may hit upon one that suits you better, for, I repeat, there is no one standard method, although it is safe to say that most modelers eventually come around to the screen-and-plaster idea.

I have never spent one cent for screening; I have used discarded door and window screens, finding the old screening easier to work with. The basic idea, of course, is to drape the screening so that it resembles the terrain you are trying to duplicate, and then cover it with a thin coating of plaster.

There has been a deal of heated discussion on the best plaster to use. The word "plaster" is herein used in the broadest sense, for many modelers use cement, arguing that it offers more strength. I have never used cement for this purpose, finding the mix I do use adequately strong. Other modelers use plaster of Paris, but this is expensive and chips too easily for my liking. However, I use it occasionally for special formations, such as a delicate piece of outcropping rock, that I want to carve carefully. Patching plaster is very popular for it works easily and dries hard. Some modelers claim that mixing a little vinegar in the mix slows down the drying. This is a very desirable quality because it allows you time to correct mistakes made in your carving. Others add a little asbestos fiber, obtainable from a furnace man, to the mix to give it a rougher texture.

After dabbling around not too successfully with various plasters, I took the advice of Frank Ellison, the venerable dean of model railroaders, whose book on model railroads I heartily recommend, and settled on a plaster known commercially by the misnomer of "texture paint." This seems to me the perfect material for landscaping, as it dries into a white, smooth surface and, perhaps even more important, it takes a couple of days to harden, allowing plenty of time to work in all the delicate detail that you may desire.

This texture paint (why it is called a "paint" I do not know) is manufactured by several companies under varying trade names. One brand is made by the U.S. Gypsum Company and it is obtainable at most building-supply houses. I get mine at the Sears Roebuck Company, in twenty-five pound bags, where it is cheaper than at most building-supply houses. Don't get too much at a time, for it is susceptible to humidity and loses its strength if exposed to too much air. By the same token, do your scenery in small batches; don't attempt to plaster the whole pike in one session. You've plenty of time.

A word of warning might be appropriate here. Don't be lured into the mistake of putting dry colors into your mix! I read of this trick in some model magazine and, because on the surface it sounded like a good idea, I tried it, mixing up a batch of beautiful, mud-colored plaster. After several-days labor fashioning a hill, I discovered to my disgust that the sameness looked appallingly unrealistic, for if you will closely observe even a small patch of earth, you will see that it is made up of many colors and shades of color. I tried painting the monstrosity, but the mud shade continued to dominate the scene, so finally I had to add a thin coat of uncolored plaster to the whole business and start over again. My advice is to leave your plaster white—we'll discuss the methods of painting it later.

The first step in creating scenery is, obviously, to decide what you want to model. If you have even the crudest ability to draw, make a sketch of what you have in mind. If you cannot draw it, get a picture out of a magazine or from an old calendar or a photograph that comes reasonably close to your mental image. Don't trust to your imagination alone, have something on paper to guide you.

The next step is to build a framework out of scrap lumber to support your screening. This doesn't have to be fancy, since it will be entirely concealed by your plaster. If you are fortunate enough to

Fig. 6-1 English Village and Tunnels

own a band saw, you can cut the necessary contours of the landscape into your wooden supports, but this isn't essential. You can hack them out roughly with a hatchet, or leave them flat and pad up the underside of your screening with newspapers or sticks.

Once the framework is erected, you tack on the screening. Small ¼″ copper tacks are preferable because they do not rust and bleed through the plaster, discoloring it. You can tack on the screening flat, if you wish, pinching and modeling it to obtain the contours, but I have found it simpler to first crumple the screening into a wad, as you'd crumple a newspaper, and when you open it flat, it has myriads of small natural contours of its own that are very realistic.

Before you tack your screening down permanently, remember to leave flat places where you will want to place your structures and buildings later. This is highly important, for you cannot place a building on a forty-five degree slope and have it look right.

The photograph in Fig. 6-1 illustrates this point, and several other items that are apropos. It was taken by Linn Westcott a few years ago and shows a then-unfinished fragment of my own HO railroad. Linn made it to show how I had blended the little English-type village into the background, which is the unfinished painting in the upper left-hand quarter of the photograph.

This angular shot reveals several things not discernible to visitors who, by the construction of the pike as a whole, are forced to view the layout head-on from a point about ten feet away. However, for the purpose of showing you how it is done, the picture serves us well.

The scene was an attempt at blending the three-dimensional foreground into the painted background, which starts at the curve of the backboard seen in the upper right of the photograph and passes along behind the village itself and continues to the right of the tiny bus and behind the rocks to the left of the photograph. Viewed from the front of the pike, visitors have a hard time deciding where the modeling ends and the painting begins.

This also demonstrates what you can accomplish in a very small space by trickery, since there is something less than eight inches between the wall and the inside rail of the first track. The most difficult part of the work was to get the road, shown just in front of the bus, to merge smoothly into the background, and the "real" trees that proceed up the slope to the left of the tunnel entrance to blend into the painted trees behind them.

As you can see, I left a shelf for the village, and another for the tiny log cabin on the hill above the tunnel. Another illusory device was in the treatment of the building. These are small plaster castings I obtained on a visit to England, and after painting them, I discovered that they took up more space than I could spare at this point. So with a hacksaw, I carefully cut some of them in half and placed them against the backdrop, after which I painted in the part I had discarded on the wall. Viewed from the front of the pike, it is almost impossible to discern that they are only false-fronts, so to speak.

If you recall, I laid great stress on consistency earlier in this chapter, and here we have a case in point. If you looked closely, you will note a small rock bridge just left of center in the photograph. Under the bridge is a stream which apparently stems from the painted mountains in the background. Now obviously a stream has to *go* someplace; it can't just flow to the edge of our hill and stop abruptly. To solve this dilemma I did what the real railroads would have done —put a culvert under the track. I accomplished this illusion by pushing a 2″ length of ¼″ copper tubing into the front of the lower hillside. The fiction is that this leads the stream down an invisible drain to a gorge out of the photograph, to the left. To the right of the culvert outlet, and above the tunnel and just in front of the hillside log cabin, you will notice some outcroppings of rock. This rock is made up of pieces of thick pine bark, stacked up and glued together to get the depth I wanted, and inserted into the wet plaster.

The half-finished hill over and to the right of the tunnel illustrates the method of framing. You can see how crude this is. Over the bend in the third track from the top, you will note a chuck cut out of the framework. This was necessary when I discovered, after the framing was in place, that I had left insufficient headroom for trains to pass under it, so I cut it out roughly with a saw. Of course, a tunnel portal goes in at this point, which will conceal the otherwise botched-up job.

In Fig. 6-2 I have sketched in the method of framing and putting on the screen.

What implements are needed for the

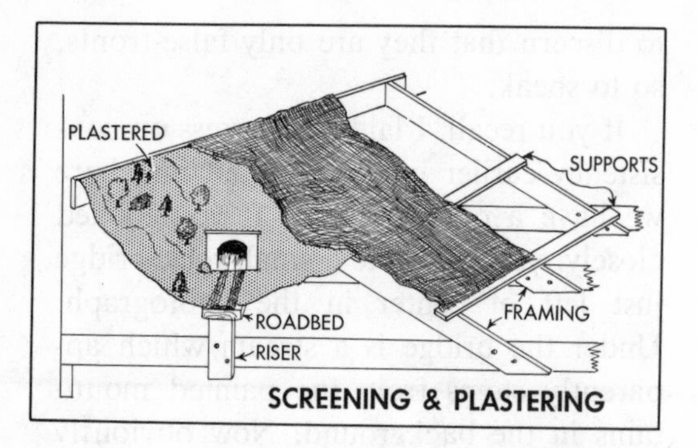

Fig. 6-2 Screening and Plastering

plastering? A small can of water, an old paint brush about two inches wide, a medium-sized spoon—I prefer a dessert spoon for the job—and a round-ended flexible-blade kitchen knife. If you can borrow one from your wife, a kitchen spatula would be even better than the knife. That's all you need—except patience and enthusiasm. The can of water is for wetting your tools so the plaster does not adhere to them while you are working.

Now before you start to mix your plaster, make sure the screen base is properly secured to its frame and that the humps, curves, and contours are the way you want them. Once the plaster is applied, it will be too late for major changes.

An old aluminum saucepan or any two- or three-quart mixing bowl will serve to mix your plaster in. Follow the instructions on the bag. Some plasters are ready for instant use when mixed, other have to set awhile. I put enough powdered plaster in the mixing bowl to do the particular job at hand, hold the bowl under the cold-water faucet and let the water trickle in, stirring constantly to break up the inevitable lumps. You must be very careful at this point, for if you get the mix too thin it will run through your screening instead of adhering to it and get out of control. If, while mixing, you find it too soupy, thicken it with a handful or more of powdered plaster.

It might not be inappropriate at this point to suggest that if you have any trackwork under your screening, you would be advised to cover it over with newspapers, or the like, to prevent the liquid plaster from falling onto it. I have learned the hard way that this is a good precaution.

As to applying the plaster, don't attempt to use a trowel, for it is almost sure to leave unnatural streaks. Put it on with your spatula or knife and spread it over the screening as if you were buttering a piece of bread. Somewhere between ⅛ and ¼ of an inch is the preferred thickness, but you can apply it more heavily if you expect to form any outcroppings of rock, or other carving. If you use your little white hands for the job, be sure to dip your fingers in the can of water, so you don't leave fingerprints on the job. To smooth the final surface, I use the paint brush, well-soaked in water, or the dessert spoon.

An ice pick, which you may also find in the kitchen, is a handy tool for carving strata in rock surfaces. In a pinch, an ordinary nail will serve.

To break up the monotonous smoothness of the final surface, there are several little tricks you can use. In the photograph (Fig. 6-1) you will see where I have embedded a few small rocks and pebbles in the plaster. On the slope to the left of the rock bridge is what appears to be a weed patch growing wild. These are nothing but the shavings emptied from a pencil sharpener. To get the effect of grass, you can use fine sawdust. The finest I have found is that from a band saw, which you can dye first with vegetable dyes, or put it on natural and trust to the final painting of the scene to cover it. If the sawdust is fine enough it gives a beautiful texture to the scene.

Remember, there are no hard and fast rules, and the only limits of what to utilize in this fascinating aspect of the hobby are the limits of your imagination. Creating good scenery is "imagineering" at its best. It is a creative art.

The far left-hand corner of my own railroad is shown in Fig. 6-3. Corners are always a problem and the good modeler tries to conceal them or utilize them so that they are not so uncomfortably obvious. Real railroads don't come to a corner and turn conveniently, but they do dodge mountains if they can. This particular scene is full of little deceptions. It is patent that the tracks couldn't head off into the waterfall, so the enforced turn to the right seems very logical. The picture also illustrates the method of blending the three-dimensional "mountains" with the background. Looking at the upper half of the photograph, the distant range of mountains in the background are painted. The part of the waterfall above the locomotive cab is a color rotogravure salvaged from a Sunday newspaper supplement and pasted on the background. The "real" waterfall is discernible between the arches of the bridge.

The realism of the rock formation to the left of the pictured waterfall has deceived a lot of visitors, who mistook it for wonderful workmanship. It isn't; it's nothing but piled-up pieces of cork salvaged from an old life preserver, found on the beach.

The rather effective-looking "foliage" growing out of the rocky surfaces was discovered in a rather humorous and dramatic fashion. I was visiting a friend whose lovely home was set in a grove of trees, and whose brick steps were covered with a fine moss, engendered by the inevitable dampness. As I was leaving the house one dark, rainy night, my feet slipped on the moss and I crash-landed on my posterior on the brick walk. My host, a very well-known modeler, rushed out to see if I was hurt. I wasn't hurt, but I was delighted. Modeling is always in the back of my mind, and I recognized that I had made a discovery. So sitting on the damp, cold bricks, I took out my pocketknife and scraped off a good pocketful of this moss and subsequently brought it home to decorate my own pike. As you can see, it is very effective.

Fig. 6-3 Waterfall and Rock Bridge

When this photograph was taken, I had not yet covered my waterfall and the river with plastic. What you see is plain plaster, smoothed down and painted blue, with white streaks where the water runs swiftest, and green and yellow in the backwashes where it is shoal. A few small rocks are imbedded in the plaster and a couple of "tree stumps" which, presumably, were washed down from the mountains. These little additions add greatly to the realism and are well worth the slight trouble it takes to insert them. But the principal idea is to place these things naturally. The tree trunk in the lower left-hand corner of the photo is, supposedly, momentarily snagged by the rock, but soon the current will carry it further along. Fortunately the current is completely static, and the stump hasn't moved in the five or six years it has been sitting there.

The trick of using the plastic and making the bridge will be covered in detail later.

While we are looking at this photograph (Fig. 6-3) it might not be amiss to call your attention to a couple of points that have nothing to do with creating scenery per se, but which are, basically, part of the overall scenic effect. I refer to the aging of the locomotive and the cars. While it is true that some railroads keep their rolling stock immaculate, the majority are content to keep them operating efficiently and let appearances take care of themselves. I like locomotives to look as if they have gone far and worked hard, so I contribute to their decreptitude by deliberately "dirtying" them. This old Mogul, much like the Moguls I used to fire, looks road-weary, as does the old freight car just emerging from the tunnel. Inasmuch as I raise Angus breeding cattle and my farm is named White Anchors, it seemed excusable for me to have a private stock car on the pike. I am currently in the process of building a "palace" cattle car for transporting my show stock—on the pike, of course.

What I am trying to impress on you is that every little detail you can add contributes to the overall realism and vitality of your layout, so long as it is consistent.

Corners are not the only bane of a realistic model layout. Nearly every modeler who has tried to build a layout in either a basement or an attic has run into the problem of what to do with pipes and vents and supporting beams that purport to support the floors above. It isn't practical to move these impediments—as I learned from bitter experience. In a small house in which I lived on the West Coast, a six by six beam rose with irritating majesty right smack in the middle of the basement where I wanted to put my shop. A fast-talking friend assured me that the beam was extraneous, and suggested a truss rod setup similar to those used under old-time freight cars. I fell for this scheme, removed the beam and put in the truss rod with the unhappy result that forever afterwards the floor above had a springiness that gave one the sensation of floating through the air.

With this background, my present advice is to try to conceal these eyesores with a magic mountain of screen and plaster. As vents and sewer pipes are usually placed in a corner of the room, the mountain can be made to appear logical enough.

If you have such a small pike that there is no space for mountains or rolling terrain, you can still dress it up with scenery. Shown in Fig. 6-4 is a scene on my first pike, which was only four feet in diameter with a single circle of track on the outer rim and a much smaller circle inside it for a trolley line. This was built on an old poker table—the average model rail cannot afford to play poker *and* indulge a love for fifty-dollar locomotives at the same time, and I was no exception. The table was a flattop, covered with a piece of Celotex, a soft fiber board which

Fig. 6-4 My First Pike

gives a pleasing effect of flat terrain. I experimented with building a small pond, shown in the photograph, using a liquid known as *water glass,* which is used primarily for preserving eggs. It hardens when exposed to air, and for a few weeks gave a splendid imitation of real water. Then for some unknown reason (I suspect some element in the Celotex) it turned a sickly white and then evaporated altogether.

WATER FOR YOUR PIKE

Inasmuch as real water is not recommended for use on a model layout, model rails have attempted various methods to simulate it. Perhaps the commonest method, and one of the easiest, is the use of plaster, molded to form tiny ripples or wavelets, then painted, and heavily covered with several coats of a good varnish. Only yesterday, I visited the huge pike of one of the finest modelers in the hobby, in Washington, D.C., and he had used this plaster, paint, and varnish technique with notable success.

But be careful of your paint job—that's the most important item. Study the color of water as it usually is. The Potomac River flows past my window; and some days it is a brilliant dark blue, but most of the time it is a dun-colored shade brought on by shallowness and erosion. My pond is usually bluer than the river; a sort of half-blue, half-green tone. So, be sure of the *average* color of the water in the area you are trying to duplicate.

If the area of your watercourse is not too large to handle in one piece, glass can be used. One of the most popular types of glass is the "ripple glass" common to office doors. Sometimes you can obtain this in a pale green that is effective as it is, or you can paint or stain the underside of it to suit. As this is translucent rather than transparent you do not have to worry about the "underwater" problem. Simply cut out the shape of your pond, lake, or stream on a piece of plywood, lay it over the ripple glass, place another sheet of uncut plywood underneath for a support, and you have it made.

Another very popular material is the ordinary smooth-surfaced, double-thickness glass, lightly tinted or stained to the color you desire. As this will be semitransparent, you will have to model in the bed of the watercourse. This method is illustrated in Fig. 6-5, and gives more scope to interesting effects. If you wish to

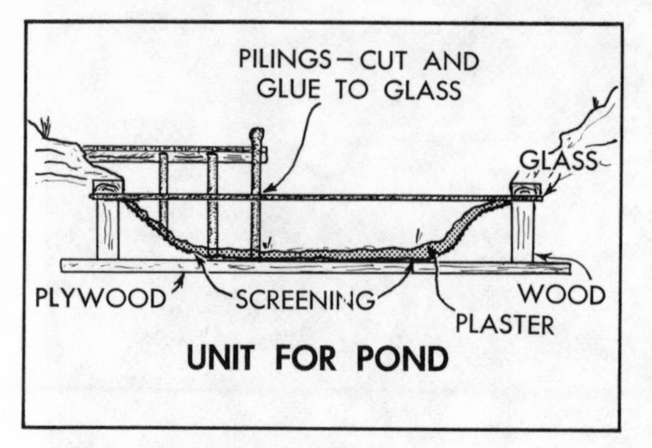

Fig. 6-5 How to Build a Pond

put a small pier or trestle in the pond, cut the pilings carefully so that the lower half of the piling is imbedded in the plaster "bed" directly under where the "above water" pilings will come. You can also insert rubbish and weeds in the bed, or even old tires gleaned from tiny toys. The whole idea is to obtain the effect of reality. One prominent model rail of my acquaintance conceived a very effective scene by modeling a water-filled quarry by this method, and in the riverbed under the glass, he put a small plastic locomotive, which is barely discernible. The story behind the scene is that the train toppled into the water from a trestle which skirts the quarry.

Fig. 6-6 Drainpipe with Water

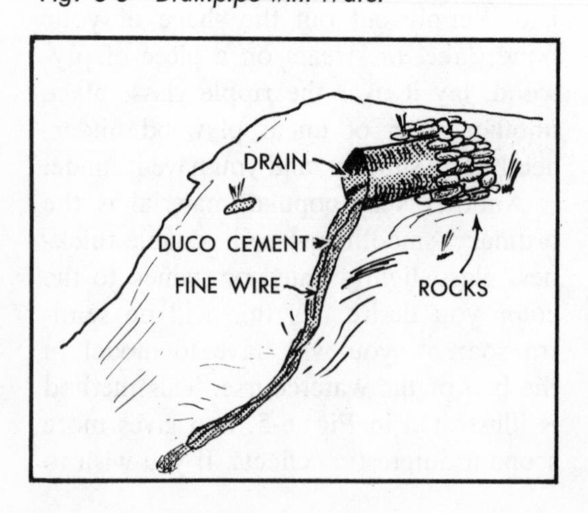

Standing water is much easier to model than a fast-flowing river or stream, for moving water is difficult to make look convincing. When I came to the point of creating my harbor scene, I was faced with the problem of size. It was too large to use the glass method, for making a joint in glass spoils the effect: I experimented with several ideas and finally settled on tempered Masonite, which proved very satisfactory. I dabbled around for a long time trying to get the right shade of green and finally mixed up my own, using tube oil colors and turpentine, putting in more yellow in the shallows. When this dried, I gave it several coats of a clear varnish. Then I modeled a few boats, cutting them off at the waterline, and set them on my harbor. The result exceeded my hopes.

For a narrow brook or stream Frank Ellison uses aluminum foil to simulate water. This is very effective if not too much of the "water" is visible.

For drains and small culverts where just a trickle of water comes out, I cement a very fine piece of silver-colored wire and then flow Duco Cement over the wire, which tends to hold the "water" in course. The wire is barely visible, and looks more like a highlight than anything else. This is shown in Fig. 6-6.

To my mind, the best "water" is realized by the use of clear casting plastic. The effect is almost incredibly realistic—so much so that most visitors try to touch the "water" with their fingers to see if it is wet. I do not know who discovered the method, but it was first brought to the attention of model rails in an article by W. S. Graves published in the *Model Railroader Magazine* in the November, 1951, issue. If you can beg, borrow, or steal a copy of this issue, I'd advise you to get it because Graves goes into the subject much more fully than I can in this book.

The casting plastic I used is a product of the Castacraft Corporation, P.O. Box 555, Palo Alto, California, and is known as Resolite 700. It is used primarily for making jewelry, novelties, and for embedding biological specimens. It is crystal clear, but can be dyed in the mixing, and hardens to a smooth glasslike finish after "curing." Wherever you purchase your casting plastic, be sure that you get instructions with it, and follow them to the letter. With the Resolite 700, the instruction book was fifty cents extra, but it was well worth it.

The plastic should be thought of as varnish; in other words, you have to completely finish the modeling of your riverbed before you apply the casting plastic. Be sure the riverbed is well dried and painted before you attempt this final stage.

The initial step in making a roaring river gorge or the like is building a firm foundation. Any flimsiness or shifting of your bed may crack the glasslike plastic after it hardens. I used ½" plywood for a base, supported by rigid uprights of thicker wood, and then covered the whole with wire screening, well tacked down. See Fig. 6-7. Next, apply the plaster bed, putting in rocks, tree stumps, piers, etc., and paint it to your liking. I'd recommend wood screws rather than nails for securing your foundation; I repeat, you need a solid foundation that isn't going to shift with the years.

In his article, Graves stressed allowing a full day for the job of applying the casting plastic; the whole process takes a long time. Also, the warmer the room, the faster the plastic will cure or set. The day I applied my plastic, I built a roaring fire in the wood stove and ran the temperature

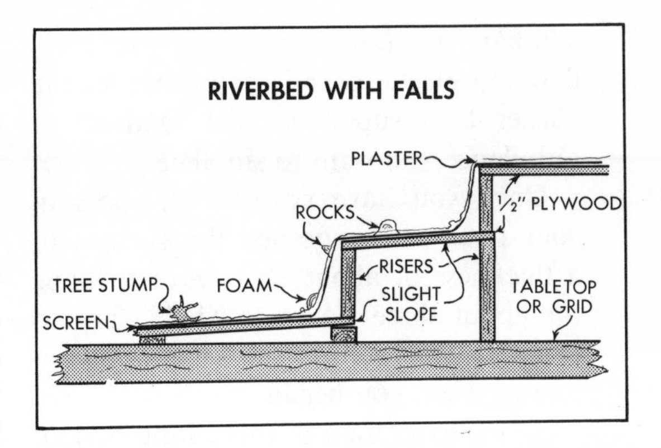

Fig. 6-7 Riverbed and Screening Method

of the shop up to about 100 degrees—and worked stripped to the waist. Don't allow any dust in the room, if you can avoid it; the dust will foul up your work.

As the directions will tell you, the plastic should be mixed in an openmouthed glass container. A liquid catalyst comes with the plastic, and you can also purchase the dyes you need from the manufacturer or supply house. I used green and blue dyes.

To get the best results, you should apply three thin coats, curing each in turn and building up to a total of approximately $\frac{3}{16}$". You can judge what you need by remembering that one pint of the casting plastic will cover about four square feet to a thickness of $\frac{3}{16}$". Mix the catalyst and the plastic in your glass mixing container and add a few drops of the dye color you intend to use. Go easy on the dye; you want to retain the quality of transparency and you should get your principal coloring from the paint you applied to the plaster bed.

The plastic may be applied without any dye, if you so desire, but a trace of coloring in the water gives it a better effect, especially in the first coat. Use a clean paint brush for spreading the liquid plastic as you pour it into the river bed. If you have any falls or rapids in your river flow the plastic over it naturally; let the plaster base supply all the "action" or turbulence you want to simulate.

Once you have covered all spots in your river and smoothed the surface to a thickness of about $\frac{1}{16}''$ leave it alone for about three hours to "jell." Try to maintain the room at the same temperature as when you began.

At the expiration of this jelling period, the river should be ready for curing, although it will still be tacky. Graves used a 150-watt bulb in a reflector, held about two inches above the plastic, and kept it moving back and forth to maintain a temperature of from 90 to 200 degrees. Don't get your lamp too close or hold it in one spot too long or you may blister the plastic.

I happened to have a 200-watt heat lamp in the house, so I used that with success. Some modelers have succeeded without using any heat, but I followed instructions to the letter. This process—and a rather tedious one it is—takes about two hours. The plastic is not very hard, more often slightly tacky—so don't leave any fingerprints in your river when you test it.

Half a day is gone by the time you get this accomplished, and you are ready for your second coat. McClanahan refers to this coat as the "special effects" coat. You can mix different batches of plastic with varying dyes to get the effect you prefer, such as yellow or green in the shoals, or white in the foaming water. However, I did not try for any such effects, being content with the job done on the plaster. If you used too little dye in your first plastic coat, you can darken it with more dye in the second application, or you can use it clear. This coat is applied in the identical manner as the first coat and cured in the same way after the jelling period.

In my judgment, the third and final coat should be of clear plastic but, of course, the choice is up to you. Here Graves recommends doubling the amount of catalyst to speed up the hardening process, otherwise the procedure of that final coat is the same as the two former ones. If you've followed the instructions, you should have a river that will amaze all visitors as well as yourself.

"ONLY GOD CAN MAKE A TREE"?

Well, perhaps, but I'll show you how to make some mighty realistic imitations. And unless you are modeling a desert layout, you'll need trees and plenty of them. For my Virginia locale, I required a lot of trees, but I got around the job by teaching my wife and children how to make them, a good trick if you can get away with it. However, it's such good fun that I bought my own sales talk and got into the act myself.

Trees are an essential part of most scenery. You can purchase ready-made trees of various kinds and shapes in your hobby shop. True-Scale is one manufacturer that makes many varieties, including fruit trees, colorful with ripe fruit, and trees of autumn shades. However, since the object of a layout is to make it individual and different from all other pikes, we'll discuss some of the many ways of making your own trees and shrubbery—and the more trees, the better the landscape.

The most popular material for making trees is a moss known as "lichen." In many sections of the country this is to be had by merely picking it up off the ground, or you can buy it already prepared and colored from your hobby shop. Before I woke up to the fact that lichen was all around me in Virginia, I bought a bale of dehydrated Norwegian lichen, sometimes called reindeer moss, from W. K. Walthers, a model railroad dealer in Milwaukee, and dyed it myself.

To prepare lichen, or any other dried weed you might decide to use, immerse it in lukewarm water to revive it. When it is fluffed up satisfactorily, drain off the water and squeeze out the surplus moisture. Handle it carefully when it dries as it is inclined to be brittle at this stage. To soften it up and ready it for use, mix a solution of technical glycerine (obtainable at any drugstore) in proportions of about one part glycerine to 2 parts water. Immerse the lichen in this solution and work the glycerine into the lichen with your hands. When spongy, set out on a screen or netting to dry. Don't throw away your glycerine mixture, you can use it many times.

There are several ways of coloring the foliage. You can use vegetable dyes, water-soluble aniline dyes, or you can spray it with a stain made of oil colors diluted in turpentine. The trouble with ordinary commercially prepared lichen or trees is that the colors are too gaudy. The tints and shades of real trees are very subtle and each one seems different. They are not a brilliant solid green or yellow but a delicate blending of many shades. Hence, I prefer to do my own coloring.

We have found the Tintex dyes, obtainable almost everywhere, to be very satisfactory both as to coloring and ease of use. If you use the so-called "forest green" dye, you may find it necessary to add a little blue or black to the solution to get a more realistic shade. Immerse your foliage in the stain, squeeze out the surplus, and set it aside to dry. If it isn't dark enough, repeat the process, at least with some of the foliage. You don't want them all the same shade of color. Ellison recommends the use of rubber gloves for this job, and I concur.

Now you can use some of the lichen you have prepared as is for clumps of shrubbery and the like. But keep the rest for the trees you wish to make.

If cost is not a major item with you, as it seems to be with many model rails, florists' wire, obtainable at any florist's shop, is probably the best material for forming your tree trunks, branches, and twigs, but it is more expensive than other types of wire. However, heavy picture-frame wire or soft copper wire will do nicely. I have used all of them, and while the florists' wire is the easiest to work, I could not see any major difference in the final result. In any event, the method of constructing your skeleton is basically the same.

Before you begin you must decide on the type of tree you hope to simulate. There are five basic forms of trees (Fig. 6-8 A): *pyramidal,* such as pines, spruce, balsam, etc.; *rectangular,* such as poplars; *square, round,* and *inverted pyramids.* Since real trees are not designed on a drafting board their forms are not mathematically perfect, so the form idea is just a general guide intended to keep you within reason. It is important, at this juncture, to remember that in creating any kind of scenery, size is relative. To maintain this sometimes delicate balance it is safe to stay on the small side because too large a tree, even if scaled down from a prototype, may well dwarf your surrounding structures or your trains. You should not attempt to construct scenery with a scale rule; you will achieve happier results by using your eyes and your judgment.

I recommend that you have a photograph or a drawing of a tree set up before you, at least while making your first

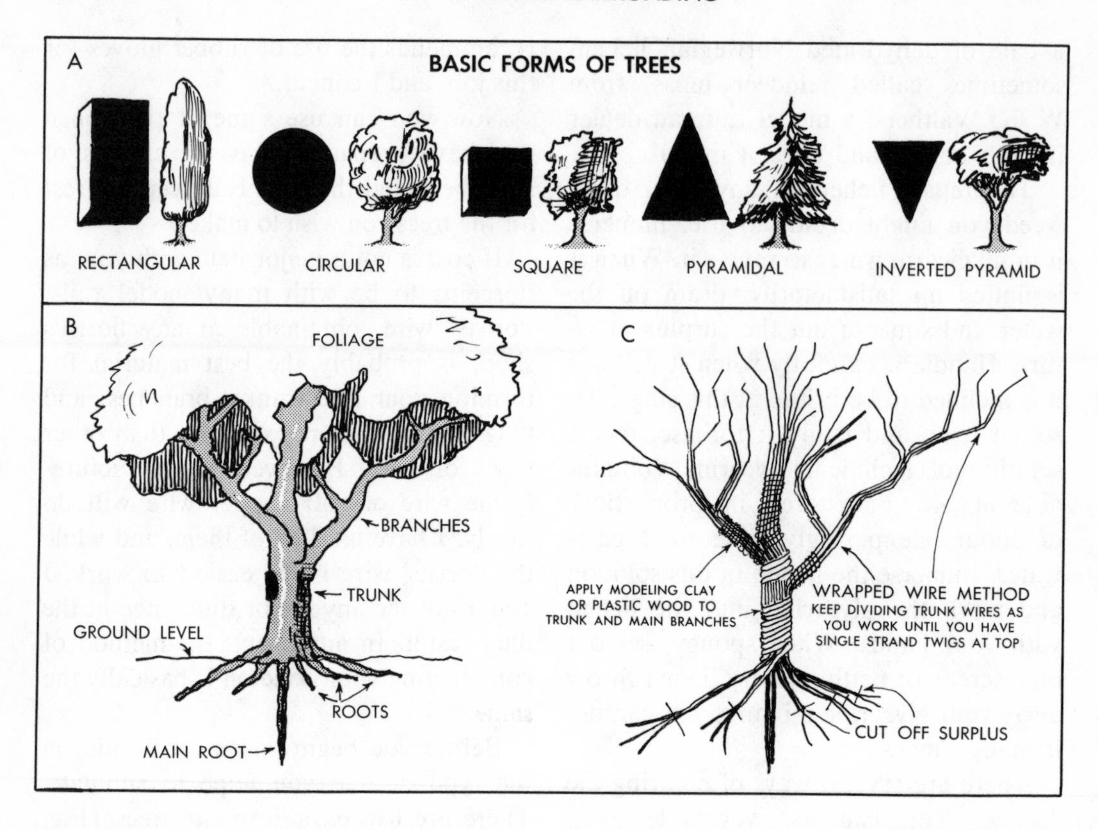

Fig. 6-8 Trees

few trees. After you've gained some experience, size and shape will be no problem. Parenthetically, when I'm working on scenery, bridges, and roads, I guide myself by a sort of mental scale, based on ⅛ inch equals 1 foot. I can gauge an inch fairly accurately by eye and, figuring it equals 8 HO feet, I proceed on that basis. It saves a lot of measuring and calculating and is close enough to achieve the final result I want.

The trunk and main branches of a typical tree are illustrated in Fig. 6-8 B. Since it is a known fact that if all the branches of a tree were bundled together the grand total would not be any larger than the trunk below the branches and, conversely, that the trunk reduces in proportion to the size of the branches that grow out from it, the wire method of building trees will keep us in proportion at least.

I deliberately did not tell you what gauge wire to use because it will depend on the type of tree you want and the thickness of your trunk. Experiment with several gauges until you hit the one you prefer. If you are using copper wire in a spool or coil, put one end in a vice and pull on the other end to straighten the wire. Then cut it into equal lengths and bundle it together to get the thickness you want for your main trunk. It may take a dozen lengths or it may take twenty; that's up to you.

If you are working in HO scale, I suggest you use six-inch lengths; make them proportionately larger or smaller for other gauges. Using very fine wire (sometimes called "hair wire"), tie your bundle about

1½″ from one end. The 1½″ will be for your roots. Continue wrapping the fine wire around the trunk until you come to the place where you want your first major branch to take off. See Fig. 6-8 C. Pull aside enough strands to make the first branch—five or six should do it—and continue wrapping to the next big branch and do the same thing. The general idea is to keep up this division of trunk and major branching until you get down to a single strand on each subdivision, which will serve as twigs to hold the lichen. Don't add the lichen yet; you still have some work to do.

When you get the upper portion of the tree to your satisfaction, go back and twist your roots. They are your supports to steady your tree when you "plant" it. Make the "straight-down" main root the stoutest; use seven or eight strands of wire from the center of your bundle and twist them into a firm group that points straight down. You plant the tree by making a hole in your plaster scenery with an ice pick, drill, or nail and shoving this main root into the hole. The other roots branch out at right angles to the trunk and serve as props to hold the tree erect.

Now some of the experts recommend coating your trunk with plaster, but I did not find this satisfactory, for it breaks too easily, especially at the intersection of the heavy branches and the prop roots. I had more success using modeling clay, sold at most general hobby shops or at art-supply houses. Plastic wood is also good. For my next batch of trees, I am going to try applying solder to the trunk with a blowtorch. This may be a bit more work, but work is the fun in modeling and the trees so made should be almost indestructible.

Whatever you use, the next job is painting the trunk. There is no one color that correctly matches the subtle coloring of a tree trunk. Artists use a combination of yellow ochre, burnt umber, blue, viridian, burnt sienna, and white. The general effect should be a darkish gray tone.

Fig. 6-9 Child's Hand with Tree

As it is very little more trouble to make a dozen trees than just one, you should set up an assembly-line procedure. Take a scrap board big enough to hold all the trees you intend to make at one time, preferably about ¾″ thick, and drill a series of holes large enough to take the main roots; then you can set out your forest in various stages of completion until you are ready to set them in place on your layout. And don't make all trees to the same pattern; keep them varied. (A tree made by my eight-year-old daughter is shown in Fig. 6-9.)

You are now ready to attach your foliage. Chiefly because it is easy to obtain, many modelers overdo the use of lichen until it becomes monotonous. There are other materials besides lichen. Fine steel wool, especially if used on trees in the background, makes a pleasant alternative to lichen, adding contrast in texture. Or

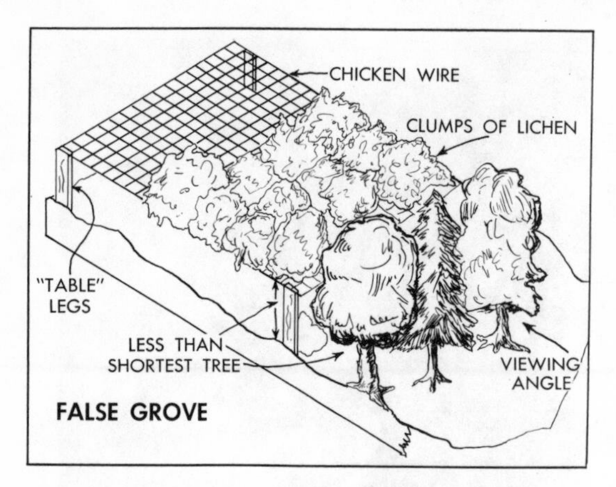

Fig. 6-10 Grove of False Trees

you can obtain a foliage from your florist known as "babies'-breath" or you might find other foliage in your backyard or on a trip to the woods or countryside. Part of the fun of modeling is discovering new materials to work with.

To attach your foliage, spread a little modeling cement on a twig, run the twig through a clump of foliage, and then bend the tip of the wire to secure it. When all the twigs are filled, stand back and admire your handiwork. If you are satisfied, plant your tree in place.

In the planting, try to view the overall effect, as an artist does. Keep in mind that your trees are a part of the whole, not an isolated scene. If the tree is supposed to lend atmosphere to a station or other structure, that's one thing; if it is on a mountain or in a valley, it may have to be viewed as a mass. But all this mass doesn't have to be actual trees.

Frank Ellison evolved a brilliant solution to this dilemma of mass. If you want to make a forest or orchard, mark out the space required on your layout and plant a row or two of trees, enough to block out the deception we are going to commit behind them. Then construct a "table" of small chicken wire or hardware cloth, whichever is cheapest and available, and support it with wooden legs to a height just slightly below that of your shortest screening tree. Figure 6-10 illustrates the general idea. Using fine wire, attach lichen or other foliage to the screening and glue a few clumps to the front of the table so it will not be discernible between the trunks of your "real" trees. When viewed from the front of your pike, the lack of form to the foliage set on the screen will not be perceptible and will look like a whole grove of trees.

However, if your pike is a walk-around or has a side viewing area, you may have to surround your fraudulent grove with complete trees to disguise the fraud. But if properly done, this device will save you a lot of work and give the desired effect of mass, so necessary for balance.

Trees can also serve the purpose of hiding such unwanted detail as too many tracks too close together, often inevitable in a medium-size pike. By screening trains for a moment as they pass behind the trees the layout appears larger than it is. Never forget that you're trying to perfect an illusion and any legitimate method of achieving it is permissible and desirable.

Wire is not the only material to use for making trees. Cuttings from hedges, especially boxwood hedges, can ofttimes be used as skeletons for trees. While walking through old pastures, I have often found roots of weeds which greatly resemble the trunks and branches of gnarled old trees. If you are lucky enough to find some, all you have to do is paint them properly and attach the foliage.

Jack Work, one of the best modelers in the hobby, hit upon an ingenious method of making trees that greatly resemble tall pines or redwoods. He takes a length of square balsa, cuts and sands it to the proper taper of a tall straight tree and pocks it with a series of small holes.

In these holes he glues tiny pieces of asparagus fern or other fine fernlike foliage.

Another mode suggested by John H. Ahern in his excellent volume, *Miniature Landscape Modelling,* is that of stacking up roughly circular pieces of thick felt to serve as a trunk, piercing them through the center with a pointed dowel, and then coloring them. If you can tear rather than cut the circles so much the better, for the final result will depend largely on the raggedness of the felt edges.

I have spent considerable space on trees because I feel they are essential to achieve effective scenery. Once you master the common methods, go on and try some of your own. Just remember that trees are not perfectly symmetrical, unless so pruned; rather they are usually ragged edged and uneven. Some modelers use those tiny Christmas trees sold in dime stores in December, often coated with "snow." The trouble with them is their evenness, which looks too artificial. If you brush off the phony snow and cut the edges ragged, bending down a few branches here and there to achieve a touch of naturalness, they can serve, especially if kept in the background and mixed with better formed homemade trees.

For hedges and underbrush, you can use tufts of absorbent cotton or small plastic sponges cut or torn to shape. Broom straw, pirated from the end of the family broom, stuck in a field of plaster gives a fairly good representation of a corn field.

ROADS AND ROADBEDS

Apeing the sour-grapes emotionalism of the prototype railroads, many model rails have generated such a contempt for the trucking industry that they seem to have a mental block against putting roads and highways on their layouts. Whether this is the actual reason or mere thoughtlessness an adequate system of roads is a rarity on model pikes. Like it or not, roads are just as much a fact of life as tracks and buildings. Wherever there are people, there are roads, therefore, no scenery is complete or natural without them. Stand on any mountainside and look down and you'll doubtless see more roads than track.

Now realistic roads are not hard to construct in miniature, but they do require planning in advance. A road serves a purpose, and it has to *go* someplace. You cannot logically stick a road in your scene that begins nowhere and ends at your station. Roads and rivers have two things in common—a beginning and an ending, although it is not necessary or even desirable to show these two characteristics. A pond, for example, can be a complete unit in itself without any explanation as to how it got there, but rivers and roads should start off-scene, wend their way logically through your scene, and quietly disappear off-stage.

In well-made scenery your roadbed should be constructed as systematically as your trackbed, with a firm base attached to your grids or table. The ideal would be to cut or form it out of soft pine boards, carefully butted and sanded smooth. There are several methods of making the road surface; we'll discuss two—plaster and illustration board. Both methods presuppose a firm roadbed.

As you know, all roads are not alike, either in substance or in width. There are four main types: dirt roads, gravel roads, asphalt roads, and concrete highways. McClanahan covers this in depth in his book on scenery, and you'll find many excellent suggestions on road construction in the model magazines.

Dirt roads are getting rarer by the

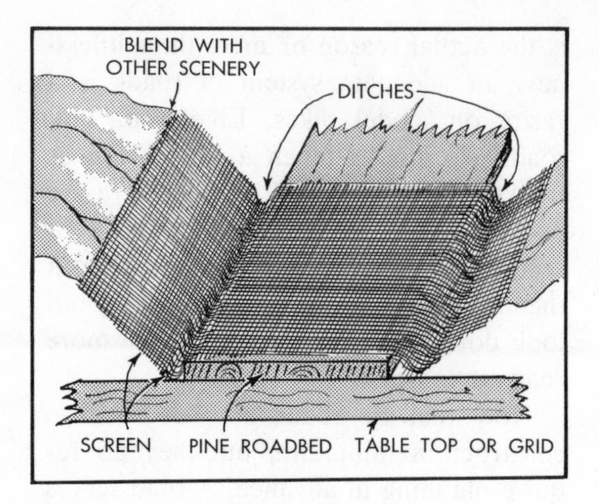

Fig. 6-11 Roadbed with Screening

year and are found mostly in mountain country or remote farming sections. Don't put a main dirt road on the edge of a city without an excellent reason for so doing. Dirt roads are narrower than paved roads and often have sharper bends, and they are invariably rougher, marked by deep ruts, occasionally full of water—a good chance for some fine superdetailing.

No matter what type of road you elect, the basic construction method is essentially the same, although with a dirt road, the baseboard is not always necessary since you can form it into the original plaster of your general scenery, modeling your ruts with a pointed stick or the wheels of a scale model automobile. Don't make them too even; remember that a lot of wheels have passed that way over the

Fig. 6-12 Roadbed of Illustration Board

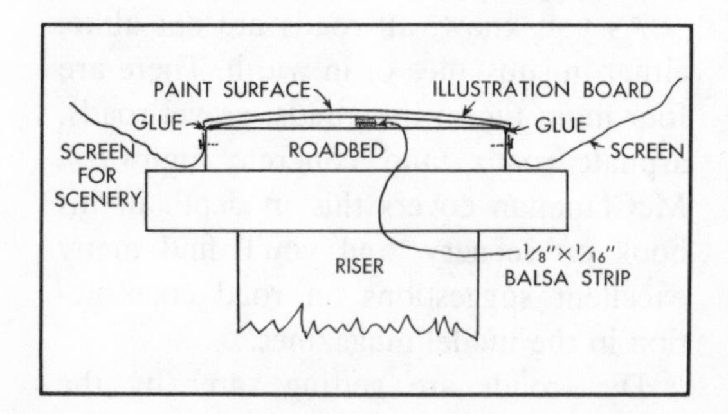

years. The basic method is illustrated in Fig. 6-11. Tack screening over the roadbed, as shown, and do not forget that a well-built road has a ditch on both sides to carry off excess water. Leave sufficient screen on both sides to merge in with your general scenery, and then plaster over it. All paved roads have a slight athwartships curve, known as a "crown," put there to drain the rainwater into the ditches, but in a model this curve should be very slight—remember, you are working in scale. Ditches are not always well kept and even and are often half full of trash and weeds.

Let me insert a word of warning here so that you don't confuse the method of making roadbeds for roads and that for tracks. *Never put screening under your tracks!* If you do, the rail spikes will cause a short that will be extremely difficult to locate. In the chapter on tracklaying, I'll show you how to attach your screening to the trackbed. Right now, we're discussing roads.

To continue: After you have applied your plaster, smooth it carefully with a wet spatula or brush until it has no unnatural marks. If you intend to make a gravel road, shake on a little sand or bird gravel (if fine enough) while the plaster is still damp and tamp it in with a wet block of wood. Try not to disturb the crown when you're pressing in the gravel.

For an asphalt road, let the plaster dry without disturbing it and depend on your coloring to get the effect of asphalt. If you are trying to create the impression of a concrete highway you will want to scribe in some expansion joints—those divisions you see between the slabs of concrete, also a center line. Don't make them too pronounced, but just plain enough to be seen. Also remember that a concrete highway will be considerably wider than a gravel or a dirt road.

We'll cover the technique of painting roads in a chapter devoted to that subject.

Many model rails prefer using artists' illustration board, about 1/16" thick, for surfacing roads. Figure 6-12 shows the general idea. Make your basic bed of pine or other suitable wood, attach your screening to the side instead of over the top to form your ditch, and join with the rest of your scenery. Then to get your crown, glue or brad a small strip of balsa wood—1/16" by 1/8" wide and as long as your road—down the center line of your base. Cut the illustration board the width of your roadbed, and of a length easy to work, and glue it to the balsa strip and to the edges of your roadbed. Weight in down with a bag of sand or pin it down at the edges until it dries. Indicate the center line and expansion joints, then paint.

The acknowledged master of model road construction is M. M. Wakefield, a professional art teacher who made the roads on the world-famous layout of the NYSME (New York Society of Model Engineers). Mr. Wakefield has had some excellent articles in *Model Railroader Magazine* over the past few years not only on road building but also on the artistry of scenery. They are well worth looking up.

Another somewhat colorful blight on the American countryside is the profusion of telephone and power poles. However much you may despise the real thing, they are part of the scene and should not be neglected. While you can obtain poles from your hobby dealer, there is a sameness to them (since they are made from a single mold) that spoils their naturalness. It is more effective to fashion them yourself out of 1/8" doweling, sanded to a taper. Attach what crossbars you require out of commercial stripwood or other small pieces of wood, and carve a few transformers out of pieces of balsa. You can make very realistic "insulators" out of tiny beads, such as they sell in hobby stores for decoration.

Unless you are running trolley lines, where you need real wire for carrying power, do not use real wire for stringing your light and telephone wires. Real wire doesn't have the proper sag and will not *look* real. The better choice is dark-gray thread. Observe the sag of the power lines the next time you go out for a drive and try to reproduce it on your models. Your eyes are the best guides to scenery; you cannot measure such things with a rule.

BIBLIOGRAPHY

Scenery for Model Railroaders, by Bill McClanahan. Pub. by Kalmbach.
Miniature Landscape Modelling, by John H. Ahern. Pub. by Marshall (England).

CHAPTER 7

Structures

The word "structures," as used in modeling, is an all-embracing term that includes such variables as water towers, signal towers, coal tipples, and all forms of buildings; in fact, nearly everything you can build for a layout that isn't strictly scenery, motive power, or rolling stock is a structure. However, they should be constructed for a definite purpose and considered not as individual features but as a part of a particular setting or of the whole scene. Too many modelers build an exquisite little structure on their workbench, then plop it down on their layout without regard for either setting or foundation. Then it looks exactly like what it is—an alien article in an alien setting.

As I stressed earlier in this book, to make things appear consistent requires "imagineering." Structures are like gears in a watch, they must be functional. For example, see the grain elevator and the little boatyard, shown in Fig. 7-1 on the harbor in my own layout. These were constructed on the workbench, of course, then they were inserted into their proper places on the layout and the harbor built around them. Therefore they become an integral part of the whole scene, not appendages put in as decoration or as an afterthought.

The whole point is one of attitude. You have to believe you are creating a real community; that real people live and work in your tiny buildings. They are not like Christmas-tree decorations; they are a vital part of your railroad empire.

One of the reasons our English cousins attain such perfection in their model settings is that they consider them as a *whole,* and often build them in just that manner. As in the movie industry, they seldom build a single structure; instead, they usually erect an entire street scene. John Ahern makes some very potent suggestions on this technique in his book, recommended at the end of this chapter.

As with the building of locomotives and/or cars, in structures there are three phases of construction: kit building, superdetailing, and scratch-building. By all means construct your first two or three

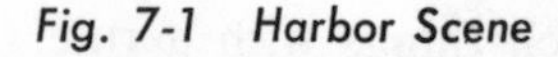

Fig. 7-1 Harbor Scene

Fig. 7-2 Wayside Station and MU Car

buildings from a kit, for it will give you an understanding of the sequence of building as well as some experience in the handling of the material.

Now there are kits and kits. There are simple snap-together kits, which advanced modelers often contemptuously call "shake-together" or "quickie" kits, the inference being that they are so simple that all you have to do is shake the box and the kit comes out ready-made. This is not true, of course, and some very nice models can be built from such kits if you do a bit of superdetailing. Then there are simple kits for beginners, and some beautiful advanced or "craftsman" kits for the modeler of some experience.

There is not much that needs to be said about building a kit, except to advise you to follow explicitly the directions supplied by the manufacturer, otherwise you may find yourself "up a blind alley." Most good kits are made to fit together in a sequence and it is easiest to build them the same way. A word of caution: Use your glue or cement sparingly, and try not to get it on the face of your model for many of the modern cements will not take paint and more models are ruined by messy glue joints than any other single fault.

Superdetailing is the term applied to putting your own individuality into a model or a scene. It is a difficult phrase to define for it covers so much ground. It is the *art* in model building, the final touch that brings the setting *alive*. It embraces such things as putting miniature people into the scene, lights in and around your structure, shrubbery and trees, and the litter inevitable around a busy industry.

For example, look at the details in the little wayside station shown in Fig. 7-2 with the White Anchors & Potomac MU car just arriving to pick up the commuters in the early evening. There are two outside lights and the interior is illuminated. A baggage truck stands on the platform with luggage on it. The station agent is hurrying out to deliver a dispatch to the engineer while two patrons sit quietly on the bench, waiting for a later train. The whole setting suggests life and movement, yet this was, originally, a beginner's kit which I "hopped-up" or, if you will, "superdetailed."

The kit was a gift from a friend, and for a while I considered it too modern for my period pike, but by adding a little gingerbread trim I made it look older. You can see this under the eaves, over the door. I got a wealth of this type of trim from a plastic fan that my young daughter had discarded. Or you can take one of those paper doilies, sold at any dime store, stiffen it with a coat of shellac, and cut out what you need. The only limits to what you can do in superdetailing are those of your imagination, and this will develop as you gain experience.

Don't depend on memory alone to superdetail a scene. Start a morgue as artists do; that is, a collection of pictures, photographs, and drawings of the type of structure or setting you are attempting to build. Two good sources for such pictures are *Railroad Magazine* and *Trains Magazine* or any of the many books published lately on the history and color of prototype railroading. Also, start a collection of the excellent catalogues put out by some of the hobby manufacturers, such as *Walthers' Reference Manual and Catalogue, Ayers Model Builder's Manual and Catalogue,* and many others. Your hobby dealer has them, or should have them, and they are worth many times the small cost for they not only give you excellent and helpful suggestions, but they indicate the wide range of supplies available to the modeler.

I mentioned miniature people. Some experts, such as John Allen, make their own figures of wire and modeling clay, but admittedly this is beyond the capabilities of the average modeler, especially the beginner. With the wide variety and excellence of the commercial figures, it is unnecessary to make them yourself. For something extra special, get your hobby dealer to show you some of the famous Weston figures; they are exquisite—sheer perfection! You can also get some wonderful miniature animals: horses, mules, sheep, even lions and tigers and elephants. Just examining them at your dealers will suggest a multitude of uses for them on your own layout.

We come now to scratch-building, the ultimate in modeling. The word means "starting from scratch," that is, without anything. When the hobby began, about thirty years ago, practically everything had to be scratch-built, trains, track, cars —the whole works. But we have come a long way since that primitive time so that now the word "scratch-building" per se is almost a misnomer, for there are so many items now available that practically nothing is built entirely from scratch. You can purchase windows, doors, siding, roofing, all types of brick and other building papers, tiny electric bulbs, and so many items it would be ridiculous to try to fabricate them yourself.

Of course, the fewer commercial parts you use, the greater the personal satisfaction you will have from the result. Let us take an example of a scratch-built structure, and follow the steps and the reasoning behind it.

The grain elevator erected to go on my harbor is shown in Fig. 7-3. It is a free-lanced version of a real elevator in our neighborhood. Free-lancing merely means that I varied from the original to serve my purpose. In the first place, the original had four more storage tanks than the model, but I deemed that too large for the space I had, so I cut it down to eight bins instead of twelve. This is a good practice in general, because many prototype building are too unwieldly in size for the average pike.

After making this decision, I photographed and stepped off the prototype measurements, then I built my base so that it would fit into the curve of the siding tracks. That done I cut a piece of

Fig. 7-3 Grain Elevator

¼″ untempered Masonite for the foundation of the actual building. Then I found a couple of mailing tubes of the proper diameter and cut eight tanks, into precisely the same lengths. These were glued into position and painted to resemble concrete. The superstructure of the original was made of sheet metal; preferring to work in wood, I chose a suitable wood from my hobby dealer and after making a drawing of the building, proceeded to cut out the necessary shapes. The windows were made of acetate .010″ thick, the panes inked on the surface with a ruling pen. The dust remover shown on the lower roof was turned down on the lathe from a piece of doweling.

When the superstructure was complete, I applied a coat of sanding sealer to it to fill the wood pores and then painted it with a thin wash of aluminum paint. The sealer gives the wood a hard finish that makes it resemble metal when painted. This is a good trick to remember when making cars and the like.

During the construction, I put tiny grain-of-wheat bulbs inside the building. Not satisfied with the final result, I built the tiny office (seen in front of the elevator) which is, in reality, a three-sided shell to house the reflector of an old flashlight. The open side faces the elevator and for a night scene I turn on the "floodlight" which illuminates the front of the elevator.

Actually, the two best features of the

Fig. 7-4 Water Tank

whole model are the waterfront pilings and the power pole with its transformers. Notice that one of the pilings has been sheared off by a careless tugboat skipper when docking a barge. The power pole was a dowel, sanded to taper, and the three little transformers were cut and filed to shape from doweling.

When working with plans, either from a kit or orginals, it is a good idea to cover them with wax paper, pilfered from your wife's kitchen. Glue and cement will not adhere to the wax paper, and it will keep your plans clean for future reference.

It is surprising how many modelers, even veterans, shy away from scratch-building, deeming it beyond their capabilities. Only last month several modelers petitioned me, as president of the Middle Eastern Region, to have a special category of kit-built models in our Regional contests so that they would not be forced, as they now are, to compete with scratch-builders.

The truth is, once you get the knack of it, scratch-building is as easy, and in many cases, easier, than building some of the quality kits. Perhaps even more important, it gives your pike an individuality that no other pike will have.

Learn to see the possibilities in various discarded household items. Start a junk pile in a box under your pike. My wife laughingly accuses me of not throwing anything away. Mailing tubes are wonderful for storage bins, water tanks, and a myriad of other things. Bath powder containers make excellent oil storage tanks, old earrings make fine clamps for miniature work, and cheap jewelry can be used in innumerable ways. I used the spout of a Jergen's hand-lotion bottle for the water spout on my prizewinning water tower, in Fig. 7-4.

White or so-called "sugar" pine and basswood are the most popular woods for structures, although properly selected cardboards will also produce excellent models. Do not use the common cardboard used for boxes and the like; get a good quality mat board or, even better, some three-ply Strathmore drawing paper, of the kind used by illustrators, which cuts to a clean edge and takes paint and scribing well. The trouble with cheap cardboard is that it warps too easily and often gets fuzzy under paint.

Some professionals are now using sheets of white plastic for model structures with incredibly realistic results. Read the model railroading magazines for latest developments along this line. Other modelers use metal, either sheet brass or some of the commercial metal sidings available at your hobby shop. To use these, however, you have to know how to solder properly or, if you prefer, you can use a glue, such as Walthers' Goo or one of the new epoxy cements.

For such delicate components as window and door trim and the like, a thin cardboard known as postcard board is excellent, or use two-ply Strathmore board. It gives a more realistic scale thickness than even the thinnest of woods.

Balsa, while not generally recommended for structures, is the easiest material to age, so keep a supply on hand. It is especially good for such old weathered structures as mills, cabins, and farm buildings.

For structure building, the tools you will need are few and simple. A steel foot rule, a supply of single-edged razor blades, an X-acto modeling knife, with plenty of new blades handy, a small saw known as a Zona saw or razor saw (because it is about the thickness of a razor blade), at least one pair of good tweezers for applying very small parts, such as window trim, to your buildings, some toothpicks for putting on glue, and a generous assortment of straight pins and those tiny pins known as "lills," and various rubber bands are all the tools necessary for building structures. A small miter box, such as the "Miter Jr.," available at your hobby store, is a great convenience for cutting clean edges and angles in strip wood.

While most model cements set quickly, they take about 24 hours to harden and attain their full strength. Therefore, when attaching the sides of a structure to the frame, it is wise to stick in a few tiny "lills" to maintain the contact until the cement sets. Sometimes I hold all four sides of a building together with rubber bands, but don't make them too tight or you may pull your structure out of line.

I have also found from experience that it is advisable to brace structures well on the inside, especially at the corners. For this job, I usually use ¼″ balsa, either in strips or in flat pieces, being careful to keep it well back from windows, doors, or other openings that might let it be seen from the outside. This is added insurance against warpage.

As I mentioned in connection with the grain elevator, I prefer to build all structures on a base. I have settled on ⅛″ Masonite as a standard for this purpose because when placed on the layout the structure appears to have a decent foundation. You can either cut or file your base to an angle to simulate ground or, better still, smooth a little plaster up to the base so it will not be noticeable. If, for instance, you are building a farm setting, you can make the base big enough to include all the necessary outbuildings and shrubbery.

While acetate is generally used to simulate windows, if not heavy enough it has a tendency to warp or bend. The best material I have found is the extremely thin glass used in medical laboratories for covering microscopic slides. It is known as "cover glass" and is almost paper thin, but will neither warp nor bend. Ask your physician for some he would otherwise discard after using.

If you desire interior illumination in your structures, you must plan for this in the construction because, no matter how careful you are, bulbs will burn out in time and if you've sealed them in, you may have to tear the whole structure apart to replace a burned-out lamp. Another point to consider is the transparency or translucency of your structure. When I built my first log cabin I found that the lamp inside showed between the chinks

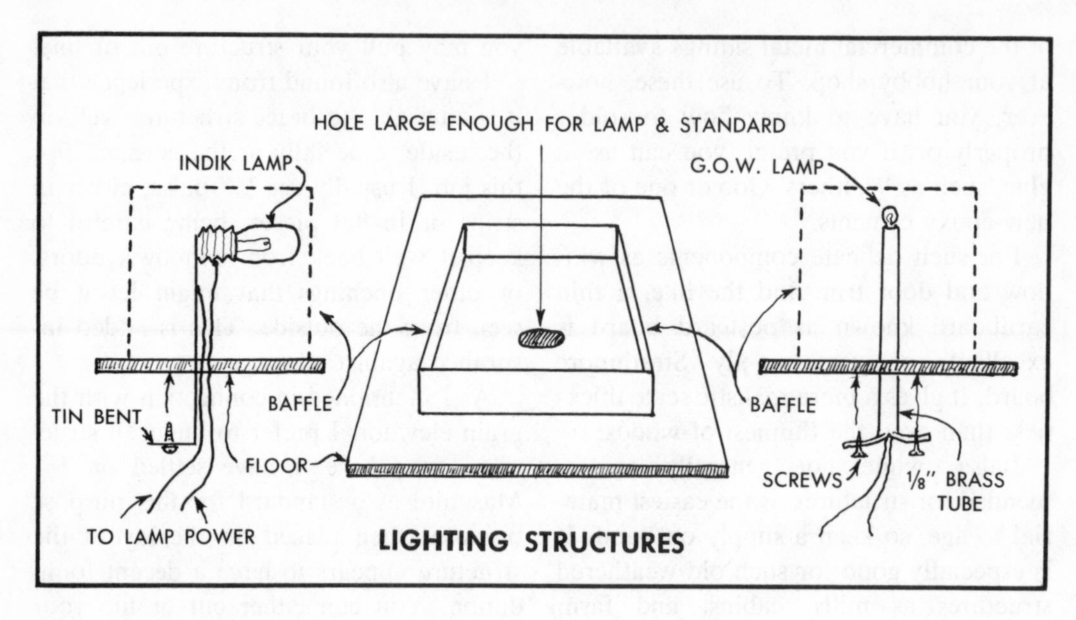

Fig. 7-5 Lamps in Structures

on the wood, so I had to remove the roof (quite a chore) and insert a little baffle or housing around the bulb.

The simplest solution to the problem of possible replacement of lamps is to have a hole in the bottom of your structure and a corresponding hole in the scenery directly beneath it so you can replace a lamp from underneath the pike. Figure 7-5 shows two methods: A, using 12-volt indication bulbs and B, using grain-of-wheat bulbs. Remember that if you use a lamp at half the recommended voltage, it will last many times longer. I use 12-volt bulbs on a 6-volt radio filament transformer. This doesn't permit the light to burn as brightly as the higher voltage would, but you don't want your building interior lighting too bright, it's unnatural. Seen through windows at night most homes and buildings appear dimly lighted.

For method "A" make a small angle out of a tin can and either glue or solder your lamp base to it. Then fasten the angle to the bottom of your structure with a thumbtack or a small screw for easy removal.

In using grain-of-wheat bulbs, known as GOW bulbs in the hobby, I take a small piece of brass or copper tubing—the brass tubing in the refill of a ball-point pen is perfect for the job—cut a slot in one end and with a pair of long-nosed pliers bend out the sides to a flare at the bottom, like a pair of wings. Punch holes in these wings to take a thumbtack or a screw, run your pigtail wires from the bulb through the tube, and fasten the little lamp standard to the bottom of your structure after pushing it up from beneath. Of course, the length of your tube will depend on how high in the structure the lamp is supposed to go.

The baffle can be of cardboard or plastic or even metal, but don't allow the cardboard or plastic to touch the bulb. There is a lot of heat generated by these tiny lamps, and you might set something on fire. Make the baffle into the shape of a square or a circle; anything to keep it from shining through unwanted places in your building.

It is not advisable to put too much strain on your power pack, so for powering your structure lamps, since alternating current is permissible, an old toy transformer or a radio filament transformer will do. I collected a lot of old radios from friends and extracted enough transformers to last me a long time.

The boatyard scene shown in the picture of my harbor, Fig. 7-1, was built by my wife, and as competent a judge as Al Kalmbach, the father of model railroading, pronounced the boathouse a little masterpiece. It was constructed, not of siding, but of individual wood planks, some broken and others bent out of shape to indicate great age and wear. This wood comes in bundles and is used by physicians as splints for bandaging injured fingers; it is known professionally as "finger splints." It comes in strips about 4″ long by about ¼″ wide and has the appearance of rough lumber which is very realistic. My wife cut these in half, which made planks about 10 scale inches in width, just right for the structure. The shingles were cut individually from ⅓₂″ sheets of balsa and applied one at a time. Sure, it's work, but that's the fun of modeling, and the results justify the labor.

Skip, my ten-year-old son, built the little prizewinning station shown in Fig. 7-6. It was also made of individual timbers and shingles. I drew the basic outline of the station on illustration board, which he then cut out and glued together, supporting the illustration board on the inside with chunks of balsa wood, to keep the corners squared. Then using ⅛″ square strips of balsa, he cut the necessary timbers, allowing enough length beyond that of the cardboard backing to make his dovetailed joints. To a ten-year old this was a tedious chore, but having already tasted blood by winning a former contest, he heroically stayed with it. After that, each timber had to be carefully trimmed and fitted at the corners to secure a perfect joint, then cemented to the cardboard backing with Elmer's Glue-All.

Fig. 7-6 Log Station

The roof was made of illustration board and then came the seemingly endless job of cutting the shingles out of 1/32″ balsa and applying them to the roof. To get a realistic aging effect, he took a burning iron and outlined both the front and side timbers and the shingles. He also used the iron for outlining the stones in the chimney. He cut up matches for the woodpile and inserted an old root to resemble a dead tree and made his platform of balsa strip wood. He won not only first in the junior division of the contest, but in the senior class as well.

In selecting prototypical buildings to model, you have to strike a compromise between what you would like and the space you have available. Don't feel frustrated by the restriction for the railroads have to do the same thing. For ease of calculation, you should get out of the habit of thinking of your space in inches and accustom yourself to figuring in scale feet. It is not necessary to carry along a conversion table or break down your measurements into fractions. Just keep in mind that 1″ in HO equals approximately 7′, thus 4″ will equal 28′, 10″ will be 70′, and so on. When you find a prototypical structure you admire, step it off and estimate at once whether or not it will fit into your space.

Bear in mind, also, that a building does not have to be a perfect rectangle. I found a picturesque old warehouse in Richmond, Virginia, that was built in the form of a narrow triangle to fit into the Y of two tracks. You can find a prototype for nearly every circumstance if you look long enough. Wherever possible, photograph all four sides of the building you intend to model, then photograph such details as windows, doors, down-spouts, angle of roof, and any signs you may hope to duplicate. Make some sketches, if you like, and make a measurement—of a door, window, or some other point of reference for taking off from your photograph—with a pair of dividers later when you actually begin construction. And make a careful note or photograph of any significant litter which may be strewn about. It is the use of these details, or, if you will, superdetails, that lend authenticity to your models.

The cardinal virtue of good structural

Fig. 7-7 Bethlehem Unfinished Station

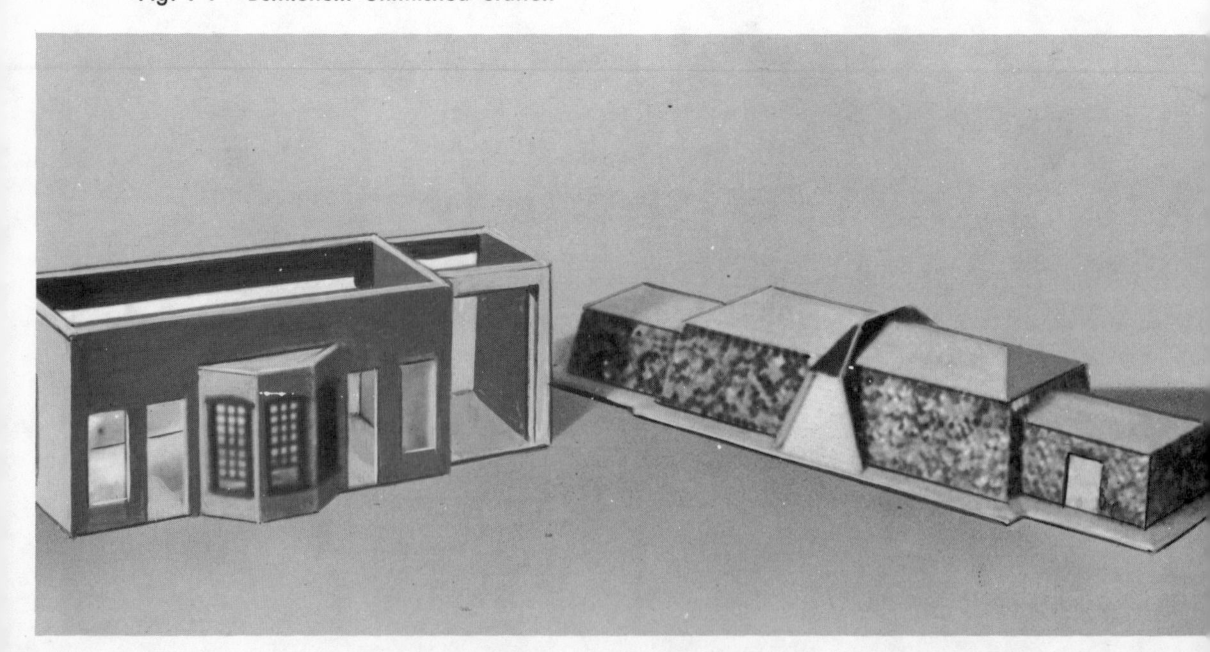

Fig. 7-8 Jerkwater Station

modeling is well-fitting joints and parts. Use a miniature mitre box when cutting strip wood, and in cutting illustration board or wooden siding keep your razor blade or modeling knife exactly at right angles to the material and keep the blade pressed flat against the steel rule. Don't use scissors. Do not attempt to cut through on your initial pass with the knife; make a very light cut first, then go over it many times. This will prevent the blade from "wandering" off the line and will give you a clean, square cut. Be sure to get well up into the corners on such openings as door and windows so you don't have any fuzz left in the corners. A ragged edge on a window or a corner can spoil a model.

Figure 7-7 shows an unfinished model of the old railroad station at Bethlehem, Pennsylvania, a colorful relic of the latter part of the nineteenth century. It has a fine old mansard roof, the sides of which are covered with octagonal shaped tiles.

I photographed the building, fore and aft, and took measurements, but for a long time the roof tiles stymied me. It was going to require several hundred tiles and the thought of cutting them out of paper with a pair of scissors overwhelmed me. Then one day I remembered an old circular ticket punch I had lying around, which on examination, proved to deliver a small paper circle just the right size for my tile. The fact that it was not octagonal didn't matter; at a distance of three feet one could not tell whether a ⅛″ tile was octagonal or round. So I found a lot of magazine covers of an approximate slate color, and bribed one of the kids to punch out a few hundred tiles for me. It was a long and tedious job to glue these individual tiles to the mansard roof (it is not completed yet) but the effect was highly gratifying, and a thin lampblack wash will stain them all to the right tone of color.

In this case, I violated one of the traditions of modeling; I made the roof of solid white pine in five sections. This was done to get the proper angles. Of course, it *could* have been done by building it up with thin siding, but it seemed less work and just as effective to cut the angles on a power saw. The gabled windows will have to be superimposed.

The frame of the building was made of 3⁄16″ balsa and faced with illustration board covered with "brick" paper. The tall windows are metal castings purchased at the hobby shop.

Some meticulous modelers frame a model exactly as a carpenter frames a house, and while this is surefire in a model contest, especially where the interior is open for inspection, it is not necessary for the practical modeler.

The hunt for structures to model is a fascinating sport. On these "protoypical junkets," as we call them, I load the whole family into the car, complete with camera, measuring tape, sketch pad, etc., and take off. It is pleasantly astonishing how much the children get out of these trips and what a help they can be holding one end of a measuring tape. You can even stand one of the youngsters up against the building, and use his, or her, height as a guide in later measurements. But take the child's measurement when you take the photograph and record it; they don't stay at a fixed height very long.

BIBLIOGRAPHY

Easy To Build Model Railroad Structures. Pub. by Kalmbach.
Miniature Building Construction, by John H. Ahern. Pub. by Marshall (England).
Ayers Model Builders Manual and Catalog #20. At your Hobby Shop.
Walthers' Reference Manual and Catalogue. At your Hobby Shop.

CHAPTER 8

Bridges, Trestles, Tunnels, Etc.

The *Britannica* describes the function of bridges as "the starting of a stream of human traffic hitherto impossible; the surmounting of a barrier, the linking of two worlds divided by a gulf." Nobody knows who invented the first bridge, but it was probably some prehistoric man who threw a log across a stream and discovered he could walk over it. Bridges and civilization are so closely related that it is almost impossible to imagine a world without them.

Aside from their utilitarian value, bridges are both beautiful and fascinating. Many are works of pure art; some have the lacy delicacy of a spider's web. To see a tall, graceful bridge with a heavy freight drag rumbling over its narrow top is something like watching a latter-day magic carpet wafting a train over an unspannable gorge.

To my biased mind, no model layout is complete without *some kind* of bridge, be it only a small concrete puddle-jumper over a stream. Interesting bridges are, inevitably, the conversation pieces of any layout. The trestle bridge shown in Fig. 8-1, on the front of my own layout, gets far more comment and attention from guests than any other feature on the pike.

While granting that prototypical bridge building is both a science and an art, as well as a lifetime study, bridges for model railroads are not difficult to construct. And they are great fun to build. However, there are certain rules which cannot be violated if you hope to have your bridge look right. Railroad bridges have to be very strong to carry the tremendous high-speed loads put onto them, and to model them necessitates at least an elementary understanding of stress and strain and compression. Also, you must choose the proper type of bridge for a particular job.

Now, inasmuch as no single volume could more than skim the surface of the subject of bridge building, I can only hope, in this chapter, to give you a few suggestions on the type of bridges suitable for the model railroader and try to whet your interest to indulge in further study. Paul Mallery, of electrical fame, has written an excellent volume on bridges and trestles, which I heartily recommend to you, and the model railroading magazines have many how-to-do-it articles on construction methods.

For your first sortie into bridge building, I would advise you to purchase one of the several excellent bridge construction kits on the market, as, for instance, the Ayres scale model kit of a modern truss bridge. These kits are made of wood, have all bridge members made of special shapes, I-beams and the like, cut to size, with a full-sized template for ease of assembly. This exercise will afford you sufficient experience to have a general understanding of a bridge's components and permit you to strike out on your own.

Remember, a bridge is a permanent fixture on your layout; it doesn't move about. It sits quietly, under the critical eyes of visitors and awaits their judgment. You cannot afford to make any glaring technical mistakes.

But even when you comprehend the intricacies of construction, you are limited to the rigid rules of scale. In other words, you cannot logically construct *any* bridge you happen to admire; it may be too big to scale down to the size of your pike. For example, I am especially fasci-

Fig. 8-1 Trestle over Gorge

nated by the famous Quebec cantilever bridge which spans the St. Lawrence, but I could not hope to duplicate it, since it is some 1,800 feet between pier centers, which, even if I made it in a scale of ⅛ inch to the foot, would make my model some 18¾ feet long. So for practical reasons, I have to transfer my affections to a lesser prototype.

For purposes of general classification, in this chapter we will first classify bridges by the material of which they are constructed, i.e. masonry, steel, and wood. Masonry will include concrete as well as stone. Then we will subdivide them into types, such as movable or fixed and whether they are *through* or *decked*. See Fig. 8-2 for classification of types.

Real railroads make their choice of type and material strictly on the basis of cost and efficiency. While the cost of a model may be only a few cents either way, you cannot logically choose a cantilever bridge to cover a small depression where the prototype roads would use a cheap trestle. It would be inconsistent and look ridiculous. Also a real railroad would never use a bridge where a fill would be possible, and cheaper. Keep that in mind in your selection of a model bridge.

Another consideration is what is below

the proposed bridge. If the land below it is extremely valuable, a real railroad may decide to build a viaduct over it, releasing the land for other uses. If the bridge is to cross a navigable river, a deck bridge may not be practical because it would interfere with water traffic or, as is often the case, a movable span to permit the passage of river craft may have to be built.

The difference between a *deck* bridge and a *through* bridge is important. Both are *fixed* bridges; that is, they do not move. But on a deck bridge, the girders and trusses are underneath the track and the trains run over the top. *Deck* bridges of the same span and capacity are cheaper to construct and, if the clearance under the bridge is not a major factor, railroads prefer them. A *through* bridge is one in which the trains pass between the trusses, thus permitting greater clearance underneath. See Fig. 8-2 A–D.

The matter of bridge supports is another factor in the selection of the proper type of bridge. If a railroad has to span

Fig. 8-2 Bridge Types

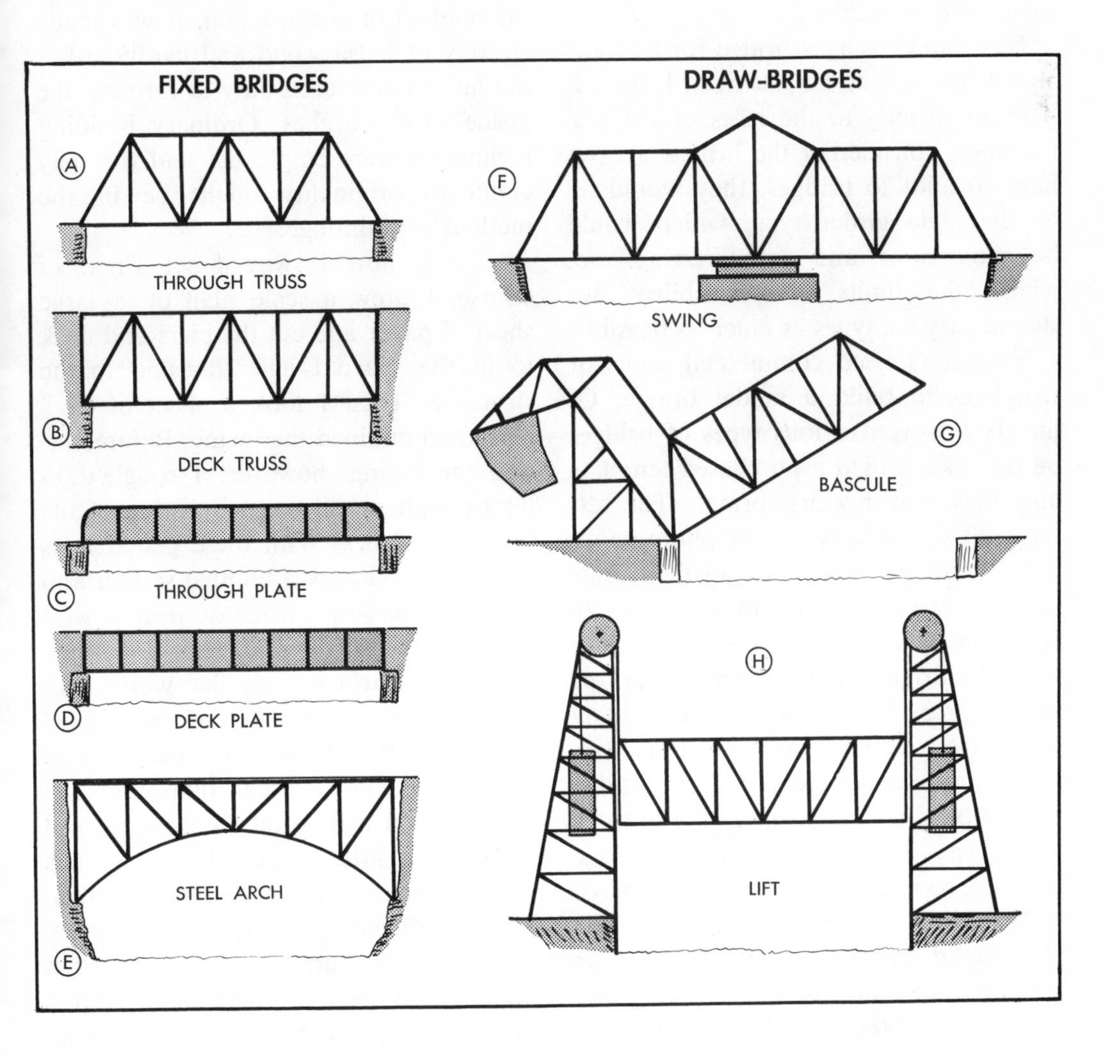

Fig. 8-3 Narrow-gauge Trestle

a deep gorge, too wide to use a girder bridge, and too deep to get adequate support for a truss type, it may have to choose an arch bridge (Fig. 8-2 E) or some other type.

Now in choosing a bridge for a model layout, we have to be practical. If we adhere too strictly to the rules of the real railroads, considering the little space we have to allot to bridges, they would all be the plate girder type, which would be montonous and uninteresting. So, within the limits of plausibility, we should vary the types as much as possible.

You don't need commercial plans or templates to build a model bridge. Of the six or seven various types of bridges on my pike, I used a purchased template only once—on my first bridge. The rest were all scaled down from photographs found in magazines. You can then draw up your own plan or template if you can find some item of scale as a starting point.

In the original photograph of my big trestle (Fig. 8-1) was a man walking across the top. Figuring him at six feet, I took my measurements for the bridge on that basis and drew up a plan to work from. The delicate little narrow-gauge bridge shown in Fig. 8-3 was also based on reasoning; I figured the timbers in the pier would average about one foot in thickness, so I measured everything else to this scale. While you have to be more mathematical in constructing bridges than in making scenery, the eye should be used as well as the scale rule. No matter how accurately you measure components, the final product has to *look* right as well as *be* right. The two are not necessarily synonymous.

The little stone bridge shown in Fig. 6-3 is a free-lanced version of the historic Thomas Viaduct, near Baltimore, originally built in 1835 and still in use today. All I had to go by was a poor photograph I had snapped from a moving train, yet it has won a lot of favorable comment from visitors and many questions as to the method of construction. It was made entirely of balsa wood and cardboard—the latter being used only in forming the inside of the arches. Ordinary building techniques were employed, and the only claim to originality might be in the method of painting.

This is how it was done: First, of course, I drew a scale plan on a large sheet of paper and cut the piers and deck to fit the space I had allocated to the structure. Then I took a sheet of 1/16″ balsa and outlined the facing. Before cutting the facing, however, I roughed in lightly with pencil the delineation of the bricks or stones. With these pencil lines to guide me, I took a blunted scriber and outlined the stone work as deeply as I could in the soft balsa. Then I painted the whole surface with flat white wall paint, making sure that the paint filled the depressions formed by the scriber. When this had dried thoroughly, I squeezed out a little oil paint on a sheet of glass—a little white, about as much yellow ochre, and a touch of burnt umber. These I mixed carefully with a toothpick, using no turps, and then rolled it smooth and thin over the glass with a rubber roller, of the type used for inking wood blocks. When I got the mix smooth enough and it covered the roller well, I rolled it on the painted balsa. This covered the high spots but did not run down into the scribed depressions, leaving the effect of mortar between the stones. The abutments supporting the piers were handled in the same manner. Later I brushed on a little of the stone color to cover a few of the mortar markings to give the effect of weathering because without doing so the bridge looked too new. All that was left to do was cut out the shape of the arches with an X-acto knife and glue the facing to the rest of the structure.

This technique is also applicable to constructing brick or stone buildings.

Another method of creating the effect of masonry is by using stout linoleum for facing your "stone" bridge. With a fine V-shaped chisel, sold at art stores for carving wood blocks, cut the outline of the individual stones, and paint each one separately. Done properly, this produces a very realistic effect.

To avoid anachronisms the modeler should choose a bridge to suit the era he is modeling. The science of bridge building has progressed greatly over the years and a model of a great steel truss bridge of the type designed in the 1940s would be as sadly out of place in a Civil War pike as a modern diesel locomotive. By the same token, a modern Class I railroad is not likely to use a wooden trestle bridge on its main line. And while there is no definite rule on the exact type of bridge you should use, there are the nebulous rules of logic and consistency.

The types of bridges most popular with model rails are, in the "fixed" group: the *arch,* both steel and masonry; the *plate girder;* the *truss;* and the *trestles,* either steel or wood. See Fig. 8-2A–E. And among the movable bridges are the *swing,* the *lift,* and the *bascule*. See Fig. 8-2F–H.

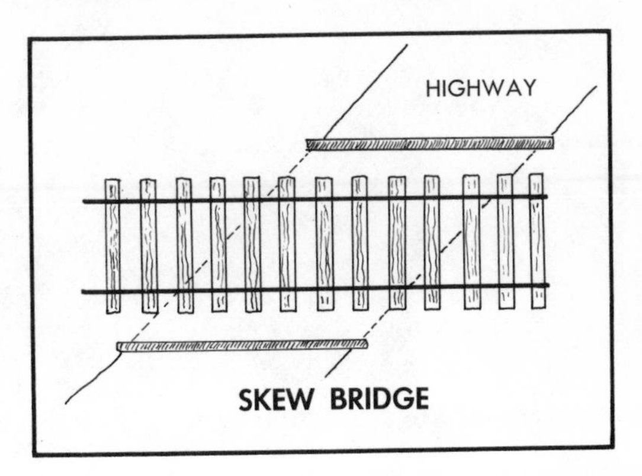

Fig. 8-4 Skew Bridge

For short spans, such as crossing over a road oı another track at other than right angles, a bridge may be skewed to reduce the length of the span, as illustrated in Fig. 8–4. Used in a logical place, this makes a nice feature on a model.

If you study the detailed plans of a real bridge, you may be overwhelmed by the array of prefabricated components designed by the bridge engineers, but you can safely disregard this and use such standard shapes as I- and H-beams, etc. These delicate shapes, in both wood and brass, are obtainable from your hobby dealer and are a great aid to ease of construction. And, best of all, they look authentic when used properly.

While most modelers construct their bridges from wood or illustration board, many of the better craftsmen prefer to work in brass. This requires a thorough knowledge of the art of soldering, but the finished product has a clean-cut look about it that is hard to equal in wood or cardboard. Before you tackle a scratch-built bridge, get from your hobby shop a catalogue of the commercial shapes available, then, after you have drawn up your plan, purchase what you need.

Fig. 8-5 Bascule Bridge

These special shapes are surprisingly cheap.

Sometimes you can combine a kit bridge with scratch-building for good effects. An example is the bascule bridge, shown in Fig. 8-5, on my own layout. Because the gap over the harbor entrance was tieing up the main line, I was in a hurry to get this bridge completed, so I built the bridge proper, that is the span itself, from an Ayres kit of a modern truss bridge, and then free-lanced the lifting apparatus from illustration board. I used pieces of Homosote to simulate the cement counterweights; while the bridge is not operable, it is so nicely balanced that off the pike it lifts beautifully on its trunnions.

Unless there is a very good reason for them, operating bridges on a model pike are not generally advisable because of their lightness; there is all too often trouble with track and electrical connections. But it has been done and it can be done, although I personally feel the trouble is not worth the effort. We have enough problems of maintenance without adding another.

Fig. 8-6 Viaduct

TRESTLES

Technically, a trestle is a series of bridges supported by piers, which are knows as *bents*. Steel trestles are sometimes used to pass the railroad tracks over a city, as the Chesapeake and Ohio in Richmond, Virginia, shown in Fig. 8-6. Wooden pile trestles are ofttimes used over swamps and shallow tidewater areas. While steel trestles are in common use by the real railroads, modelers seem to have a great affinity for the old-style wooden trestle, either pile or frame. The difference between the latter two types is that the piles are driven into the ground, or swamp, with a pile driver to obtain a firm, hard footing (Fig. 8-7), often at an angle for better bracing, while the framed bents rest on concrete piers or mudsills. See Fig. 8-8.

Fig. 8-7 Pile Trestle

You may hear and even read about modelers who build their trestles on location "as the real railroads do it," but to my way of thinking, this is going to a lot of needless trouble to have something to brag about. The real railroads do it because they have to. It is much simpler and more efficient to construct your bents on a workbench. Perhaps the best method of doing this is to make a cross-section template of the terrain where your bridge is to go, see Fig. 8-9, holding it in place and cutting until it fits the landscape perfectly, indicating on it the position of your bents or piles, then transfering the template to your workbench and cutting the bents or piles to the exact length. It's a tedious enough job to do it this way, without trying to sink your piles in the plaster ground, just because the real railroads have to.

Fig. 8-8 Mudsill for Bents

The NMRA Data Sheets cover the standard procedures in depth on the subject of bridges, both wood and steel. But

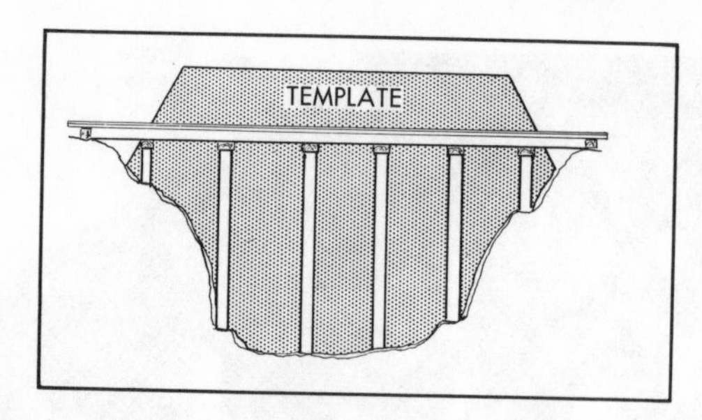

Fig. 8-9 Template for Bridge-making

if you will browse through a book of old-time photographs, you will find fascinating trestle bridges that are far from standardized. The two wooden trestles on my own pike, Figs. 8-1 and 8-3, are cases in point.

When the originals of these two bridges were constructed, there were few standards and very little federal inspection. If a gap or gorge yawned in front of the track, it had to be spanned, one way or another, and the bridge engineer had to tailor a bridge to suit a particular need. If the design was unorthodox, nobody cared, so long as it did the job. Doing a job was the only criteria. Therein lay their charm. Ofttimes they were never duplicated but stood alone, real works of art, until age and modernity destroyed them.

TUNNELS

Tunnels are extremely popular on model pikes, and every tunnel requires one or two portals to protect the entrance and/or exit. In very rocky country, the portal was sometimes hewn out of solid rock, and left that way. In the Far West, and in parts of the country where timber was readily available, wood portals were used on occasion. Figure 8-10 illustrates such a portal, as used on my pike. Also, some of the early portals were built of brick or stone, as shown in Fig. 8-12, but modern portals are almost universally constructed of concrete.

The two-track portal shown in Fig. 6-1 is a commercial portal cast in plaster, which a friend gave me. The rest on my pike are scratch-built, since I prefer individuality. A very simple "concrete" portal can be made in a few minutes with a piece of ¼″ balsa and a piece of postcard stock. See Fig. 8-11.

Fig. 8-10 Wooden Tunnel Portal

In designing the opening be sure to allow plenty of clearance for your largest locomotive or other equipment which may have to pass through it. Then cut the opening with a jigsaw, a band saw, or modeling knife, cement on your cardboard "facing," cut a piece of balsa or pine for your "cap," and you have it made. Or, if you prefer, you can rough out a portal from a piece of ½″ or ¾″ pine, cover it with screen and plaster, carve your rock, or whatever facing you choose. You can do the same with a piece of linoleum.

For support, and as a preventative against erosion and falling rock, railroads customarily add headwalls and wings to the front of a portal. Notice the long headwall on the little tunnel shown in Fig. 8-12.

The finest exposition I have seen on the subject of tunnels and portals was a two-part article written and illustrated by M. B. Wakefield, published in the April and May issues of *Model Railroader Magazine* in 1954. They are well worth the trouble you may have in obtaining them.

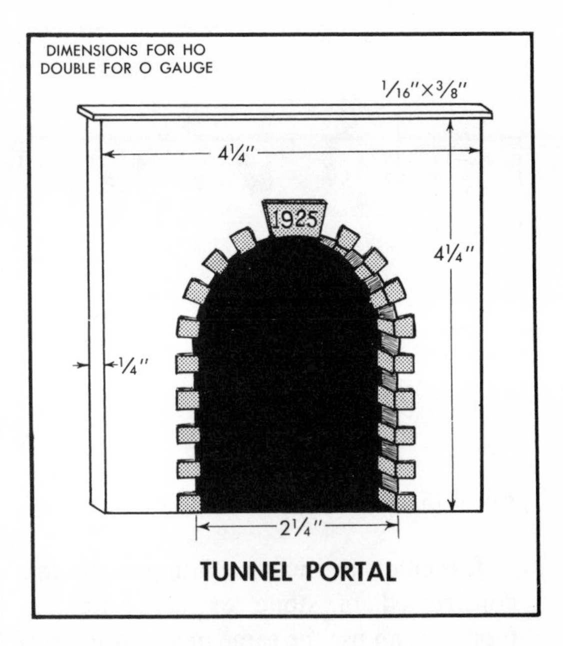

Fig. 8-11 Tunnel Portal

Fig. 8-12 Tunnel Portal in Richmond

RETAINING WALLS

Whenever a real railroad makes a cut through a piece of land, they try to cut back far enough to slope the terrain to what is known as the "angle of repose," which means simply that under normal conditions, the earth or rock will not roll down on the tracks. But where either the value of the land is too high to make this long slope feasible or if there just isn't enough room, the railroads resort to the only device left to them—retaining walls or cribbing. On a home layout, where space is always at a premium, retaining walls are even more necessary than on the prototype.

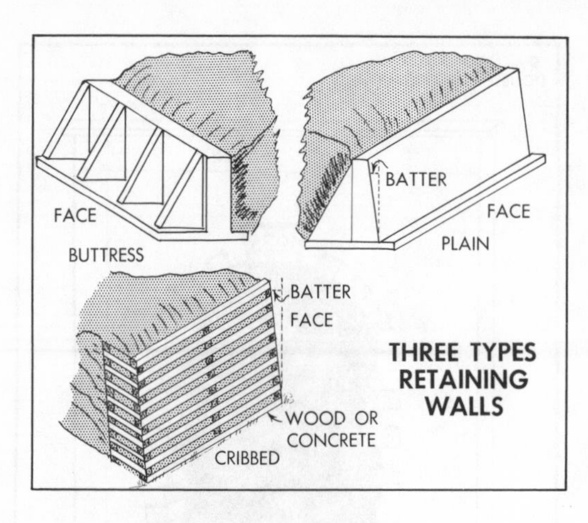

Fig. 8-13 Retaining Walls

Inasmuch as most retaining walls are constructed of stone or concrete, the modeler can use the same methods of construction as used in building stone or concrete bridges and portals. Use wood, linoleum, or plaster, whichever you wish. Figure 8-13 illustrates three popular types of retaining walls.

Figure 8-14 is a photograph of a portion of the well-known Brooks Valley Railroad of Douglas S. Smith. Shown is an excellent retaining wall of "stone" made by Doug's artistic wife. It is made of sheet linoleum, scribed with a linoleum knife and painted with oil colors. A fine piece of prototypical workmanship.

Cribbing belongs to an earlier age and is, perhaps, even more picturesque and just as simple to build as other retaining walls, although it is a retaining wall itself in the proper sense of the word. As the name implies, cribbing is formed by making "cribs" of timbers or, in many instances, of reinforced pieces of concrete molded in the form of timbers. These cages, or cribs, are then filled with rock, gravel, or a mixture of both with earth, and serve to hold back erosion and the like.

To fully understand the principle take a few wooden matches and lay two parallel to each other, about an inch and a half apart. Then lay two more across the first pair, at right angles and about the same distance apart. Add two more, running the same as the original pair, and again, two more the opposite way. That's the basis of a crib.

However, since your plaster terrain is not likely to erode, you do not have to build an actual crib, merely the *appearance* of one. So your first step is to cut a piece of illustration board to the exact size of the wall you wish to retain. Paint this board an earth color or a Van Dyke brown and build the face of your cribbing on it.

For an HO pike, 3/32″ strip wood or balsa would be a good size for your timbers—proportionately larger or smaller if you are working in another gauge. Prototype timbers would be about nine inches square, so you can scale it on that basis. Cement a length of timber horizontally along the bottom of your painted illustration board, then cut a lot of tiny pieces from another piece of 3/32″ strip wood, about 3/32″ long, to use as inserts which will represent the lateral timbers supposedly buried in your fill. Cement these about an inch apart and then glue another long horizontal timber above them, as shown in Fig. 8-13, and continue this process to the top. In placing the finished product in place on your pike, allow for a slight slope, technically known as the "batter," as indicated in the drawing.

UNDERPASSES

Railroad underpasses are so common, and the construction so similar to that of tunnels, there is no need to dwell on

Fig. 8-14 Retaining Wall

them, save to get them on record to remind you that they, too, should be part of your scenery. Fig. 8-15 shows a typical highway underpass.

COVERED BRIDGES

Utility, cost, and efficiency have to be the standards for a prototype railroad, but not necessarily so for a model pike. Charm and scenic interest—within the realm of plausibility—should be considered for a model, for it is individuality that will make your pike different from all others. And when it comes to charm and interest, few structures can equal a well-made old covered bridge.

These relics of the past always attract attention, whether on a model or "for real." While not commonly used as railroad bridges, some were used in the "golden age," although it might be difficult to find one these days. Yet there are still a few lingering on, like old memories, for road traffic and they lend a nice touch of the picturesque to any pike. Figure 8-16 is a drawing of an old-timer.

In concluding this piece on bridges, trestles, and the like, I might add that whenever I go on a bridge-hunting junket, I set for myself three standards: the colorful, the unusual, and the beautiful. The accompanying photographs, taken recently, will illustrate my point.

Fig. 8-15 Underpass

Fig. 8-17 Little Stone-arch Bridge

Fig. 8-18 Two-type Bridge

Fig. 8-19 Three-level Bridge

Fig. 8-20 Two Shots of Bascule Bridge

Fig. 8-16 Covered Bridge

Figure 8-17 is a charming little stone bridge over a placid creek in Richmond, Virginia, which would make (and will make) a beautiful model.

Figure 8-18 is a most unusual structure. Apparently part of an old bridge had been swept away, so the railroad added a through-plate girder bridge to the remnant of the old structure and put it back in service. This would make a good conversation piece on a pike.

Figure 8-19 is one of the most-photographed structures in railroading fan literature—the famous-three track crossing in Richmond. One track goes under it at ground level (the tracks are just this side of the automobile), the Seaboard Railroad has a bridge over that track, and the Chesapeake and Ohio Railroad built their viaduct above the Seaboard's route. And, of course, there is a highway viaduct above that.

Figures 8-20, A and B, are photographs of a small and unusual type of bascule bridge over the James River canal. It would make a fine model for a pike.

Figure 8-21 shows an ordinary truss bridge over the approach to my yard tracks on the WA&P. It also shows the tunnel portal, illustrated in Fig. 8-11, in

Fig. 8-21 Truss Bridge and Tunnel Portal

Fig. 8-22 "Bark" Tunnel Portal

the hill in the background, just over the cattle sale barn. You will notice that the upper face of the tunnel has been blackened by locomotive "smoke." This was applied with a piece of absorbent cotton dipped in powdered charcoal.

Figure 8-22 shows a tunnel portal on the WA&P "carved out of solid rock," but actually made of pieces of stacked up pine bark. The locomotive is a Mantua Mikado, with a superdetailed and built-up front end.

BIBLIOGRAPHY

Bridge and Trestle Handbook for Model Railroaders, by Paul Mallery. Pub. by Simmon-Boardman Co.

CHAPTER 9

Aging, Painting, Lettering, and Decals

These are highly controversial subjects in the model railroading hobby and I approach them with circumspection. While the suggestions made are not original with me, I give them as my own preference and choice, not as standards you have to follow. If they sound reasonable to you, accept them; if not, try another method. So leaving myself an avenue of retreat, I'll proceed.

Aging is inevitable in man and in machine. As an intelligent human being usually grows old gracefully, so does a piece of railroad equipment. Aging ofttimes engenders respect and affection, and an old road-weary locomotive, its steam chest and steam dome encrusted with boiler compound and its smokebox streaked with rust, is a greater attraction for railroad lovers than a shiny locomotive just out of the paint shop. Therefore it is not strange that once you do a really good job in aging one of your locomotives, you'll discover it has become your favorite.

There is no disputing the fact that aging and painting in general is an art, but it is not a hard art to learn. What it chiefly requires is a familiarity with the originals and a sharp faculty of observation, either from originals or from good clear photographs, although the latter will not supply the subtlety of color.

The best explanation of the art of aging and weathering was in an article written by the old master of the art, John Allen, in the January, 1956, issue of *Model Railroader Magazine*. By all means, obtain a copy if you can.

It is safe to say that more good models are ruined by poor paint jobs than for any other reason. You must remember that paint has scale, as do structures and equipment, so house paints and the like have no place in modeling. Your hobby shops stocks specially made lacquers and paints for models, but even these should be chosen with extreme care. I'll grant you that real locomotives are painted black, but they are viewed in the brilliant sunlight which permits you to see their detail clearly. But if you will observe carefully, as you back away from a real locomotive and view it at a distance, it will appear a dark gray color, not black.

Viewed in the relatively subdued lighting of a pike, a model locomotive painted flat black loses most of its detail and become something of a silhouette, as John Allen phrases it. I have painted a lot of locomotives and even yet have not altogether satisfied myself as to the proper method. The best finish I have found is not a paint at all but a stove polish known by the trade name of Black Silk. To the best of my knowledge this technique was discovered by John Armstrong, a former editor of *Model Railroader Magazine*. It is easy to apply and gives a nice dark sheen, a delicate patina that permits the details and piping to show up nicely, and has a genuine metallic appearance. I shake the bottle well, then brush the Black Silk onto the bare metal, letting it dry and then polishing with a dry one-inch paint brush. It requires about three coats, all applied in the same way, to get the best effect. It is not as substantial as regular model railroad paint, but I have one Pacific, which handles the local train, which was so colored

Fig. 9-1 Old Mikado Loco

about four years ago, and is still in good shape.

If you prefer to paint use a medium to dark gray; the locomotive will appear black in the general lighting of your pike. Bear in mind what any artist will tell you —there are no absolute blacks in nature! Atmosphere and dust tend to lighten the black of a prototype locomotive until it appears at a distance to be a warm gray.

Since passenger locomotives are usually kept daintier and cleaner than the old workhorse freights, I paint my passenger locos with Black Silk and weather the freight locomotives with a gray wash —made by mixing white oil paints in turpentine. This kills the dead black look, and gives the effect of dust and grime. Now if you will look at the old road-weary locomotive in Fig. 9-1 you will notice that the smokebox, the firebox, and the pop valves are covered or at least heavily streaked with a composition known as "boiler compound," which is a whitish-gray substance caused by escaping steam. This will gather around the steam dome and, if not frequently washed off, will run down the sides of the boiler and the smokebox. To simulate this boiler compound, I make a mix of white with a touch of red or brown to give it a warm tone, and thin it down with turps. Then I brush it on, following the course it would naturally take as it leaks down the sides of the locomotive. Be careful not to make your wash too thick, and don't overdo it. Keep the effect of transparency if you can. John Allen recommends stroking in a touch of red or brown paint to give the effect of rust.

Freight cars can also be improved by weathering. Stock cars are usually washed down with a disinfectant or a lime wash which discolors the flooring and the lower side planks to a whitish tone. I obtain this effect with the white oil paint mix.

A nice effect of weathering passenger and freight cars can be easily managed by the use of men's shaving talc, especially the type known as *neutral tint,* supposed not to show on the face. I apply this with a swab of absorbent cotton and find it very effective for getting rid of the shiney "store-boughten" look which so often plagues ready-to-run equipment. While the talc is not very permanent, it will wear well if the cars are not handled too frequently, and is simple to reapply when necessary.

A few years ago, I won a first prize in a rather large model contest with a simple little water tower. The success was due entirely to the aging. See Fig. 7-4. Leaking water forms a white crust on the outside of such towers and also stains and rots the wood. This effect was achieved by the judicious use of oil paints.

The kind of paint to use is a matter of personal preference, but be very careful in mixing it. Most model railroad lacquers will dissolve oil-base paints or other lacquers like a paint remover. So, before you apply one paint over another, make a test first to see if you're headed for trouble.

I prefer oil paints because I'm most familiar with them, but many fine modelers use casein colors, tempera paints, and even water colors. But you'd be well advised to stay clear of ordinary house paints or the like.

Most model railroading paints are lacquers, preferred because they dry quickly and adhere to almost any surface. But their quick-drying quality makes them rather difficult to apply with a brush. Therefore many hobbyists and nearly all professional model makers use a spray gun because the paint goes on faster, dries quicker, and is thinner than if applied by a brush. Thinness is a desirable quality in that it does not obliterate fine details, such as rivet markings and the like.

Fig. 9-2 Paint Spray Gun

Some of the finer craftsmen use an artist's airbrush, a rather expensive piece of equipment for the average amateur. But for less than five dollars, you can get a hobby spray gun at your hobby shop, made by the Stewart/Lundahl Company, which is made to fit onto the end of a vacuum-cleaner hose. See Fig. 9-2. I use one of these little gadgets myself and have found it very satisfactory within its limitations.

While we all strive toward perfection there is a chance of carrying it one step too far. Recently I was a judge at a large model contest and one of the entries was a beautifully made articulated steam locomotive. The builder had painted and aged this gem with an airbrush, and a beautiful job he had done. It looked as if it had just that moment come out of the railroad paint shop. Unfortunately for the contestant, real railroads don't age their locomotives in the paint shop, so the prize went to another builder whose locomotive looked as if it had just come in from a long cross-country drag. Its firebox appeared encrusted with boiler compound, streaks ran down the boiler sides from the pop valves and the smokebox was dirty and rusted. Perhaps it wasn't as well-made or did not have as *perfect* a paint job, but it had that priceless quality of absolute realism. You could almost feel the heat, smell the hot oil of its drivers, and touch the boiler compound.

The most important part of painting a locomotive is the preparation. If you neglect this, your paint may peel off later, for metal surfaces have to be thoroughly cleaned before apply paint or lacquer. The safest course is to disassemble your locomotive and wash the superstructure thoroughly to remove all fingerprints and specks of dust or oil that may be clinging invisibly to the surface, for these may lift off your paint if you do not remove them beforehand. There are several methods for removing this unwanted surface film. Naphtha and benzene are good—I know one professional model painter who uses aviation gasoline, obtained from the local airport—but I prefer washing the superstructure in a mixture of water and a household detergent such as Tide. Some experts recommend brass locomotives be cleaned in a solution of one part white vinegar to ten parts water. The important point is not the method but the thoroughness of the cleaning job.

Many modelers prefer using an undercoat, such as automobile painters use. I tried this method once, but felt that the undercoating made the final paint job too thick to give me the transparent effect I desired.

Whatever paint or lacquer you apply, allow the model plenty of time to dry. It may *appear* dry in an hour or so, but paint of any kind needs at least 24 hours to "set" properly before handling or lettering. So, in your enthusiasm, don't attempt to hurry the job. Remember that patience is a prerequisite to good craftsmanship.

Decalcomanias are most popular with hobbyists for numbering and lettering rolling stock and locomotives because they are relatively easy to apply. You can purchase them at your hobby shop or get a set made up to your own design. Follow the directions that come with them. Trim each letter or word before soaking, and don't soak them too long or you will wash off the thin coating of glue. Work slowly, doing each letter or word before going on to the next. When you have applied your decal let it dry thoroughly, then brush or spray it with a thin coat of varnish (I prefer dull varnish) or a clear lacquer. This will not only help the decal to adhere to the surface but will protect it against the inevitable handling.

I used decals extensively when I first started in the hobby but after attending a few model contests and exhibits, I noticed that nearly all the finest craftsmen did their lettering by hand. I felt this art was beyond my capabilities until I had a surprise visit from Bill Rau, a former president of NMRA and one of the top car builders in the country. Bill had some of his exquisite hand-lettered models with him and when placed beside my models, mine looked very amateurish indeed. Bill then showed me the tricks of the trade, and since that time—no more decals.

Rau uses poster paints, obtainable at any art store and many hobby shops. He applies the paint with a fine lettering pen, although many craftsmen prefer a very fine red sable-hair brush for the purpose. As the poster paint would not normally flow off a pen, Bill thins it a bit with, of all things, *beer*. First plot the lettering carefully on a sheet of paper to serve as a guide and for spacing, then letter directly on the equipment. After the lettering is thoroughly dry, cover it with a coat of varnish.

Of course, as with any other phase of art, practice makes perfect, but even my earliest attempts exceeded my expectations and, to my way of thinking, even a fair job looked better than the absolute precision of the decals. Give it a fair trial, and I think you'll agree with me.

A word about brushes. A cheap brush

is an abomination, and a good artist-quality brush is well worth what you pay for it. A good brush has enough body to carry plenty of paint and the hair will not pull out and ruin your work. I have fallen for bargain paint brushes often enough to have learned that lesson well. And keep your brushes clean while you're working. Lacquers especially have a tendency to gum up a brush, so if the going gets rough, pause and clean your brush in the thinner supplied by the manufacturer of the particular paint or lacquer you are using. The same requirement goes for spray equipment.

For painting nonmetallic models, such as wooden or cardboard structures, bridges, and the like, you have a wider choice of paints. And since this book is based largely on my own experience, a sort of how-I-do-it type of thing, I'll stick to what I know best. As I said earlier, I prefer oil paints, but I do not mean to imply that they are the best. In fact, the finest background scenery I have ever seen was the photographs of the work of Paul Detlefsen, a famous professional illustrator, shown in the December, 1961, issue of *Model Railroader Magazine*. Mr. Detlefsen's work is so exquisite it is almost discouraging to the rest of us. And he uses casein colors rather than oils.

Because my own pike is on the large side and I have a lot of painting to do, I outfitted myself with a good supply of colors. In most cases, it is not necessary to use expensive artist-quality oil paints; I bought most of mine at the local paint store. But as Frank Ellison so aptly put it: "The truth is there are no short cuts or slap-happy methods to finishing a good landscape." Since you are reading this book, it is fair to assume that you want to do as good a job as you are capable of, so we'll proceed on that basis.

It is safest to purchase colors by name, rather than by appearance. And since you will undoubtedly use more white than any other color because of mixes, you will be advised to get a large-sized tube of this, usually known as titanium white. My collection of tubes include burnt sienna, burnt umber, lamp black, raw sienna, raw umber, viridian, yellow ochre, Van Dyke brown, Prussian blue, cobalt green, and ultramarine. And be sure to purchase plenty of pure turpentine and a little linseed oil. With such a stock, you can tackle almost anything. And oil paints are very good for applying to gypsum-based plaster.

For coloring scenery I use a muffin tin as a palette, squeezing out a little—from a quarter to a half inch—of earth colors into each compartment and adding a lot of turps to make a very thin stain. Earth is not a one-color monotone but a blending of many shades of color. To apply, use a good-quality paint brush, from a half to an inch wide, and take a brushful of one color mix, say burnt umber, and press the brush against the side of your mountain or slope and let the color run freely downhill. Before it has a chance to dry, take a brushful of another of the earth colors, such as raw umber, and daub it in the same fashion in almost the same spot so that the colors blend and run together. Keep this up with the various colors until you get the effect you desire. The earth colors are the umbers and the siennas with a little scarlet and Van Dyke brown thrown in. Inasmuch as there are no true blacks in nature, you can use Van Dyke brown to give a blackish appearance. Prussian blue, well thinned, is especially to be recommended for shadows.

Experiment freely. If you don't get the result you want the first time, you can always modify it later with a second coat; that's the beauty of these thin washes.

No one can give you hard and fast directions for painting scenery, but at most art stores you can obtain, for a few cents, a guide to color mixing which will help you in your selection of colors and the blending of them.

Limestone rocks and granite cliffs can be simulated by a thin wash of lamp black with overwashes of ultramarine and burnt sienna. Shale is produced by a wash of burnt sienna, second-coated with a thin wash of Van Dyke brown.

Except for a few extremely well-tended city lawns and golf courses, grass is seldom an evenly colored green. If you get out into the countryside where the wild grasses grow, you will discover that such grasses have more grays and pale yellows than greens. The general effect appears green at first glance but when you train your eye to observe nature as she really is you'll note the subtleties of color.

Roads are peculiarly deceptive. We know that asphalt, for example, is black, but on closer examination, unless freshly applied, it is more often a pale brownish gray. Recently, I drove over a hundred miles on an asphalt highway and was amazed at the variety of colors blended into it. The highway looked like a patchwork quilt, running in shades from a dirty white through varying browns to near-black patches where repairs had been made. It's these details that make a layout realistic, so don't overlook anything.

For coloring dirt roads made of plaster, a mixture of burnt umber and burnt sienna will give you a rich brown earth color, with traces of Van Dyke brown in the deeper ruts, or even a touch of thinned Prussian blue to simulate shadows.

There is no single color that I know of which properly looks like concrete, although a popular brand of model paint has come out with a shade they *call* cement. To the casual eye, concrete appears a light gray, but closer inspection will show a yellowish or light brownish cast. Light gray with a little yellow ochre mixed with it will come reasonably close to the real thing.

Inasmuch as nothing around a railroad—buildings, equipment, or locomotives—remains spotless, especially in the days of coal and steam, bright, new, and shiny equipment and structures look like anachronisms. Grime and soot are inevitable and are washed off the roofs by rain and drip down the sides of the buildings and cars.

To get this dirty effect, you must first paint your buildings as they were when new. Never use shiny enamel finishes; always use thin flat colors. When the structure has dried thoroughly, it is time for dirtying it. Parenthetically, this is sometimes a heartbreaking chore, especially when the newly finished structure looks so nice and clean. But you must harden yourself and regard each structure not as a unity in itself but as a part of the whole scene.

For this job I use a very, very thin wash of lamp black and turps if the structure is light colored or an equally thin grayish mix of white and turps if it is basically dark, for example a black coal hopper. Don't try to achieve your effect with one coat; you may get it on too thick. Weathering is a slow process in nature, so you want to gain the same effect by numerous thin coats, permitted to dry beween washes. My roundhouse is made of illusration board covered with "brick" paper. It took about a half a dozen thin washes before I got the weathering I was striving for.

In applying "grime" and "soot," try to streak it in the same direction that rain running off the roof would take, that is, from the eaves downward.

You will doubtless have some "old" buildings from which the original paint has long since flaked off, leaving bare boards. If the boards have silvered with age, use the white mix, otherwise use a very thin lamp black and turps mix.

The same goes for wood that never was painted, such as log trestles, timbered retaining walls, and railroad ties. Apply your colors sparingly and always keep them transparent, so that the wood texture shows through the stain.

Most of my own prizewinning models have been timbered structures of one kind or another, and I attribute my luck more to the weathering and finishing than to the craftsmanship of making the models. Most good modelers use bass or pine strip wood, which is undoubtedly stronger and nicer to work with than the despised balsa. But where strength and rigidity is not essential, I like balsa because you can achieve such delicate weathering effects with your stains.

My ten-year-old son carried off top honors, in the junior *and* senior classes in structure, in a recent regional contest with an "old" timbered station house. The station itself was made of 1/8" balsa strips, and the shingles of the roof were individually cut from 1/32" balsa. The planked station platform was formed of 1/16" x 1/8" balsa strips. To weather the structure, he used common school-type water colors—mostly black, thinned down with water. It required about three or four coats to get that "silver" effect of age, and after coloring it to his satisfaction—and mine—he emphasized the whole by burning between the shingles and between the timbers with a small burning iron. A small soldering iron would do a similar job. The finished effect was almost incredible. Unhappily, some of the viewers were unkind enough to say the boy hadn't made it at all, that it was my work. It was not; however, I grant I couldn't have done it better myself. See Fig. 7-6 for a photograph of this model.

The whole secret, if there is any *secret* about it, lies in the thinness of the coats. It is a matter of *stain,* not *paint*.

Another good trick in coloring structures and freight or passenger cars is to paint as much as possible *before* assembling them. This is especially true about such delicate detail as window and door trim, which is very difficult to do properly when construction is finished. You may have to touch up the otherwise-finished job with paint, but you'll get a clearcut line in your trim if you paint it separately, before you glue it in place.

And speaking of glue: Most model cements dry to a hard, shiny surface, like clear ice, and will not be covered by paint. For that reason, I prefer such casein-type glues as Elmer's Glue-All because they dry to a flat surface that is easily covered by paint. I grant you that the expert isn't supposed to let glue or cement ooze out onto the surface of his model, but I never met a modeler that doesn't have it happen enough to be a headache.

Nearly all glue and cement manufacturers claim to have the all-purpose glue, but I haven't discovered it yet. In my "adhesive" box, I keep Duco and Ambroid cements, which have the principal virtue of quick-drying, Elmer's Glue-All if there is any possibility of getting it on the face of my model, Pliobond for glueing rail to ties in trackwork, some of the new epoxy cements for really tough jobs, such as joining metals, Walthers' Goo for the same type of job, and a large can of Weldwood powdered glue for big jobs, such as binding roadbed together, fastening the grids of the framework, laying a base for ballast, and that type of work.

For painting passenger cars, Bill Rau uses Tuscan red, in the standard railroad lacquers, darkened with a little black, to achieve a most effective rich brown, such as the color of the Pennsylvania Railroad's cars.

The edges of my harbor are "planked" with balsa strips, and "creosoted" with the same thin wash I use on other timbered surfaces. Then I darken this above the waterline where the seepage of the water would normally take place.

Let me repeat, because a prototype railroad uses a certain paint it doesn't mean that the same paint will look right on a miniature model! I know of modelers who have gone down to the paint shops of real railroads and chiselled or promoted a can of the real paint the road uses. And then they wonder why their own cars, so painted, do not look right. Not long ago, a friend of mine, spent several months making a beautiful bridge for a contest. Since the original was creosoted, he argued that you couldn't get anything that looked so much like creosote as creosote itself. Well, that sounded logical enough, but the result was disasterous. The excellent model looked as if it had been dipped in black paint, and didn't even place in the contest. The moral is: Don't worry about what the original was painted with; strive to get the same effect with your own mixtures.

The painting of backgrounds is a very controversial subject, especially when it comes to perspective. Even a professional artist runs against the hard fact that the scale of a train in the background is the same as a train in the foreground, and while it may seen a trifle smaller in the limited distance of the average pike, it still defies the whole premise of perspective. Then, too, there is the plaguing question of shadows. The shadows formed by the three-dimensional structures and scenery in the foreground depend largely on the angle from which you view them, but shadows on a painted background never vary. McClanahan gets around this by not having any structures on his backdrop, but even that doesn't solve the problem of shadows formed by hills and mountains.

This may seem like technical quibbling, but it is disconcerting to see the sun on the right side of your background and on the left side in your three-dimensional scenery. You can whip this dilemma to some extent by arranging your pike lighting so that the sun of your foreground comes from the same direction and angle as your background lighting does.

By the same token, you can sort of "straddle the fence" on the problem of perspective. I accomplish this by building the structures in the background to a scale slightly smaller than HO, about 1/8″ to the foot. The little English-type village against the back wall in Fig. 6-1 is a case in point. Then I painted the background to a limited perspective. Now when you look at a distant range of mountains you will observe that those farthest away are dimmed by an atmospheric haze. This same effect of the background receding in the distance can be achieved with the help of a spray gun. Mix an "atmospheric haze"—composed of white, a bluish-gray, and a touch of brown—make it very thin, and when your background is perfectly dry, apply it in a very fine spray. I cannot overemphasize this business of thinness in applying color. The reason my background is unfinished in the photograph is that I put on the original coat too thick and had to paint it over with white paint to begin over again. You are not painting a house to protect it against the weather; you are trying to achieve an artistic effect.

Frank Ellison and many other good modelers do not make four-sided buildings, reasoning that since the pike cannot be viewed from the back, the back of a building is superfluous. John Ahern, in his excellent book, *Miniature Building Construction,* shows how to make whole streets of backless buildings. So far, most of my buildings have been built complete, chiefly because I enjoy the construction and because I like to put electric lights in my structures. But backless buildings would undoubtedly save time.

Ellison is also famous for his "flats," that is, structures cut from magazine illustrations and cemented to flat pieces of illustration board. Placed in the background and viewed from the front angle only, these are very effective. Or you can paint the building on the illustration board yourself, if you are talented enough. Flats representing low hills and placed just an inch or two in front of your painted backdrop can also be highly effective and help to create a feeling of depth. There are no standard rules; all that counts is the final result.

Another assist to realism is to remember that most real railroads adopt a standard of coloring; most of their stations are of one color, their trackside structures another, and so on. On the WA&P we have settled on a pale yellow for company stations, although some of the older wayside stations, erected before the WA&P "gained control," are painted other colors. It is just a device to achieve a real railroading atmosphere.

CHAPTER 10

Special Effects

A few years ago I had the privilege of being present on the opening night of a Broadway play that was to become famous. The rising curtain opened on the scene of a dry riverbed in California, beautifully illuminated by blue light to represent nighttime. As the audience stared in wonder at this magnificent setting, a coyote was heard howling in the distance. There wasn't a living person in the scene, yet the audience rose spontaneously as one and gave the setting a standing ovation that any famous star would have envied.

When the actors came onstage later they were superb, but for many of us the setting "stole the show." It established the mood, the locale, the atmosphere, and that intangible quality—the reality. It was a powerful and impressive lesson for a would-be model railroader.

For just as a good stage production depends heavily on special lighting and off-stage sound effects, so should a good model railroad. The ideal is to bring your pike to life, and it's asking too much of the movement of trains alone to accomplish this. Of course, if you mean to concentrate on operation alone, you will be concerned primarily with the general lighting of your layout, so we'll start with that.

All too many model rails are satisfied to have a couple of bare, unshaded lamp bulbs hanging over their pikes, but this gives a flat uninteresting light that is hard on the eyes. Fluorescent lights are better, but have the disadvantage of being undimmable if and when you want to create night scenes. The basic principle of lighting is to illuminate your railroad to the best advantage without making the lighting itself intrusive.

It is impossible to set up standard rules for pike lighting, since there is no such thing as a standard pike. Each individual layout is "an island unto itself" and the only way I know of to get the effect you desire is by experimenting with various types of lighting—overall lighting, spotlighting with various colored lights, or fluorescent lamps. A lot depends on the coloring of your scenery and the structure of it; and whether it is an around-the-wall type of pike, a walk-around, or whether you and your visitors view it only from one angle, as in a stage play.

Before you begin, it is essential to have a clear concept of what you are striving for. And inasmuch as I have no way of knowing what *your* concept is, I can only tell you about *mine,* in the hope that it will give you enough ideas to go ahead on your own plan.

As I have said elsewhere in this book, my pike is viewable only from the front, in the manner of a stage setting. That makes the problem of lighting simpler. And as the traditional footlighting used in stage productions is not adaptable to a layout, I reversed the procedure and put the footlights above the scene instead of below it. I built a valance, using a six-inch board, across the front of the pike and hid my lights behind it.

This worked fine—for illuminating structures and scenery well toward the front of the layout, but it was too dim further back. And inasmuch as parts of my layout are fifteen feet in width, I had to install two more valances; one about two feet from my backdrop and the other halfway between the front and the back valance. Each valance has its own row of

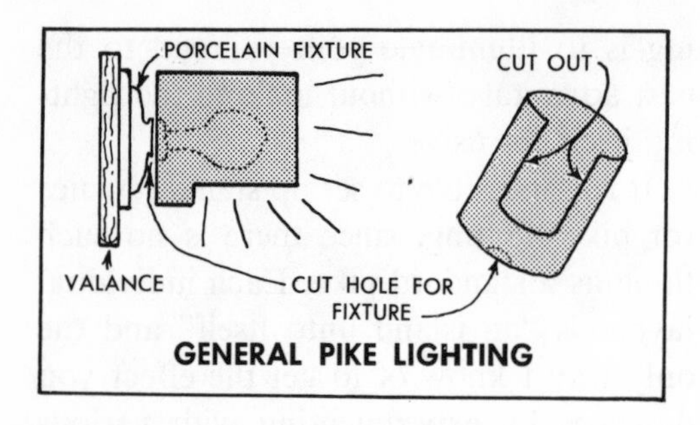

Fig. 10-1 Valence Lampshade

five bulbs, shaded by cutdown tin cans, as shown in Fig. 10-1. I used ordinary tin cans, about five inches in diameter and about six inches in depth, and cut out about a third of the can as shown in the drawing, cutting a hole in the bottom to fit over a cheap porcelain fixture. The can serves to concentrate the light and direct it where I want it to shine, much as the reflector does in a flashlight or an automobile headlight.

As some parts of the pike required more light than other parts, I controlled this by the wattage of the bulbs. Some are 100 watts, others 50, but the average is about 75 watts. As with the height of your table, which should be adjusted to your own height, I placed the valances at what I deemed a comfortable height; high enough to afford a clear view of the whole pike, and sufficiently low to conceal the bulbs themselves from my eyes. It has proven very effective and gives a fine even light for general operation.

That's how the matter stands at the moment on the WA&P but the plan is set for further development. Between each of the white lamps will go another fixture to carry colored lights for special effects, such as night scenes, dawn breaking, and the like. A percentage of this second bank of lights will be blue, with red and amber mixed in as experimentation dictates.

The next step will be to install two variable transformers or heavy rheostats; one for gradually cutting off the white bulbs, the other for turning on the colored lights to give the effect of day fading into night.

It was this latter scheme that negated the use of fluorescent lamps which will not function on variable voltage. If you do not care to have dimming effects, fluorescent lights are fine, especially if you use the cool white tubes.

The marvelous effects you can obtain by lighting alone are limited only by your desires and your imagination. Some model rails achieve the effect of an electrical storm by sudden flashes of lightning on distant hills. You can install a moon by using a light-blue spotlight, or with a spot you can attract attention to a particular structure or bit of scenery. You can install working headlights on your locomotives, which not only give a nice effect but will improve your control, as mentioned in the chapter on electricity. Or, if you are clever enough, you can install high-frequency lighting in conjunction with your track power to light up your passenger trains. Paul Mallery, in his electrical handbook, describes how to build a high-frequency oscillator for this purpose but it is too complicated for inclusion in this book.

There is one simple little piece of detail on my pike which never fails to attract visitors—a small camp scene, placed on a flat area of a mountain. This is, presumably, a hunter's camp, with a tiny wall tent constructed of paper and a roaring campfire in front of it. There is a pack mule standing nearby and a few tiny figures of men warming their hands by the fire. But it is the fire itself which makes the scene; it is the focal point of interest. The fire is simply a grain-of-wheat bulb, stained to a light red, set on the ground with logs of split matches glued into a cone-shaped pile over it. The light from the bulb glows between the logs like a real fire. Obviously, you don't want to pile the wood so thick around the bulb that you block out this flame effect.

Now as the dominant characteristic of a railroad, especially a steam railroad, is *sound,* you cannot very well ignore it and hope to achieve a sense of reality. Whistles, bells, the thunder of pop valves, the hiss of steam are so essential to the setting that we must find a way of duplicating them.

This is not difficult for at least a dozen specialized companies are putting out recordings of railroad sounds: switching, passing over trestles and bridges, passing standing trains in the night, or a long freight drag laboring up a hill. For a list of such record makers, you have but to look in almost any issue of one of the model railroading magazines. Columbia Records also has a number of sound effect records available.

To get the full benefit of these sound effects, you will of course need a record player or, better still, a tape recorder, and a few speakers arranged judiciously around your pike, with suitable controls for cutting them on and off as needed.

Perhaps the best method of elucidating the possibilities of sound is to describe the plans for such effects we have for the WA&P. First, there will be a series of general railroading sound effects. We are getting some of those very tiny speakers, available at any large radio-supply house, which can be inserted into the tender of almost any HO locomotive, since they measure only about 1″ in length and width and ¾″ in depth. By means of an appropriate tape, this will give out the sounds of a locomotive in actual operation—the sound being piped to the speaker in the tender through the tracks. The complete details on how to achieve this seeming miracle are revealed in an article by Herbert Chaudiere in the May, 1959, issue of *Model Railroader Magazine.* While somewhat complex, it is not difficult, and is well worth the effort involved.

With such a set-up, you will be able to hear your engine thundering along the rails, whistle blowing, pop valves barking, and the drivers pounding as she comes to a stop in a hiss of steam.

As a starter, we have achieved a very satisfactory effect by buying a couple of those toy "whistling stations," discarding the station part and setting the sound-making apparatus at strategic points under the pike. Then by means of doorbell-type push buttons, placed on the side of my control panel, I can flash the proper whistling from trains as they near a station or a crossing. As the sound is somewhat diffused, it seems to emanate from whatever train happens to be moving in the vicinity of the source.

Other small speakers will be inserted in some of the structures which lend themselves to sound, such as saw mills, cattle barns, churches, and the like. All this will necessitate a sound-effects panel, separate from the main control panel, so that the sounds can be cut on and off as required.

The *pièce de résistance* will be when we invite a visitor to climb into a locomotive cab and take an imaginary journey around the layout. Then he will hear all the sounds of a locomotive from the inside, including the conversation between the engineer and the fireman, and over this he will hear the sounds presumably emanating from whatever building he is passing, the whine of a saw biting into a log as the train passes the sawmill, church bells and perhaps a choir singing as he rolls past the church, cattle bawling in the cattle sale barn, that peculiar rumble as he rolls by a string of empties in a siding, and so forth.

All this will call for careful synchronization of both recording and of the speed of the train. For example it would ruin the effect if the music of the church came in clearly as our passenger passed the sawmill. I mean to make up a careful chart of the exact instant the train will pass each structure at a prearranged speed and then write up a script of the precise timing when the different sounds must be cut in, much as the sound effects are timed for a TV show or a stage play.

Even more so than with lighting effects, the possibilities are endless. You can bolster your lightning effects with a recording of a thunder storm. Wakefield, the scenic artist, even has crickets chirping in the night scenes on his pike. If you have access to a portable tape recorder, there are no limits to what you can achieve. Dogs barking, crickets chirping, a wolf howling in the distance, the bellowing of a station master announcing outgoing or incoming trains, the crow of a cock at dawn—anything to increase the dramatic effect of realism. Wakefield has also installed tiny fans that blow on the faces of visitors during a thunder storm. Small rheostats or potentiometers inserted in the lines to your tiny speakers can create the effect of the sounds dying away in the distance.

If you are fortunate enough to have a radio ham or a recording bug among your acquaintances, he'll be able to help you over the technical hurdles. All I can hope to do in this book is indicate the possibilities.

One thing that has long troubled scale model fans is the lack of smoke emanating from their locomotives. But recently this problem has been overcome. Certain manufacturers now build small units which can be inserted in your locomotives for creating smoke effects. The tiny devices can also be installed in factories and residences if desired. They use smoke pellets or smoke-making fluid you can obtain at your hobby shop. Or, if you prefer, you can make your own smoke unit out of one of those electric bottle warmers mothers use for heating baby's formula. I made one out of an electrical "insect killer"—a small gadget about the size of a house lamp socket which had a small heating coil in the base and a tiny tin can to heat the repellant. Although it wasn't much good as a fly killer, it did an excellent job cooking the small smoke pellets I dropped into it. I fastened it under the pike and ran a small metal tube, painted to resemble a tall smokestack, through a factory on the pike. Dropping a smoke pellet down the stack puts it into the warming pan and the resultant smoke that issues from the stack is very realistic.

Another special effect which can afford you a lot of fun and satisfaction is experimenting with animation. Some of the toy train manufacturers have developed all manner of strange and unprototypical contraptions in this line, so be careful not to overdo it; you don't want to downgrade a good scale pike to the level of a toy train layout. But a few touches here and there are not only permissible but desirable.

You can do a lot of tricks with an old Model T spark-plug coil if you can lay hands on one; they are not hard to come by—I got mine from a junk dealer specializing in antique car parts. The first time the possibilities were shown to me was several years ago when visiting the pike of a well-known model rail in Ohio.

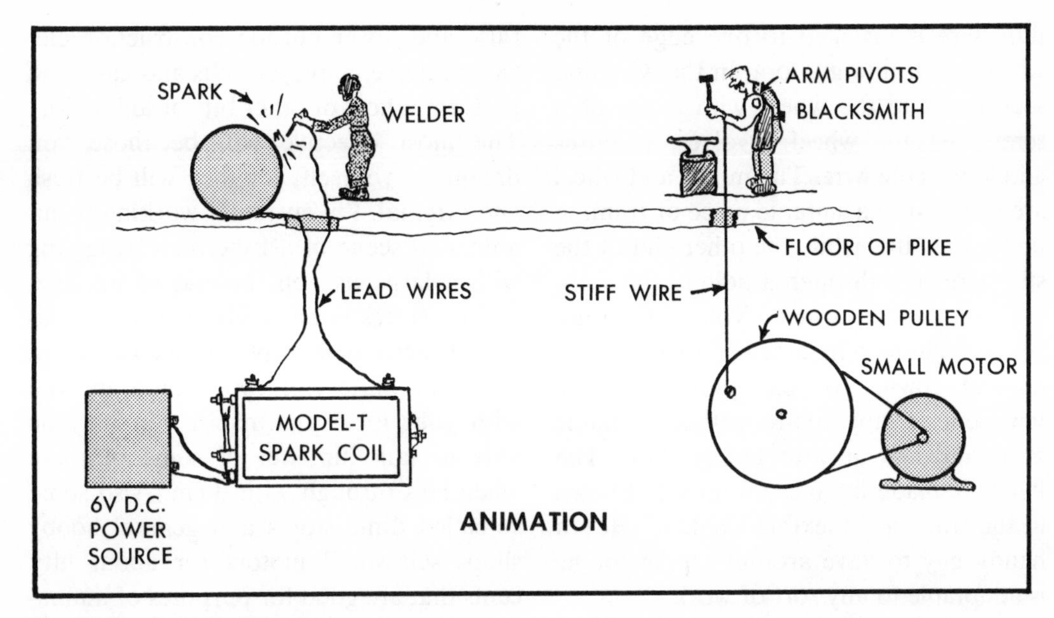

Fig. 10-2 Animated Figures

He had put his trains through their paces and just about the time we were thinking of taking our leave, there was a loud cracking and a spurt of blue flame from the overhead wires on his electric trolley line. It was highly effective. I thought it was a genuine short circuit or something of the kind. My host said he would have to rush a work train to the scene, and in a moment he had a work train hurtling around the track in the direction of the trouble. It was a dramatic little episode and, when I realized it was staged, I wanted to know how the trick was done.

He had, of course, deliberately planned a gap in his trolley-overhead wire and hooked it up to a Model T spark-plug coil. The modern automobile coils will not serve, since they require a distributor whereas the old-type coil did the job of producing a spark by itself.

Later I saw the same basic idea used in another fashion. Near a model roundhouse a tiny metal figure, complete with face shield and gloves, was in the act of welding a broken piece of machinery. From the miniature electrode in his hand blazed the typical blue-white flame of a welding torch.

The hookup is simple. Both the welder and the machine to be welded should be made of metal. A wire from one side of the spark coil goes to the electrode in the welder's hand, the other to the machinery. When you press your effects' switch the circuit is complete and the spark jumps from the electrode to the machinery, creating a lifelike spark. You adjust the length and intensity of the spark by the distance between the electrode and the object being welded, and/or by adjusting the thumb nut on the top of the coil.

I have seen a blacksmith forging a horseshoe on his anvil and a man cutting logs, both actions being controlled by the same or a similar device, such as illustrated in Fig. 10-2. It's just the old drive-wheel principle, similar to the treadle on an old-style sewing machine. A small, slow motor—or you can gear down a faster motor if you prefer—has a wooden wheel attached, and a length of stiff but thin wire is fastened to one edge of the wheel but forming a loop in the wire and securing it to the wheel with a pin or a screw. As the wheel revolves, it raises and lowers the wire. The motor and wheel are fastened to a suitable piece of framing under the pike, while the other end of the stiff wire goes through a hole in the scenery to a flexible arm on your tiny figure which, holding a hammer or an ax, moves up and down. You can purchase for a few cents a tiny figure with detachable arms and legs at your hobby shop. The figure is made by Weston, and is known in the trade as "Flexible Freddy." He's a handy guy to have around a pike for he is adaptable to any sort of work.

As you experiment, many new and unusual ideas will occur to you. The treadle principle is good on animated signboards or for many other purposes. You can raise and lower outside construction elevators, move conveyor belts and cars, and perform a host of other bits of animation. The most effective will be those you dream up yourself, for they will be fresh and original. I'm currently working on an animated scene of a fisherman struggling with a large fish on the end of his line.

Drugstores in particular use many animated signs with tiny motors run by a flashlight battery. If you stand in well with your local pharmacist you may be able to talk him out of some of these when he's through with them. Also some so-called dime stores and general hobby shops sell small motors for about fifty cents that are good for purposes of animation. Sometimes you can salvage some helpful machinery out of discarded toys. The list is endless once you get the general idea of what you want and need.

CHAPTER 11

Steam Locomotives and Other Motive Power

To any small boy of fifty or sixty years ago, the steam locomotive was easily the most glorious and wondrous creation of mankind. Every normal boy with red blood in his veins wanted to be an engineer and guide one of these mastodonlike monsters to its ultimate destination in the Big Rock Candy Mountains, the Valhalla where such heroes go to dwell through eternity with the other heroes of history and the old gods. It is impossible to exaggerate the effect of the steam locomotive on life in America about the turn of the century.

To the average man of fifty or thereabouts, no memory in life is quite so poignantly ecstatic as his first introduction to one of these giants of yesteryear. I can still recall with awful clarity the evening my mother and I stood on the planked platform of the little station at Chaudiere, a division point on the Canadian National Railroad about nine miles west of Quebec, waiting for the Ocean Limited to come in from Montreal. This was a very special occasion, not only because the Ocean Limited was one of the two fastest trains operating in Canada, but also because the engineer was my uncle—imagine such a hero being one's very own uncle! I was all atremble with anticipation and clung tightly to my mother's reassuring hand.

Darkness settled over the scene, but that was all right; the train wouldn't be late. My Uncle Will would as soon have denied the existence of God as bring his train in thirty seconds late. *On Time* was a religion with him, as with all his breed in those days.

"She'll be along in a couple of minutes now," remarked the kindly station agent.

The observation was extraneous, for a moment later we heard the imperious blast of *her* whistle, far away to the west. Was there ever such a heavenly sound? It came rolling out of the forest, sprang lithely over the intervening river, and rolled down upon us with a blast that seemed to set the planks atremble under our very feet. My mother was a great lover of classical music and had sought vainly to inculcate a similar love in me, but I thought then (and still think today) that nothing of the feeble compositions of Brahms could compare with the throaty scream of a locomotive whistle on a frosty autumn night. Even the legendary trumpet of Gabriel is a sickly imitation.

Soon the Cyclopean eye of the locomotive flashed its yellow radiance down the shining rails and the thunder of the drivers became audible. The very ground began to quiver and I thought I would have to run away, not in terror but in sheer excitement. The thrill was almost more than one small boy could endure.

We moved back slightly from the edge of the platform and stood trembling. The station agent had told us where the locomotive would stop and at long last she pulled up precisely where he said she would. I was more impressed than ever. How could one man bring this snorting monster to a stop where he wanted it?

Although Chaudiere was the end of her run, as another locomotive would haul the train to the next division point, the locomotive did not relax and act as if she was glad her work was over for the nonce, like a livery horse coming back to the stable after a hard day. On the contrary she stood hissing and snorting as if impatient over the delay. In a way, she made me think of the big lead dog of a team of giant Malemutes I had sometimes seen bringing furs in from the Far North—savage, eager, panting with exertion, yet anxious to get going again.

Then I saw my uncle looking down from the right-hand window of his little (by comparison) cab. Like all railroaders of that early day, he was a confirmed individualist. He recognized my mother and with a surprisingly nonchalant wave of his black-gloved hand, he climbed down out of his cab in the imperious manner of some pirate chieftain swinging to the dock from his ship. Was it possible that this ferocious looking moustached giant was the same kindly man that had so often dangled me on his knee? I marveled that he would dare leave this monster even long enough to salute us.

He took me by the hand and led me closer to the drivers. I was both loathe and eager to go.

"She's breathing hard," I said nervously.

"Oh, that's only the compressor pumping air for the air brakes," he said with a smile.

But I knew different. The monster was alive, and that panting came from its living body. The great drivers towered above me. I had seen other locomotives, Moguls and Consolidateds, but this was my first close-up of a Pacific-type locomotive. It was said that in the United States they had even larger locomotives, Mikados and Berkshires, but I knew this was a lie on the face of it. No locomotive *could* be bigger that this giant. That was impossible!

He lifted me into the cab, where the fireman was readying the engine preparatory to turning it over to the hostler, the lucky man who would guide it to the roundhouse. My uncle stepped on the pedal that opened the butterfly door of the firebox and I glanced inside. Then I knew that what the preacher said on Sundays *was* true—there was a hell! I sprang back in terror; it almost made a Christian out of me. Then my uncle explained the vast myriad of valves and controls; a waste of time because I didn't see how any one man could possibly understand that great complexity of equipment. He let me sit in the engineer's seat and put my hand on the throttle that controlled the speed (he said) and touch the great Johnson lever, which put the monster in reverse. All this time the fireman was fussing with the fire. I watched him out of the corner of my eye, jealous because I knew that someday he would be an engineer. In the awesome glow he looked like an imp of hell stirring up the eternal fires. I little thought that someday I, too, would be a fireman.

It is difficult in these days of giant trailer trucks and diesel locomotives to realize the grip these steam locomotives had on the heart of America in an earlier era. When the Virginia Railroad appealed to the commission to abandon its money-losing Orange branch, a farmer testified in the inevitable opposition suit that he and his cattle liked the sound of the train's whistle and therefore didn't want operation suspended.

Now, unhappily, the steam locomotive has all but vanished from the American scene, but the spirit lives on in thousands of model pikes throughout the country. True, these tiny replicas do not heave and pant when they pull into a miniature station; the little Pittman motors wait quietly for another turn of the rheostat. But the imagination can vivify that model and any oldster will tell you that *he* hears the puffing and the snorting and the hiss of

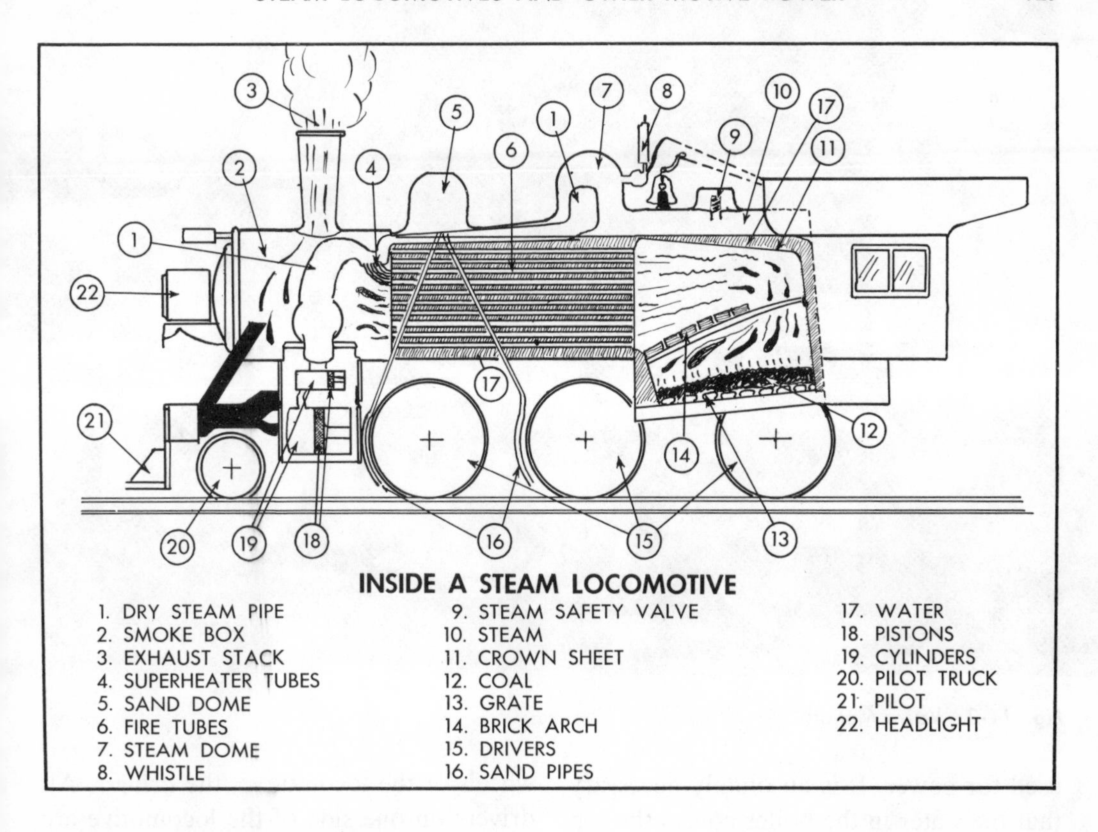

Fig. 11-1 Interior of Locomotive

steam escaping from the steam chests. That's where the real thrill of model railroading comes to the man over forty.

While it is possible to operate a scale model locomotive without any knowledge of how a steam locomotive works, it is much more fun if you do know, and every model rail worthy of the name is interested in the prototype. Figure 11-1 will give you a basic idea of what is inside a typical steam locomotive.

The discovery of steam as a source of energy is usually attributed to James Watts, but in truth it goes much further back in time than that. In the *Pneumatica* of Heron of Alexandria (*ca.* 130 B.C.) is a description of an *aeolipe* which was, in effect, a primitive steam turbine, but it was put to no practical use at that time. Most of us make our first discovery of steam by watching a water kettle vibrating on the stove and watching the live steam escaping from the spout. Steam, then, is the vapor of water and in its pure state is an invisible gas. If you plug the spout of the kettle on the fire, the lid will dance to allow the steam to escape. If the lid is fastened down, the kettle will explode because the power of expanding steam is fantastic. It is this power, or energy, which makes a steam engine, such as a locomotive, operate. This is the basic principle.

Refer again to the illustration of the steam locomotive in Fig. 11-1. As you will see, the locomotive is, essentially, divided into three main sections—the smokebox, the boiler, and the firebox. Our locomotive is, in effect, a giant kettle which produces steam, which, in turn, is

Fig. 11-2 Valve Motion

used for power. It is absolutely necessary that the water in the boiler covers the top of the firebox, the *crown sheet* (No. 11 in the drawing). This is the responsibility of the engine crew, for if this crown sheet became dry, the boiler would explode, causing almost certain death to the men in the cab.

To make the locomotive go, the engineer pulls the throttle which opens a valve in the steam dome (No. 7) which passes the steam into the dry-steam pipe (No. 1) which, in turn, feeds the steam into the cylinders (No. 19) forcing the pistons (No. 18) to pump back and forth driving the crosshead (not shown in the drawing) which manipulates a complexity of small rods known as the *valve motion* or *valve gears* for feeding steam into alternate ends of the cylinders. There are several different types of valve motions but, as they are beyond the scope of this book, let us just say that the crosshead also operates the main driving rod to the big wheels of the locomotive, the *drivers*. All drivers on one side of the locomotive are linked by big *connecting rods* or *side rods* as they are called, which force the wheels to revolve in unison. See Fig. 11-2 for valve motion of a Norfolk & Western Y6B.

When the engineer wants to back up, or reverse his direction, he throws the reverse lever, which, by a complicated linkage with the valve gear puts steam into the opposite end of the cylinder, causing the pistons to function in the opposite direction. In earlier days, this was a huge lever, known as the Johnson bar, which functioned much as does the reverse gear shift on your automobile. As I recall from my own days as a fireman, it used to take a real *man* to manipulate this giant reverse lever.

In more modern types of locomotives, however, the elbow grease is supplied by compressed air and the reversing is as easy as in a modern automobile.

IDENTIFYING STEAM LOCOMOTIVES

Most newcomers to the hobby are confused by the multiplicity of types of steam locomotives and by the easy glibness which experienced model rails use when speaking of Berkshires, Pacifics, 10-wheeler, Moguls, *et al.* This difficulty was anticipated years ago by a man named Whyte, and he evolved a very simple method of classifying locomotives by their wheel arrangements, a method used not only by model fans but by the real railroad companies as well.

You doubtless know already that the small wheels under the front end of the locomotive are the pilot wheels, that the large wheels are the drivers, and that the smaller wheels under the cab are the trailing wheels. This is the basis of the Whyte classification system.

To identify any steam locomotive, you simply count the wheels, starting always at the front end. See Fig. 11-3. If it has no pilot wheels or trailing wheels, it is a switch engine. If it has three drivers on one side it is an 0 (for the pilot wheels) 6 (drivers) 0 (trailing wheels), in other words, an 0-6-0 switcher. If it has four drivers to a side, it is an 0-8-0 switcher, and so on.

Logically, a locomotive with a pair of pilot wheels, four drivers, and a pair of trailing wheels will be deemed a 2-4-2. You call the shots by counting the different styles of wheels as you look at the locomotive, but you will have to memorize the *type* of locomotive which the wheel arrangement signifies—in this case, a 2-4-2 is a Columbia type.

Figure 11-2 will give you a working premise to start on, and covers the most popular types, but it is by no means complete; there are many more types than I can hope to cover in this book. But the principle is the same in any case. Remember—you do *not* count the tender wheels; only those of the locomotive.

DIESEL LOCOMOTIVES

As "president" of an HO gauge railroad and, therefore, not concerned with the eternal problem of revenues, I can afford to indulge my whims of the romantic and the picturesque. Hence I have only steam locomotives on my roster. No diesels are tolerated.

Admittedly that is turning one's back on reality—permissive in a hobby. However, the diesel is here to stay, and if tomorrow I were appointed to the presidency of a real railroad, the first thing I would do is to make certain the road was completely dieselized. Of course, I would care lovingly for any steam locomotives in the roundhouse, and keep a few in good running order for those emergencies which often crop up on railroads where, for reasons of flooding, sleet storms, and the like, which incapacitate the modern diesel, I would need steam.

There is no disputing the fact that the diesel is a money-maker, and has taken many a railroad out of the red side of the ledger and placed it comfortably in the black. Though it pains me to concede it, the diesel is more efficient than the steam locomotive, costs less to operate and much less to maintain. Hence its popularity with the accounting departments of railroads, if not with the bulk of railroad fans. Real railroads have stockholders to satisfy as well as fans.

There is no simple method of classifying diesels, such as the aforementioned Whyte system used in identifying steam locomotives. You have to identify a diesel largely by its silhouette. To further complicate the matter, diesels are chiefly multipurpose locomotives; that is, the same

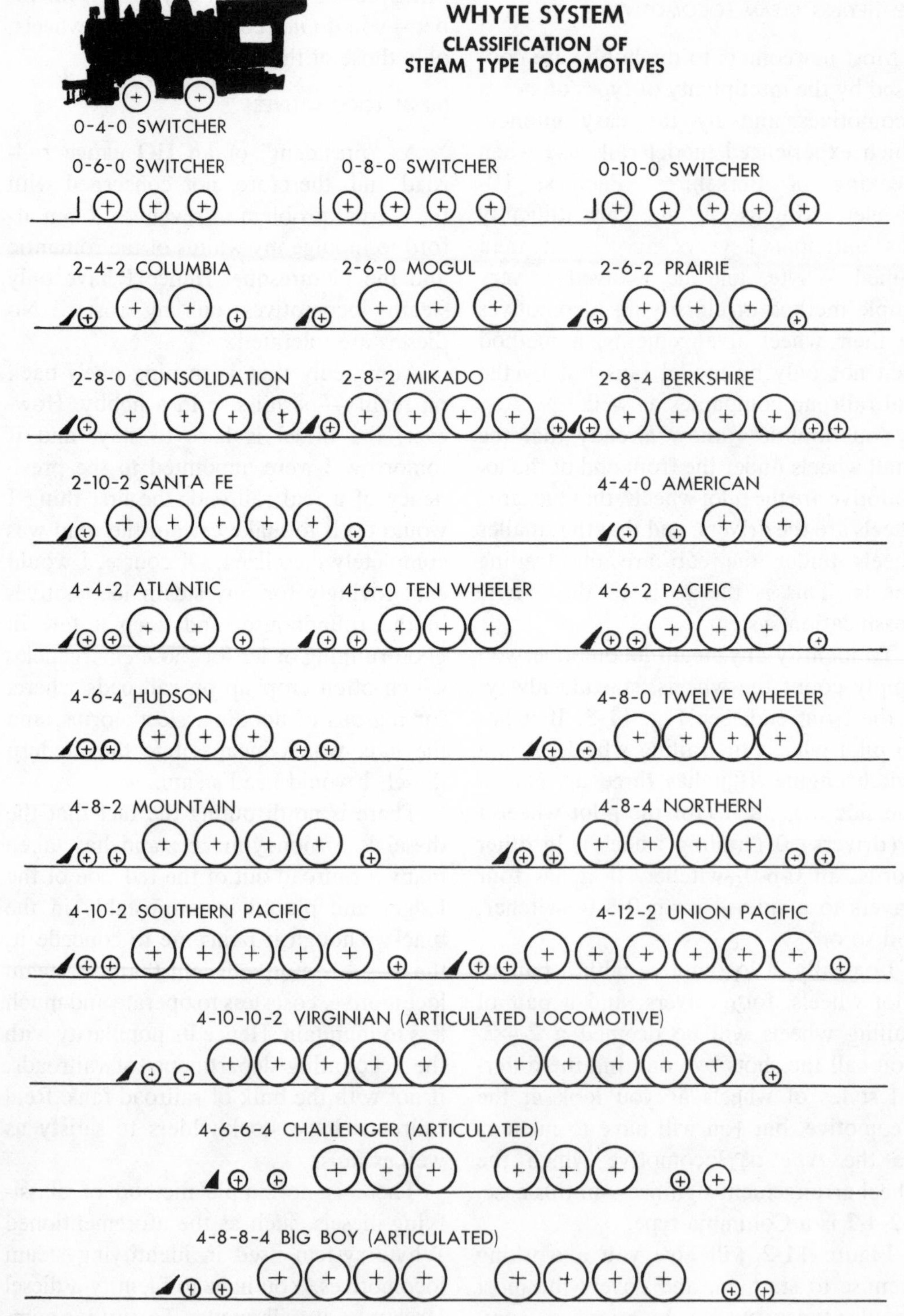

Fig. 11-3 Identifying Locomotives (Steam)

locomotive can be used in either slow freight or fast passenger service—one reason for their popularity with the motive-power departments of the railroads. The NMRA Data Sheets gives you drawings of these silhouettes, with the proper designations.

Electric locomotives are used by many railroad companies, especially by those with big terminals in major cities which do not permit steam locomotives within their limits. The straight electric, like the diesel, is built for all kinds of service, from main-line operation to switching service. They too are identified by their silhouettes.

ACQUIRING LOCOMOTIVES

To the best of my knowledge there are only five ways of obtaining locomotives, aside from receiving them as gifts: buy them RTR (ready-to-run); buy kits and put them together yourself; buy them secondhand, a risky procedure; scratch-build them; or, if price is no object, have them custom-built for you by a professional.

In the RTR field, there are some beauties on the market—and plenty of monstrosities. They run all the way from the frankly toy market, to the exquisite miniatures imported from Japan. Many of the American and European models fall into the former class, with too-large flanges and out-of-scale sturdiness. Many have plastic bodies which make them too light in weight, thereby losing traction power and adhesion. Their principal virtue—if it is a virtue—is cheapness, a poor criterion to use in the choice of a piece of motive power. If you have found an honest dealer, ask him for his candid advice; and, if you have joined the NMRA, as I advised, you will have been given a scale gauge for whatever scale you are in. I wouldn't consider buying a locomotive or any rolling stock without applying this gauge to their wheels, for all too many imports and some American-made equipment will not measure up to the standards.

American-built locomotive kits are an economical way of adding to your motive-power roster. It is grand fun building a kit locomotive, and wonderful experience. They all come with detailed, easy-to-read-and-understand instructions; and in the end you have a piece of your own workmanship to show for your efforts. It is not my intention to praise one manufacturer over another but from my own experience I have found Mantua and Penn-line kits to be well worth the money. Of the dozen or so locomotives on my own pike, four were built from Mantua kits; another four are Japanese imports, RTR's, from Pacific Fast Mail; one is a custom-built Atlantic from the bench of Joe Dorazio, of Morristown, Pennsylvania, one of the best professionals in the business; and the rest are odd jobs I picked up here and there.

There's nothing I can say about kit building that won't be said in the instructions that come with each kit, so my only advice is to follow these instructions to the letter. If you do this, you shouldn't have any major difficulty although there are inevitable adjustments which must be made. Just be certain that your wheels run free in their slots and that the gears mesh properly. If you get them too tight you will be headed for trouble.

Buying secondhand equipment is always risky. You may get a honey or you may get a lemon. You'll have to use your own discretion, but base your judgment on the integrity of the seller and on his model-making capacity. I've seen all too many modelers take a good kit, and by careless or sloppy building, utterly ruin it. However, model rails, like all humans, eventually die, and sometimes you can obtain excellently built and cared-for models from their estates. But get either a guarantee from the seller or a good demonstration of the locomotive's capabilities before you invest.

Scratch-building your own locomotives is the ultimate! But it is no job for the novice. Occasionally I read in the model railroading magazines an article on "kitchen table" scratch-building of locomotives; how some fellow with a file and an assortment of brass builds a locomotive without any machinery. I won't state categorically that it can't be done, but the odds are a thousand to one against it.

A model locomotive is a delicate piece of machinery, with extremely narrow tolerances, and must be as precise as a fine jewelled watch; everything must be in absolute alignment or you'll have a bind. In the planning stages of this book, I took a tape recorder and visited Joe Dorazio, a professional locomotive builder, and recorded the step-by-step procedure in the construction of a model, for I intended to put in a chapter on building your own locomotives.

That did it! I doubt if there are twenty model rails in the country with sufficient equipment and machinery to do a good job. Joe uses two milling machines—a vertical mill and a horizontal mill—a metal lathe and innumerable hand tools, not to mention a large assortment of taps and dies, special soldering equipment, and, an important ingredient, oodles of patience.

A lot of so-called scratch-built equipment is built on professionally made running gear—either assembled from kits or built by a professional, for this running gear is the most difficult and precise part of a locomotive.

Figure 11-4 illustrates what I'm driving about; it is the running gear of one of Dorazio's locomotives. Once you have the running gear in perfect order, the rest of the locomotive, the boiler, superstructure, cab, etc., are basically decoration and relatively easy to build.

Some of Dorazio's finished products are shown in Figs. 11-5, 6, 7, and 8—finished except for painting and superdetailing. As you will notice, Joe puts on a minimum of trimmings, feeling that the purchaser can "doll up" the locomotive to suit the characteristics of his own line. But the important part, the operation, of these locomotives is incredible. You'd have to see it to believe it.

You know, the real test of a locomotive is not how fast it will go, but how *slowly*. Joe demonstrated a small Atlantic that went so slowly you could not be sure whether it was actually moving or not. It was fascinating! The side rods moved so slowly you had to watch carefully to see the movement. No jack-rabbit starts or stone-wall stops! Just perfection of control.

This is not meant as a plug for Joe, so much as an explanation of what to seek in a locomotive. I don't profess to know all Joe's secrets, but one, obviously, is the perfect traction, caused by the weight of the locomotive. Even Joe's smallest locomotives weigh seven pounds or more, for he fashions them of heavy brass. Then the gears mesh perfectly and the friction of the wheels and other driving mechanism is so precise as to virtually eliminate friction, or at least reduce it to an absolute minimum. You can do much to improve even a kit-built locomotive by working it up with the same care.

For superdetailing locomotives, or

Fig. 11-4 Running Gear of a Locomotive (Model)

Fig. 11-5 Dorazio Locomotive

Fig. 11-6 Dorazio Locomotive

Fig. 11-7 Dorazio Locomotive

Fig. 11-8 Dorazio Locomotive

Fig. 11-9 N&W Y6B Steam Locomotive

Fig. 11-10 N&W 12-wheeler

modernizing them, you can find plans and photographs in the model railroading magazines. A splendid book is the *Model Railroader Cyclopedia,* published by the Kalmbach Company, which supplies priceless data on nearly 70 steam locomotives, diesels, gas electrics, interurbans, and trolleys, not to mention freight and passenger cars, and right-of-way structures. It is a must for the ambitious modeler.

I am including in this chapter four more photographs which I feel are apropos. Figure 11-9 is a photograph of one of the Norfolk & Western's famous coal haulers, a Y6B, constructed in their own shops. Pacific Fast Mail has an excellent Japanese model of this famous loco.

Figure 11-10 is the N&W's wonderful little 12-wheeler, #475, which is one of the loveliest locomotives I have ever seen, with her neat lines and gleaming brass trim. Someday I hope to make a model of this prototype.

Figure 11-11 is a shot of an articulated locomotive on the turntable in front of the roundhouse on the Baltimore Society of Model Engineer's HO pike. Figure 11-12 is included because it illustrates the massiveness and power of the front end of a giant articulated. By competent workmanship you can simulate this feeling of heft and power on a model. I did it by superdetailing a Mantua Mikado.

Fig. 11-11 BSME Turntable and Roundhouse

Fig. 11-12 Front End of an Articulated

CHAPTER 12

Short Lines, Narrow-Gauge Railroads, Interurbans, and Trolleys

Model railroading is a diversified hobby, with numerous facets to explore. Like the great Mississippi River, it opens into many deltas, each with its own channels, vistas, and adherents. Traction, which includes trolleys and interurbans, is one of these fascinating variants. Today, traction, like steam, has all but disappeared from the American scene, but it will live long in the memories of thousands of city-bred males who look back with nostalgia at the screech, the clang, and the sparking of the colorful old-time trolley.

Though gone from our streets, trolleys and interurbans live again in replicas on thousands of pikes throughout the country and no group within the NMRA is more enthusiastic than the traction fans. Recently, during the planning stage of this book, I asked Bob Noel, one of the hobby's most ardent traction enthusiasts why he preferred trolleys to trains. His answer is so concise and apt that I give it verbatim.

"I can give you three good reasons," Bob said without hesitation. "First is the matter of cost. If I buy a locomotive, I have to buy passenger and freight cars to make up a train. But if I purchase a single trolley car, I'm in business. Second is the question of space. A trolley will operate perfectly on a 7½" radius curve in HO, but it takes a 24" radius to get a locomotive around a standard curve; furthermore, trolleys, being double-ended, require no turning tracks or turntables to reverse themselves." Then he paused, and grinned. "Lastly, well, I guess I just like stringing trolley wires."

Of course, he could have merely said that he liked trolleys best, but his logic is irrefutable. Aside from their individual charm, trolleys do take less space, cost less to "get into business," and getting your juice through a fragile trolley pole is fun.

But you do not have to give up locomotives to enjoy traction; the two can live together in peaceful coexistence, as compatibly as ham and eggs. They do on WA&P, where two old-time trolley cars wend their erratic way through the town of Camelot, the principal town on my own pike. And because of a nostalgic affection for the big red cars of the Pacific Electric, which used to serve southern California communities, I'm putting in an interurban line from Camelot to the harbor town of Embarcadero.

Shown in Fig. 12-1 is the trolley loop on the huge HO layout of the Baltimore Society of Model Engineers. The gentleman in the picture is Irving Kopp, a former president of the BSME.

While you do not have to string trolley wires, for the tiny cars will run just as well on two-rail, the same as your locomotives, you will miss much of the fun and thrill without the typical overhead wires. It used to be quite a chore to run the wires over the sharp radius curves, but now it's a cinch, for your hobby shop stocks special pole sets, complete with the proper wire, to do the job. After you instill a few of these and taste the fun of traction, you may want to experiment with making your own poles and stringing your own wire. These trolley-pole sets come with complete, easy-to-understand directions, so you can't go wrong.

Fig. 12-1 BSME Trolley Line

We usually associate the trolley exclusively with passenger carrying and that was their prime function up until the tin lizzie began to clutter up the city streets. Many trolley lines had combines, that is a car that carried both passengers and freight. Then there were those wonderful little open cars in which you could tour the city on a balmy summer evening to escape the heat. There were special cars for charter and, when I was a kid in Ottawa, I remember a big, black, ornate car that carried something else—a hearse car that solemnly carried the dead to the cemeteries on the edge of the city.

Yes, trolleys played a tremendous role in American life 50 years ago and they deserve perpetuation on a layout. Some modelers build their own, but you can purchase inexpensive and beautiful trolley kits. The Mantua Company manufactures an excellent little four-wheel trolley and Penn Scale Models puts out a marvelous old-time Brill-type that will twang the strings of memory. Try a trolley on your layout and I'll wager you'll get the bug!

INTERURBANS

The interurban was a logical development of the city trolley car; a sort of big brother, bringing the thrill of the trolley to the surrounding countryside, linking the city with the farms and outlying towns and villages. A ride on one of these giants was an unforgettable adventure to a small boy. Usually leaving from the center of town, it proceeded through the city with a great deal of caution, as though half-afraid of its own strength and power, but on the edge of town, where it turned into its own private right-of-way, the motorman notched up his controller and the big car picked up speed.

Sometimes it was a single car, probably a combine, carrying passengers, mail, express, or daily papers for the rural communities it served. Often it was a two- or three-car train. Occasionally, the interurbans hauled sleeping cars on long night runs, but they were never a complete success. There were a few private trolleys, as plush and luxuriant as any on the major railroads, with staterooms and all the gaudy trimmings, for those were the days when multimillionaires lived in the grand manner.

It is difficult to overestimate the value of the interurban on rural life in America; they literally brought civilization to the boondocks and linked the countryside to the city. Now those halcyon days are gone, the interurban has been superseded by diesel trucks and the automobile, but there is no reason why they cannot live again on your pike. All that was said before about space saving and cost of trolleys is applicable to the interurban line. And for operational action, you'll get an incomparable thrill from keeping two or three interurbans shuttling in both directions on a single-track main line.

You have a wide variety of choice in interurbans. The Walthers Company manufactures a number of different types, and Suydam & Company stocks a line of exquisitely made interurban imports. Figure 12-2 A and B shows one of the Suydam imports. B is the model of a Pacific Electric, while A is a photograph of its prototype. The detail on these models is fascinating.

SHORT LINES

The short line, or branch line, is a small general carrier that brings produce from the back country to a junction with a main trunk line, where it will be transshipped to all parts of the nation. While chiefly a freight carrier, it usually hauled a few old-time open-ended coaches discarded by the bigger railroads; more often they carried a combine, if passenger traffic was light. Never big money-makers, they operated on a penny-pinching budget, skirting hills instead of tunneling through them and, wherever possible, using wooden trestles instead of steel bridges. But to the railroad enthusiast, they had that priceless ingredient—*color*. Their old tea kettles were kept running by farmer-mechanics and their track was something to behold, but they were content to do a specific job without worrying too much about modernity. But modernity caught up with them, and today steam has all but vanished from the short line as it has from the trunk lines. For a while the interurban took their place; but now, what short lines are left use a gas-electric, called a "doodle-bug," or a diesel-electric at the head end.

The doodle-bug is a self-propelled combine, carrying both passengers and freight. It may haul a mixed train, made up of a reefer or two, a tank car, and, perhaps, a couple of hoppers. Quite possibly at its

Fig. 12-2 Suydam Kit and Prototype

countryside terminus it may make a connection with a private lumber railroad and haul a few lumber cars back to the interchange with the trunk line. Or it may pick up the hoppers of a coal mine. The operational possibilities are endless.

Frank Ellison explores these possibilities thoroughly, as well as operation in general in his excellent little book, listed at the end of this chapter. By all means, try to work a branch line into your layout design, for it will lend excitement and color to your future pleasure.

NARROW-GAUGE RAILROADS

Probably no phase of railroading has fired the enthusiasm of the hobbyists as that of the narrow gauge. It has become something close to a religion among its adherents. Understandably so, for it has an attraction that is unique.

But narrow-gauge model railroading is not for the beginner. Narrow-gauge modelers are a hardy and peculiar breed of men; they have to be, for relatively few parts for narrow-gauge equipment are available in the hobby shops and most equipment has to be fabricated from scratch. But therein lies the challenge and the attraction.

What is narrow-gauge railroading? To answer that we have to go back to the early days when the railroads were first seeking a toehold in the complex business of transportation. In that bygone era there were few rules and fewer standards. The builders of railroads arbitrarily selected their own width between tracks, a width that ran anywhere from two to seven feet. But there came that inevitable day when standardization, that bogey of American life, caught up with these independent moguls of the iron rails and, about the time of the Civil War, the standard of 4 feet 8½ inches—the width between the wheels of Roman chariots—was ordained the official gauge by federal decree for main-line public carriers in interstate commerce.

However, the 4 foot 8½ inch gauge was expensive to construct and necessitated curves of larger radius than many small branch lines could afford, so that many of the small railroads clung to their narrower gauges. The state of Maine was famous for her two-foot gauge lines, and the three-foot gauge, even a three-foot six-inch gauge, continued in existence, to the great joy of railroading fans the country over. Many standard-gauge roads had dual-gauge interchanges. Dual-gauge, as the name implies, means that the track permits the use of two gauges. This is accomplished by laying three rails. One rail is common to both gauges, while the other two are separated from it for the two gauges required.

Though I have heard that there are rugged individualists who build in the two-foot gauge, I have never encountered them nor do I know of any equipment or trucks manufactured in the two-foot gauge. But both O and HO gauge have a number of enthusiasts working in the three-foot gauge category. These two gauges are officially known as On3 and HOn3, the "n" designating narrow gauge and the number being the gauge itself. For HOn3 there are a few locomotives available, a very few turnouts, and a limited supply of car kits and trucks. There is, to my knowledge, no fabricated narrow-gauge track obtainable, but you can buy Code 70 rail, in either nickel, silver, or brass, and lay your own track.

But it is this scarcity of materials that challenges the real craftsman and whips up his enthusiasm for something unique. Narrow gauge captures the true spirit of old-time railroading as no other phase of the hobby can. It has an air of independence and unorthodoxy; it seems to defy all standards and makes its own rules as it goes along. Its cars and locomotives are ofttimes improvised, and its locos will assault a grade that would stop even a UP Big Boy cold in its tracks.

And like trolleys and interurbans, a narrow-gauge branch line will fit into almost any layout, or it will make an ideal layout by itself. I have had a taste of narrow-gauge railroading, and sometimes think that if I ever build another layout, it will be entirely narrow gauge.

My own narrow-gauge line is named the Virginia Central and is a privately owned lumber road. It winds up into the mountains and brings down logs which it delivers to its own mill pond; the resulting lumber is brought to an interchange at Profane Junction where it is transferred to the standard-gauge WA&P for transshipment off-stage.

The two railroads are in sharp contrast. The WA&P is a Class I railroad with a large engine terminal, a big roundhouse, and all the facilities that go with it, while the little Virginia Central has a primitive one-stall enginehouse with offices in an old passenger car set on ties. For motive power, the VC has a Shay geared-type locomotive and a vintage model 0-6-0, with a slope-backed tender. In addition to logging cars, these old tea kettles haul a once-a-week open-end passenger car up to the logging camps beyond the mountains to transport loggers to or from work.

The Shay is shown in Fig. 12-3, waiting on the ready-track beside the one-stall enginehouse.

If you go into narrow gauge, you should take advantage of the opportunity offered for the use of such old-time equip-

Fig. 12-3 Model Shay at Enginehouse

ment as the vintage stub switches and the colorful old harp-switch stands and the picturesque stacks on the locomotives.

You don't need a lot of space. To climb high mountains, you can do as I did, utilize the almost-forgotten switch-back method. See Fig. 12-4. The idea is neither new nor original. Goats and cattle have climbed steep hills in this zig-zag fashion since the beginning of time. And when I was a boy, before the days of fancy mechanical ski lifts, we laboriously climbed up the steep slopes in this way.

The early railroad builders seized upon the same device for surmounting mountains, and I gleaned the plan from an old book, written in the last century by one of that hardy breed. Of course, the fact that a locomotive cannot run around of its own volition, like a goat or a skier, necessitated some refinements, as illustrated in my sketch.

Let's follow this for a moment: Our train leaves the junction and proceeds along the dual-trackage marked "A" in the drawing, then cuts over to all narrow-gauge trackage "B." At turnout #1, it pulls into the stub marked "X." It is essential that all these "X" stubs are long enough to hold your entire train, which will not be very long because your locos won't pull many cars up so steep a grade. On my pike this "B" track is a 7½ per cent grade.

When your train is in the stub and your caboose has cleared the #1 turnout, the switch is thrown, and the train *backs* up the "C" track, passes through turnout #2 and into the second stub. Once again the #2 turnout is thrown, and the train proceeds up to the "D" track to the next switchback, and so on. The only limit to how high you want to climb is the amount of space you can devote to the operation.

You may well ask: What happens when you get as high as you want to go? My solution was to put a hill in front of the end of track, so that the train seems to be going into a cut, and is screened from view. There I leave it; the show is over, for it is presumed to have gone off into the distant Big Candy Mountains, painted on the background.

If you use Code 70 rails for your narrow gauge and standard prefabricated track for your main line you will, of course, have to shim up your Code 70 to the same height as the standard to get a smooth transition. Also, for the dual-trackage, you'll have to use the standard-sized rail for your third rail. This presents no particular difficulty and is merely a matter of common sense.

Making a dual-gauge turnout may present problems for the novice, but if dual-track is an on-again, off-again affair, as mine is, it is not necessary to have a movable turnout at all, since only the narrow-gauge trains will use it. Figure 12-5 offers a solution used by African railroads that have narrow-gauge interchanges. This is the device I have settled upon and is used by many narrow-gauge fans.

If you use Code 70 rail be sure to get the special narrow-gauge spikes sold for the purpose. The regular HO spikes may give you operational troubles because of their larger heads. Frankly, I depend on Pliobond Glue to bind my narrow-gauge rail to the ties, using spikes only here and there to keep the rail in gauge until the glue hardens. Be sure to have several track gauges if you attempt the glue method, but if you do goof, a touch of

Fig. 12-4 Switchback

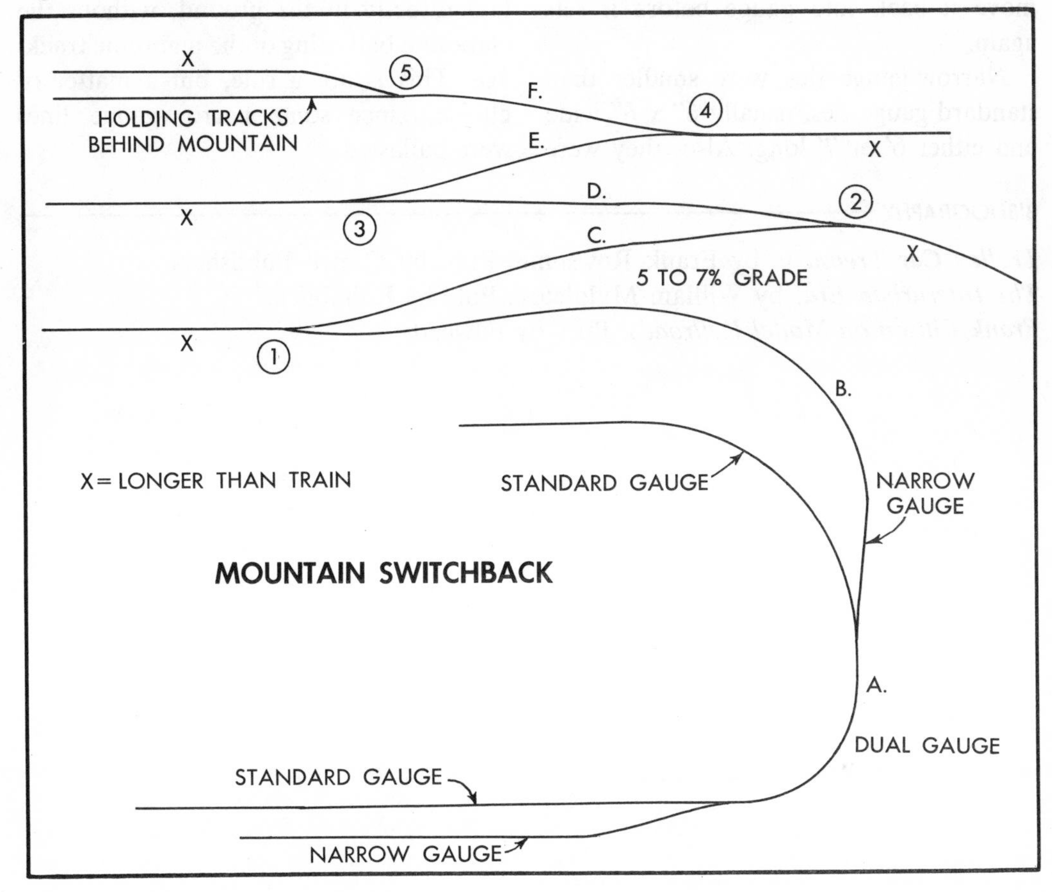

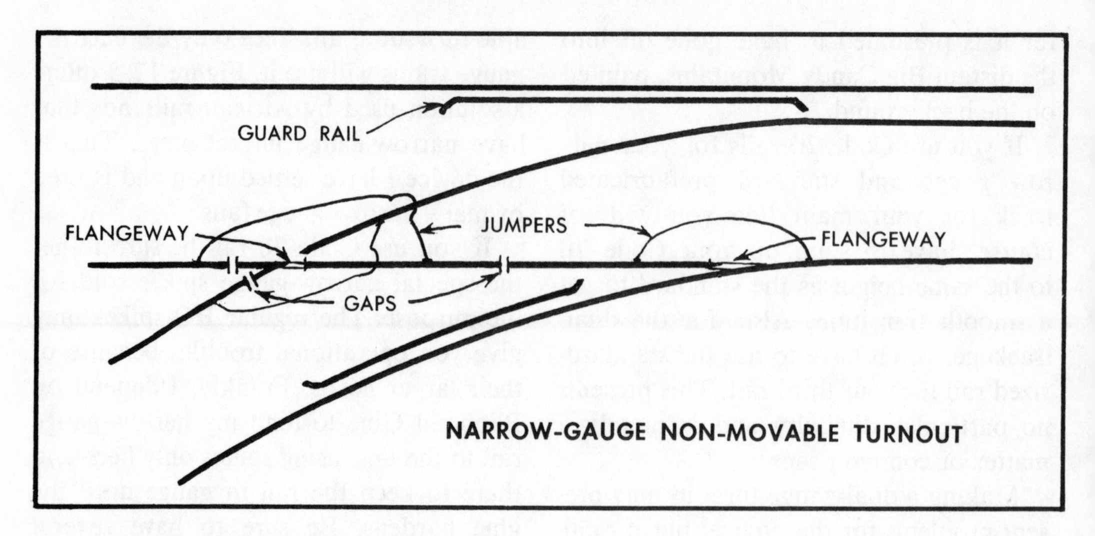

Fig. 12-5 Narrow-gauge Turnout

a hot soldering iron to the rail will soften the glue momentarily, permitting you to move it back into gauge before it sets again.

Narrow-gauge ties were smaller than standard gauge ties, usually 6″ x 6″ wide and either 6′ or 7′ long. Also, they were spaced farther apart, averaging about 21″ from center to center of the ties, and often laid directly in the ground, without the elaborate ballasting of the main-line trackage. This is not a rule, but a matter of choice, since some narrow-gauge lines were ballasted.

BIBLIOGRAPHY

Trolley Car Treasury, by Frank Rowsome. Pub. by Crown Publishers.
The Interurban Era, by William Middleton. Pub. by Kalmbach.
Frank Ellison on Model Railroads. Pub. by Fawcett.

CHAPTER 13

Operation

Now we come to it, the crux of the hobby—*railroading!* If you have faithfully performed your homework, you have a properly wired layout, with scenery and buildings in place. Visitors gape and marvel as your trains go around the loop or whatever you have, and you're pretty proud, as you have a right to be. You've proven yourself a real modeler.

Nevertheless, deep inside of you is a vague feeling of disappointment. True, your trains circle the track without a hitch, but they don't *do* anything. Every circuit of the track is the same old thing. It *looks* like a railroad, but it doesn't *act* like one.

What's wrong? Nothing is wrong! You've merely reached the second stage of the hobby; you're ready to put the *railroading* into model railroading—with operation. Operation in model railroading is where the action begins; it's the *raison d'être,* the ultimate excuse for the pike's existence.

But are *you* ready? Do you have the necessary equipment, cars, markers, couplers, and so forth, necessary to make up a train? And just *what is* a train? The *Rule Book*—the bible of all railroaders—defines a train as "An engine, or more than one engine coupled, with or without cars, displaying markers."

The key to that sentence is the word *markers*. What are markers? They include the headlight on the front end, properly colored flags, and small lamps that are set on the front of the locomotive and on the rear end of the last car of the train. The color of both the flags and the lamps designates the class of train that is carrying them.

Railroad rule books are hard to come by, and if you can promote one from a railroad official or employee, by all means do so; you'll have a treasure mine of information for realistic operation. I'll give you enough rules to start off with, taken from the *Operating Rules and General Regulations* of the Grand Trunk Railway System, published in 1911. Later rule books may be worded slightly differently but I haven't discovered any essential changes since that time.

Now let us pause a moment so the rules I quote will have some meaning to you. We have to do some paper work at this point and make some decisions. We have to conceive a *concept* of where our railroad is to go and what it is to do. Will it have passenger service with name trains or is it strictly freight? A train is more than a collection of cars hooked behind a locomotive; it is a service, a distinct entity, it has to *go* somewhere and *do* something. That's why the point-to-point type of railroad, with a separate and distinct division point at each end of the line is so popular with model rails who really go in for operation. Real railroads don't just meander around in a circle; they serve a purpose, and to operate realistically, you have to simulate this purpose.

All right, we'll assume you intend to have a passenger schedule with all the trimmings. Now if you will recall, I spoke of the convention of *direction* in Chapter 5. We must go back to that for the moment, for we have to set up a superior direction for our trains, east or west, north or south.

Let's say you choose *east* as the superior direction; you'll learn what this term *superior* means in a moment. Real railroads usually number their trains by direction; even numbers for eastbound and odd for trains going the opposite direction, and railroad men always refer to the train by number, rather than by name, no matter how famous and how much publicized it is. Thus the New York Central's famous Twentieth Century Limited is Number 26 when going east, and Number 25 when westbound. But remember, only scheduled trains (that is, trains operating by timetable) have official numbers, whether freight or passenger.

Remember, too, that when I speak of timetables, I am not referring to those summarized lists of trains that the companies hand out to passengers, but rather to the official timetables used by railroad men, which are much more detailed and complex and list all scheduled freight trains as well as passenger trains. Try to talk your local General Agent out of a copy; it will help you in making up a schedule for your own railroad.

In the social strata of trains there is a caste system as rigid as human society in medieval times. There is no argument about all trains "being created equal" or "having equal rights before the law." The high-wheeled fast-stepping name passenger trains are the "princes of the blood" and, unless otherwise directed by the dispatcher, have precedence over all other trains.

Now back to our definitions from the rule book:

Regular Train: a train authorized by a timetable schedule.

Section: one of two or more trains running on the same timetable schedule, displaying green signals or for which green signals are displayed.

Extra Train: a train not authorized by a timetable schedule. It may be designated as:

Work Extra: for a work train.

Passenger Extra: for an extra passenger train.

Extra: any other extra train.

Superior Train: a train having precedence over another train.

Train of Superior Right: a train given precedence by train order.

Train of Superior Class: a train given precedence by timetable.

Train of Superior Direction: a train in the direction in which regular trains are superior to trains of the same class in the opposite direction, as specified in the timetable. *NOTE:* Superiority by direction is limited to single track.

Timetable: the authority for the movement of regular trains subject to the rules. It contains the classified schedule of trains, with special instructions relating thereto.

Timetable Schedule: that part of a timetable which prescribes the class, direction, number, and movement of a regular train.

Yard: a system of tracks within the limits defined by yard limit boards, or indicated by timetable, provided for the making up of trains, storing cars, and other purposes, over which movements not authorized by timetable or by train order may be made subject to prescribed signals and rules.

One of the common questions which plagues the beginner is: How many and what kind of cars do I need to make up trains? There is, of course, no pat answer to that; it depends on a number of variables, such as the size of your layout, the type of operation you hope to have, and, perhaps, your pocketbook. Most of us, when we start out, get a number of various types of cars according to our whim of the moment, or the attractiveness of the cars. But if you're going to operate realistically, you must have a plan. That doesn't mean that you have to buy a full complement of cars at once, but you should draw up a plan of what you will need and acquire them as circumstances permit. See Fig. 13-1 for various car designs.

Always bear in mind that model railroading is the art of condensing the fundamentals of real railroading, not following the prototype to the letter. A real freight drag may have 125 cars in its string, but eight or ten will look more appropriate on your pike. And a name passenger train, like the Super-Chief may carry 15 or 20 Pullmans, whereas three or four will serve you just as well.

In an attempt to solve the dilemma of car needs, I obtained from the Association of American Railroads the percentage of the numbers of different cars the real railroads used, but the proportions were too great to help me much. So after a great deal of thought I drew up my own roster of rolling stock. I still don't have all the cars on my list, but I add to it as often as circumstances permit. Narrow-gauge equipment is not included. I believe this is a fair list for an average-size pike, and I offer it to you for your consideration. Just remember that my railroad specializes in coal and cattle traffic, so you may not need as many hoppers and stock cars as I have listed.

Freight Cars	
Box (all types)	20
Gondola	6
Hopper	15
Flat	4
Stock	4
Reefer	3
Tanker	2
Work and Service	6
Caboose	4
Special (circus, etc.)	6
Total	70

Passenger Cars	
Coach	6
Pullman	4
Baggage	3
Mail and Express	3
Express reefer	2
Combine	2
Diner	1
Private	1
Observation or Lounge	2
Total	24

Motive Power

For heavy freight: a 2-8-2 Mikado, and/or a 2-6-6-2 articulated.

For light freight: a 2-8-0 Consolidated and/or 4-6-0 10-wheeler, also a 2-6-0 Mogul.

Switching: 0-4-0 switcher.

For heavy passenger duty and name trains: 4-6-2 Pacific.

For light passenger trains: a 4-4-2 Atlantic and/or the 2-6-0 Mogul.

For light commuter service: a gas-electric doodle-bug, with or without a trailer.

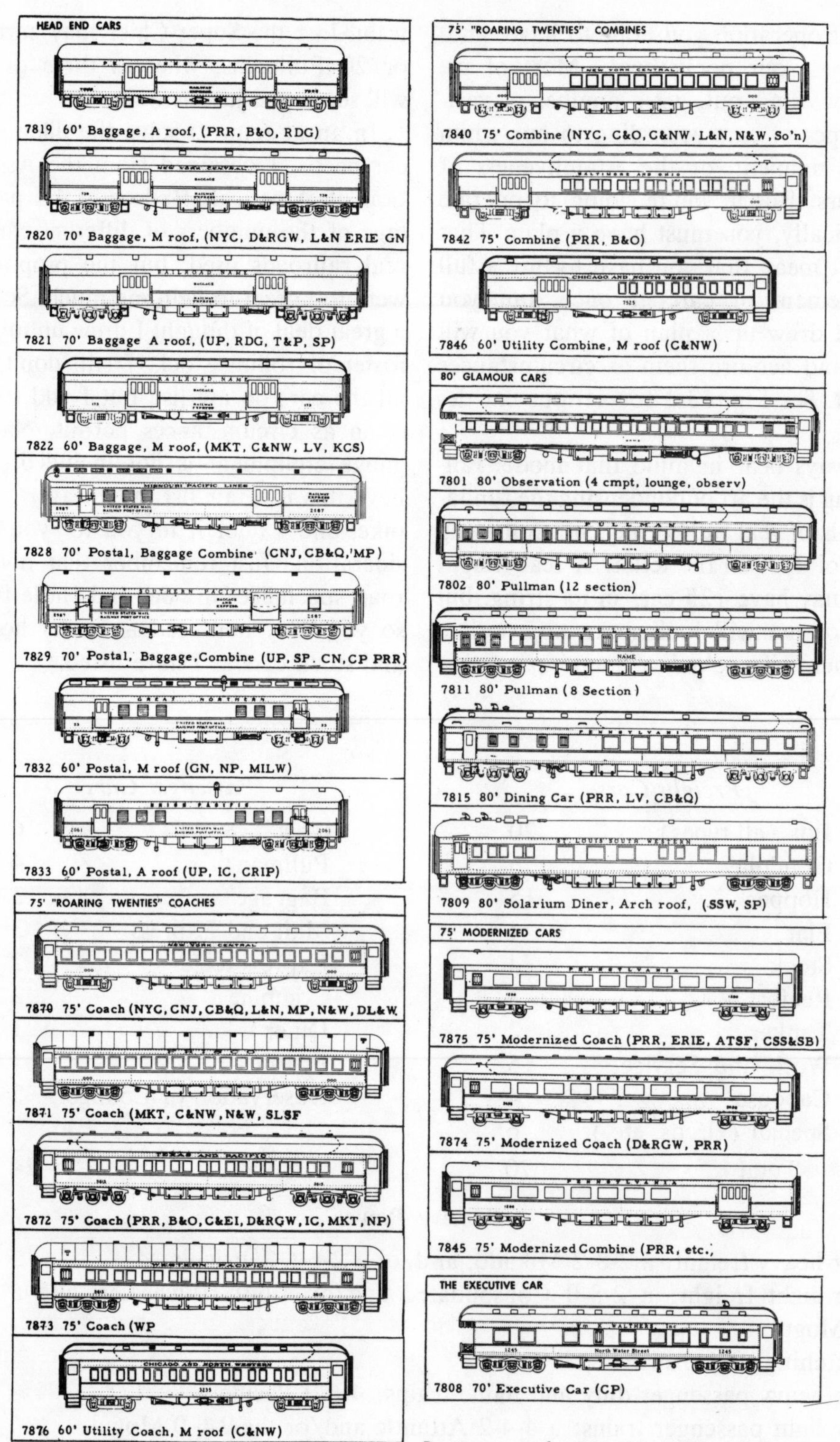

By courtesy the Wm. K. Walthers Inc.

Fig. 13-1 Passenger and Head-end Cars

With such a roster of motive power and rolling stock, you're ready for a lot of fun and activity. But first let's set up an imaginary schedule, complete with name trains. You have to have this schedule in black and white, otherwise your operation will have no purpose. It's the "concept that makes a railroad go," as *Model Railroading Magazine* phrased it in an excellent article on the subject.

If you already have a roster of cars and locomotives similar to mine, you can make up your own schedule; if not, let's use the roster of the WA&P, and make up an imaginary schedule for my road.

First, we want a couple of glamorous name trains to give our road some *éclat*. Suppose we pilfer the name of a famous train of yesterday, the Blue Comet, a luxury train that used to run to Atlantic City. We'll establish *east* as the superior direction on our road and designate it Number 26 eastbound and Number 25 westbound. This will be our crack daytime Limited, leaving Camelot every morning at 8:45, on the button. It will be hauled by a well-cleaned Pacific, with most of its cars painted a bright dark blue to give it a touch of class. Behind the tender will be an express reefer, perhaps carrying fresh meat to its destination, then a full-length RPO car (Railway Post Office car), a baggage express car, a couple of coaches, a diner, and a lounge or observation car if you have one. If the "brass hat" (the president of the railroad) chooses to go along, he may order his private car coupled on the rear end. This train will have precedence, both by direction and schedule, over all other trains on the main line, unless it is modified or annulled by the dispatcher in an emergency.

Our other name train we'll call the Ocean Limited, another fast-stepper that leaves Camelot at 6:30 every evening; Number 8 eastbound and Number 7 westbound. It starts out westbound, and therefore does not have superior direction, but otherwise it is a first-class scheduled train and superior in everything but direction. It, too, will carry a full-length RPO car at the head-end, followed by an express car, a combination baggage and smoker, a single day coach, and two or more 12-section Pullman sleepers, a diner, and also a lounge or observation car.

Now these two name trains do not stop at every whistle-stop or rural station, so we must have a *local* train that serves all communities. We'll give this chore to the 4-4-2 Atlantic, or in a pinch to the 2-6-0 Mogul, because it won't be a heavy train. It will consist of a combination mail and express car, a combine for baggage and smokers, a coach or two as required by traffic, and, on occasion, it will carry a stock car or reefer if so ordered. Though operating by right of timetable this will be a second-class train, with the responsibility of keeping off the main line when the name trains are due. The "meet" or place of passing is usually designated in the schedule, but in case the name train is late or delayed, the local will get its order from the dispatcher for a meet at another station or siding.

To add a bit of tone to our freight trains, we'll start off with a "hotshot." Perhaps it is a fruit special carrying perishable fruit from the South, coming over our line from another railroad; or it may be carrying stock cars loaded with cattle that must get to the stockyards before they lose too much "drift," or weight, en route. In any event, a hotshot is a freight train in a hurry, and it must go through with all possible speed.

There are several ways to do this. You can schedule a regular hotshot on your timetable, you can run it as an extra train, or, as the real railroads so often do, you can run it as a section of a fast name train, so it won't be subject to constant orders from the dispatcher.

This section business is not complicated. Back in the halcyon days of railroading, when passenger traffic was a sought-after commodity instead of the headache it is today, name trains often went in sections, each with its own locomotive and train crew. In the 1920s, the famous Twentieth Century Limited sometimes ran as many as six or seven sections —all referred to as number 26 by railroad men, but distinguished on train orders as second 26, third 26, and so on. But each section had all the rights and privileges of the original train. The only outward difference was in the markers they carried. The first and all subsequent sections, *except the last,* carried green flags and markers, to indicate to towermen and station agents that another section was following. When these men saw a final section come along without the green indications, they knew it was the last section, and were governed accordingly. See Fig. 13-2 for a sketch of how and where these flags and markers were displayed.

Fig. 13-2 Marker Lights and Flags

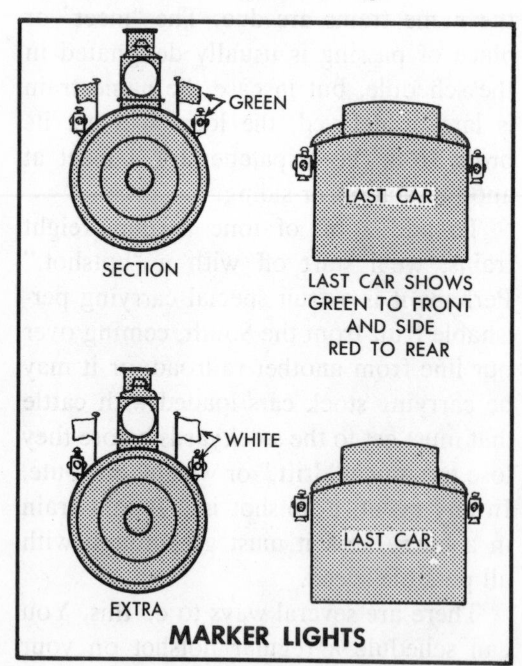

Since the hotshot will have to maintain the schedule of our Limiteds, we'll have to haul it with adequate power to pull the load and keep to the timetable.

An extra train, as the name implies, is one which is not listed on the operating schedule or the timetable. It may be an extra passenger train, necessitated by a large convention of some kind; it may be a fast mail extra, rushing Christmas mail across the country, made up solid of Post Office cars; it may be a strawberry special, loaded with perishable fruit for the market that could not make the scheduled hotshot. Or it may be a work train, called out in an emergency, such as a derailment, a collision, or a length of torn-up track.

Whatever the consist, an extra train carries white lamps and white flags, as illustrated in the lower part of Fig. 13-2. And it moves through the tortuous labyrinth of scheduled trains only by a myriad of train orders issued by the dispatcher. Whenever practical, such a train is put on the road as a section rather than an extra to save the confusion of multiple orders.

Work trains are the peasants of a railroad and have to keep their lowly place in the scheme of things, getting out of the way of all other trains, except in an emergency. Even the haughty name train makes way for the work extra when there is serious trouble on the main line.

This gives the model rail an opportunity for some spectacular operation. Word comes into the dispatcher that the trestle over Mud Creek has washed out and the Ocean Limited is held up. What to do? The dispatcher immediately notifies the Ocean Limited to go into the hole (siding) at the Clementine Station and clear the line for Extra 43, a work train which is already high-balling toward the scene.

The little work extra may have a couple of flats loaded with pilings, a crew car for the section hands, a pile driver, and an old locomotive tender to bring water for the pile driver's steam engine. For the time being #43 "owns the railroad," as they say; that is, she has unlimited right over all other trains, and as she waddles on her errand of mercy, she passes the hotshots and name trains waiting docilely in the various sidings.

Now we come to the lowly way freights, sometimes called "peddlers" or "hucksters." Frank Ellison says (and who should know better?): "The little wayfaring freight is the daddy of all model railroading. By all odds, it offers more down-to-earth railroading per minute than any other type of train."

As usual, Frank is right. The way freight is the logical type of train for a pike, especially a small pike, because it operates in a very limited area, rarely exceeding 50 to a 100 miles in a working day. The little peddler is a switch run, delivering and picking up freight cars on the various industrial sidings and spurs between towns. It is usually run as an extra train because of the exigencies of its work, for its schedule is unpredictable. It may have to pick up a grain car at the Northern Neck grain elevator, and drop a flat at Captain Al's boatyard for the loading of a newly built cruiser and/or a stock car at the Tidewater Beef Cattle Sale Barn. Its consist will be varied and variable but at the end of a working day it will probably return with a string of empties for the switching crew to distribute in the yards.

Way-freight operation is a science, and we'll get back to it in a moment or two, but first let me anticipate an almost inevitable query: "Where do all these special trains come from and where do they go?"

The answer to this calls for a little "imagineering." Some modelers pretend that their railroads connect with one or more of the real railroads, such as the New York Central or the Santa Fe. Other rails form a loose agreement with model railroading friends, conceiving imaginary interchanges between their railroads to give an excuse for incoming and outgoing traffic. The WA&P belongs to the latter group.

In open violation of all antitrust laws, four of us modeling brass hats got together and formed what we called "The Unholy Alliance" to divide up all rail traffic in the eastern United States. Don Burdick, with his H-Y Lines empire covers the South and a good part of the Middle West, Bill Rau's BA&P covers the mid-North, and Bart Crosby figuratively puts the New York Central and the Pennsy out of business with his NC&F railroad. My WA&P fills in the middle ground.

Burdick generously built an imaginary branch line to the WA&P so that if he gets a hotshot grapefruit special from Florida, he brings it to our mutual interchange and I highball it through to Profane Junction, where Rau's railroad hurries it to northern markets. Of course, that all takes place in our imaginations, but at least it affords a fictional explanation as to how a Florida hotshot can abruptly appear on the WA&P, which otherwise "serves all Virginia from the tidewater to the mountains." To further the illusion I have "holding tracks" inside one of my mountains, a stub siding where a train supposedly going on to another railroad can lie quietly out of sight until I'm ready to bring it back onstage.

If your layout is large enough and has sufficient industrial tracks to make it worth while, operation is most realistic when you have a group of men working at it. That calls for a number of cabs so that each man can operate his own train and it requires enough rolling stock and industrial sidings to keep them busy. Frank Ellison is perhaps best known for his fabulous operation on his famed Delta Lines, where for fifteen years or more, a group of eight or nine operators have met once a week for these operation sessions. It must be very fascinating, for one of the men has been with him for 13 years, and several others 8 and 10 years. Men are not prone to give up a night a week for years on end without being rewarded by fun and excitement.

Another prerequisite to precise timetable operation is a scale clock. Since model railroads do not have the scale distance between stations, making in seconds a distance that would take a prototype railroad perhaps hours to cover, it is almost imperative to have some means of keeping to a schedule. As you know, real railroads adhere strictly to the timetable, and *time* means exactly what it says, and calls for accurate watches and clocks. So you cannot ignore one of the basic essentials of the real railroads and hope to have realistic operation.

What you need is a clock that is speeded up about twelve times so that it will run an "hour" in from four to five minutes. There have been numerous suggestions in the model magazines on how to accomplish this, but the easiest, and in my judgment the best, is the method proposed by the MR staff in the February, 1960, issue of *Model Railroader Magazine*. We haven't space to go into the intricacies of this operation here, but if you are interested, I recommend you obtain a copy of this issue. It will greatly increase your fun.

Other requirements for operation are good couplers and uncoupling ramps. On prototype railroading, coupling and uncoupling is done by hand, by the brakemen. In the early days of railroading, link-and-pin couplers were used, but these were hazardous and vicious devices, that lopped the hands and arms off brakemen with frightening regularity. But in the 1870s a man named Janney developed what might be termed a "handclasp" type of coupler which cut down the rate of amputation considerably. This Janney-type coupler was made mandatory by law and, with few modifications, is in use today on nearly all Canadian and American railroads.

The matter of couplers in model railroading, especially in HO, is a highly controversial subject. Inasmuch as the tiny brakemen in model railroading are purely decorative, being made, not of flesh and blood, but of either plastic or metal, we have to have couplers which will couple and uncouple automatically. There have been many such couplers manufactured for model railroads and each has its ardent adherents. But no matter how efficient the different couplers were, there was always the problem of interchange. A model rail, taking some of his equipment to operate on a friend's pike, too often found that the friend used another make of coupler that would not work with his own. And as the Association of American Railroads had standardied on the Janney coupler, it seemed only logical that the National Model Railroad Association should do likewise. So a technical committee was set up to explore the possibilities of a coupler that could be made a standard.

The subject was a ticklish one. A model rail with a couple of hundred cars was, naturally enough, loath to scrap all his couplers and put on new ones, so when the NMRA Coupler Committee finally came up with a coupler known in HO as the X2F type, there was such an uproar that it almost caused a schism in the ranks of the NMRA. That was several years ago but the clamor of protest has not subsided. The X2F was *not* made a standard, although many manufacturers of ready-to-run equipment adopted it.

As the surest way to lose friends in the model railroading fraternity is to publicly champion one coupler over another, I'm not going to stick my neck out. I started out with a well-known make of coupler, but was never satisfied with it because the fitting was too critical and because it would not couple well on curves. So I switched to the X2F and found it to my liking. Later, Kadee Metal Products came out with their famous "Magne-Matic" couplers, which uncouple by a small magnet installed between the rails.

The Magne-Matic caused a great furor in the HO ranks and many modelers, including my two friends, Burdick and Rau, changed over to them. Then Paul Mallery, of electrical fame, developed an X2F magnetic coupler, which is interchangeable with the old X2F, which seems to hold great promise, although I haven't tried it yet.

To get around this interchange business with other rails, I have a couple of so-called "interchange cars." These have an X2F on one end, and another popular make of coupler on the other. So when I want to run a friend's equipment on my pike, I place this interchange car with the X2F coupler hooked onto my tender and he can couple with his equipment on the other end. This is highly satisfactory, and settles the coupler squabble insofar as I'm concerned.

To uncouple with the X2F you can purchase both plastic and metal uncoupling ramps which set neatly between the rails on your sidings and industrial spurs. These ramps squeeze the low-hanging spurs on the couplers which open them for uncoupling.

I use the fixed type of uncoupling ramp, but some model rails use ramps that are raised or lowered by electrical remote control. Your hobby dealer can show you both types and explain the difference. Naturally, the controlled ramps are more expensive and usually require electrical components.

In summation, let me say that it doesn't make any difference what make of coupler or uncoupler you use so long as they are dependable and efficient—that's the essential criterion.

WAY-FREIGHT OPERATION

Way-freight operation is essentially a group operation, somewhat like card playing, but, if you must, you can play solitaire. It is a matter of shuffling and dealing. Try it just once and you'll discover that it is not child's play. With high-speed scheduled passenger trains and hotshots roaring around your pike at about four-minute intervals, you'll find that it takes plenty of nerve and a cool hand to dodge in and out of your sidings between all this traffic. Even without the timetable traffic, it takes a lot of skill and know-how just to make your switching moves.

This was proven at the last Mid-Eastern Regional Convention at Camden, New Jersey, when the Silver Valley Railroad Club put on a switching contest. This was set up on a small board, with about four tracks and crossovers and a number of industrial sidings. Contestants were given a switch engine and a caboose, with orders to pick up so many freight cars and redistribute them to other specified industries in a given number of moves in a given time. It looked painfully simple, but it was amazing how many supposedly hotshot operators, including myself, fell flat on their figurative faces in the attempt. See Fig. 13-3 for this problem. Talk about advanced chess! I used to be a pretty good chess player, and I thought I could visualize all the necessary moves in advance, but in the limited space allotted, I was soon hopelessly entangled in the maze. An ex-professional switching engineer beside me took his turn with confidence, and while he eventually completed the cycle, he took nearly twice as many moves as was necessary and nearly twice the time permitted him.

The switching game is not standardized. Each move is a problem in itself and each one is different. If the siding on which you have to deposit a car is a facing switch, that is, if the turnout points are toward you, it may be advantageous to couple a car at the head end, in front of the locomotive, so you can push it into the required siding and back out. While most roads operate with the caboose at the rear end of their trains, a peddler freight engineer may decide to couple it up behind the tender so as to permit greater maneuverability in distributing his string. Real railroading is a blend of rules and expediency, and the engineer of a way freight is permitted to use his judgment on how best to shuffle his cars.

Now Doug Smith, the brass hat of the Brooks Valley Railroad, is an operational authority. He has written many articles for *Model Railroader Magazine* and put on a clinic on operation at the NMRA National Convention. Like Frank Ellison, he meets regularly with a group of experienced cronies for operational sessions on the Brooks Valley R.R. With Don Peck, one of these regulars, Doug evolved what they call the "PS" system of prototypical way-freight operation.

The bogey of most systems is the amount of paper work involved for the shuffling and dealing of cars, and the PS system cuts paper work down to a minimum. They claim this system will work as well on a one-man layout as on a large club pike.

Real railroads maintain a large clerical staff; railroads may be said to operate on paper—manifests, train orders, switching orders, and all the rest of it. But model railroaders want to be engineers, not clerks, and therein lies the crux of the problem, for cars are not shuffled here and there at the whim of engineers. There must be written orders from somewhere. For if the Northern Neck Grain Elevator requires a couple of grain-carrying freight cars, the manager doesn't call the engineer; he calls the railroad company, explains his needs to the proper official, who in turn sees to it that orders are passed on through the clerical chain to the Yard Master who then passes along the orders to the conductor and engineer of the way freight.

Doug Smith examines and covers the whole field of his own and other systems of way-freight operation in a lengthy article in the December, 1961, issue of *Model Railroader Magazine;* a piece I can heartily recommend because it will save you many headaches and disappointments if you try to concoct a system of your own without sufficient experience.

As with any workable system, the initial job is to list every industry in your empire, and then dream up what sort of shipments these industries could conceivably receive or ship, and the type of railroad car needed for the job. My Croton Oil Company, for instance, would receive bulk oil in tank cars, with an occasional shipment of oil or grease drums and the like in a freight car. The Tidewater Beef Cattle Sales Barn would use stock cars primarily, but it would also use baled hay, sacked grain, and concentrates which would come in a box car. Captain Al's Boatyard would use lumber and fittings and ship cruisers and sailboats in flats or gondolas. Only *you* can draw up such a list to fit your own layout.

That done, you should make up a set of car cards, listing every freight car on your roster, with the name, type, and number; one card for each car. Next you make out waybills for each item that can possibly be shipped by the customers in your empire. If you have team tracks in your towns, the industries do not have to be located on a siding; we can assume they have trucks to convey their shipments from the team tracks to their place of business. So don't pass up a good bet and exclude off-track industries. The more the merrier!

On these waybills—which you can have printed or mimeographed—put a "To" and "From." You fill this in as required. For example, one waybill might read: From, Northern Neck Grain Elevator, loaded with mixed feed; To, Tidewater Beef Cattle Sales Barn. Return empty to yard. Or, From, Burdick Hot Air Plant, gondola of air conditioners, To, Embarcadero Station Agent for transshipment, supposely by water.

When you get enough of these waybills made out, you're ready to operate. Guided by the waybills, the Yard Master knows how many and what type of cars to sort out on the ready track. Then your little bob-tailed locomotive hooks on and goes off about his busy business of spotting cars, picking up empties, bringing in loaded cars to be put on the regular scheduled freights, or perhaps enough to make up an extra train for through freight to off-stage lines.

This, greatly over-simplified, is the basis of the PS system. You do not throw away your waybills; you can use them over again at another operating session. But it is the best system I have as yet heard of, for it offers a maximum of switching with a minimum of paper work. Try it, and you'll never again be satisfied just running trains around your layout without purpose.

Another device for adding color to your operation is to have special trains, passing through as "extras," made up of interesting cars. On the WA&P we have a coal drag of about fifteen hoppers loaded with coal, tailed by a little four-wheeled crummy (caboose) and hauled by a road-weary Mikado, that comes down out of the mountains (from a hidden storage track), makes its slow and majestic way over our trackage and again disappears off-stage. We are currently building a circus train, with a flat toting bright animal cages, stock cars with elephants aboard, and all the other colorful paraphernalia of an old-time circus train, for on our empire is the winter quarters of the Helenbach Circus, a feature which always fascinated visitors. These maneuvers

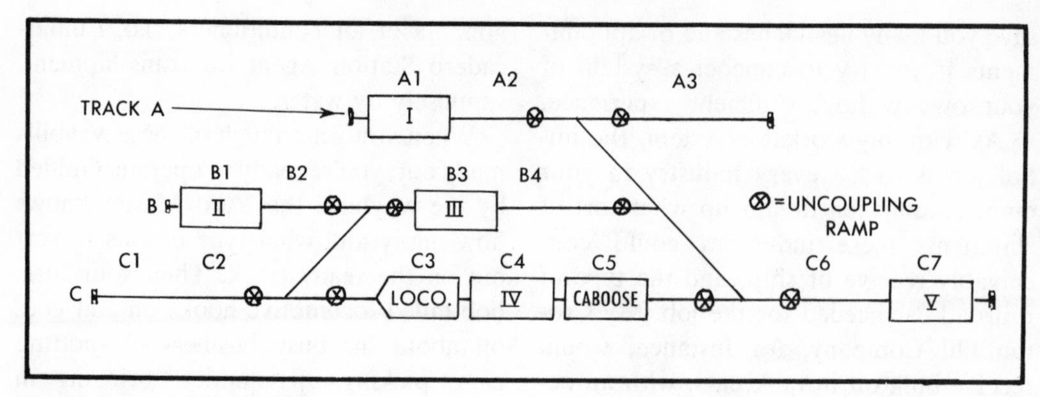

Fig. 13-3 Switching Problem

are not strictly operation in the technical sense, but their passage over the pike lends color and interest, especially to non-railroaders.

In short, operation puts the railroading back into model railroading and justifies the name. You can make it as simple or as complex as you like, but either way, it's no game for morons.

If you still think way-freight switching is "kid stuff," try your hand at the switching problem worked out by the Silver Valley Model Railroad Club for the recent Mid-Eastern Regional Contest, mentioned earlier in this chapter.

Figure 13-3 represents a track plan of an industrial area with four sidings and a passing track, serviced from a main line at left (not shown, but the entrance is just left of track C). The spotting positions are indicated by a letter and a numeral (A-1, B-2, C-3, etc.). The uncoupling ramps are designated by an X enclosed in a circle. The freight cars to be shifted are labeled with Roman numerals (I, III, V, etc.).

The object is to shift the freight cars, as explained in the table, in the minimum number of moves and/or time. A "move" is defined as a change in the direction of the locomotive.

The shifts are:

From (Track and Spot)	*Car No.*	*To (Track and Spot)*
A-1	I	B-1
B-1	II	C-4
B-3	III	A-3
C-4	IV	A-2
C-7	V	B-2

Loco and caboose to be reset on original spots.

Now try this out before you look at the following solution. I'll give you just two tips: you're supposed to complete the chore in 5 minutes and to do it in 29 moves or less.

Operating Contest Solution

Move No.

1. Loco, IV, and caboose move right and pick up V from C-7.
2. Proceed left, drop IV, caboose, and V on C-3 to C-5. Loco moves to C-2.
3. Loco through turnout onto Track B, picks up III, continues to C-6 and C-7.
4. Loco and III proceed left to pick up I at A-1.

5. I, loco, and III back down to clear Track B turnout.
6. Proceed on B and drop I at B-4.
7. Loco and III back right to clear Track B turnout.
8. Proceed to Track A.
9. Loco and III right. Drop III at A-3. (Car III finished.)
10. Loco moves to A-2.
11. Loco backs down to C-6.
12. Loco moves forward to pick up V from C-5.
13. V and loco back to C-6 and C-7.
14. V and loco proceed to Track B to pick up I at B-4 and then pick up II at B-1.
15. II, I, V, and loco back up to clear turnout at B-3.
16. Move left and drop II at C-2.
17. I, V, and loco back onto Track B.
18. Forward to drop I and V on B-1 and B-2. (Cars I and V finished.)
19. Loco backs down to C-6.
20. Loco proceeds on Track C. Pushes II and IV on to C-1 and C-2.
21. Caboose and loco back up. Spot caboose on C-5. Loco to C-6.
22. Loco forward onto Track B. Picks up IV at C-2.
23. IV and loco back down to C-6 and C-7.
24. IV and loco forward to Track A, drop IV at A-2. (Car IV finished.)
25. Loco backs down to C-6.
26. Loco forward on Track C. Picks up caboose and II.
27. II, caboose, and loco back up to drop II and caboose on C-4 and C-5. Loco backs into C-6.
28. Loco forward on Track B to C-2.
29. Loco backs to C-3. (Problem completed.)

Well, how did you do? I grant that it sounds complicated written out like this in detail, but it's a typical switching situation such as a way-freight crew handles every day. Jerry Crosson, assistant chairman of our Regional Contest Committee, who evolved this particular problem, assures me that the Silver Valley operators "run through it in less than five minutes."

If you still find this "kid stuff," all I can say is you are accustomed to smarter "kids" than I am.

BIBLIOGRAPHY

Operating Manual for Model Railroaders, by Boomer Pete. Pub. by Kalmbach.

CHAPTER 14

Model Railroading Is Shared Fun

When you first get into model railroading, you may not be interested in the social side of the hobby, but if you stay a "lone wolf" you'll be passing up a good bet. I learned that lesson the way I learn most things—the hard way. Of course, I joined the NMRA because only that association could give me the data and information I felt I needed; but as to the social side—that was *out*. I felt I had all the friends I could keep up with, and I wasn't interested in making new acquainances. However, I did want to see a finished pike, so I got the address of an active modeler in a nearby city and wrote him, asking if I might visit his pike. As he was a total stranger, I addressed him as "Dear Mr. So-and-so," and signed the letter with my full name.

By return, I received a letter which began: "Dear Les: The first thing you have to learn about model railroaders is that there are no 'Misters,' " and he went on to invite me down.

My wife and I had a wonderful evening and this chap and his wife became very good friends of ours. Nonetheless, I refused to join the Region, which is chiefly for getting model rails together. Then somewhat to my embarrassment, our new friend signed up both my wife and me into the Region and sent us our membership cards. As the next regional convention was reasonably close we attended because we felt obligated to.

To make a long story short, we had such a wonderful time I haven't missed a regional convention in the past eight or nine years. In the first place, I discovered that model rails are really first-rate people—the sort of folks you like to know. And the clinics, lectures, pictures, and the model contests are all extremely stimulating. Heretofore, my experiences with conventions were disappointing, with too much drinking, too much cheap horseplay, too many off-color stories, and too much general carousing. Model railroading conventions are neither prissy nor dull, but they are family affairs where a man is not ashamed to take his wife and children.

The clinics alone are worth the trip. Usually there are three or four at regional conventions, where an expert on some phase of the hobby demonstrates or lectures on his specialty. At our last Mid-Eastern Convention we had a clinic on route-cab control, another on scratch-building with wood, and a third on scratch-building with metal. In each case the expert putting on the clinic demonstrated in detail how he did his work and answered questions from the audience.

For me, the model contest is the main dish of a convention. Here you see exquisite models competing with each other. The contest is divided into categories: locomotives, freight cars, passenger cars, structures and scenery, and "other" equipment. They are judged for workmanship, scale accuracy, appearance, painting and lettering, ingenuity, and operating qualities. The competition is keen, and judging them is an ordeal. I was one of a panel of three judges at a recent contest and it took us six straight hours to make our decisions.

The banquet is always a highlight of any convention. Sometimes there is a prominent railroad man, often the president, as the speaker to discuss the problems of prototype railroading. Usually there is a trip through some local railroad facilities—such as yards, roundhouses, repair shops—and often a fan trip, sometimes with steam. There may be visits to local model pikes or the host club may put on an operational evening.

Helpful and educational as these activities are, it is the friendships you make that are the real treat. They've forced me to reverse my former position—for after twenty-odd conventions, I've seen all the prototype facilities I want to, so of late I just remain at the hotel, talking shop with the friends I've made over these wonderful years.

I've mentioned taking children to all these affairs, so a word of caution may not be amiss. Nearly every parent thinks his own little darlings are faultless models of perfect behavior. I have no such illusions, but of one thing I am sure—neither of mine will put their hands on another man's pike. I've taught them *that,* if nothing else, because I long since learned that it is a statistical fact that more friendships have been broken in model railroading because of the conduct of children than all other reasons combined.

If you join NMRA—and I strongly advise you to—you will receive a directory giving names and addresses of all other members in the world. Beside each name is a code, telling you whether visitors are welcome, and under what conditions. Many modelers signify "adults only," due to some unfortunate experience in the past. I've lost a couple of good friends because they would not make their children keep their hands off my pike, and resented it when I corrected them. That's too bad, but after I—or any other modeler—have spent months building something, such as a delicate trestle bridge or the like, I have cause to be upset when some untrained child pulls it down. The moral is—if a model rail invites you and your family to view his empire, see to it that your children *keep hands off!*

Aside from the child problem, there are certain rules of etiquette you should observe. Always telephone in advance to make sure whether or not it is convenient for the host to receive guests, and tell him the number in your party. Then make your first visit short; a half hour is long enough. Don't touch any of his equipment without his express permission, and then handle it with extreme care. Don't ask to operate his trains, but if he invites you on his own, run them more slowly than you would your own; you don't know all the foibles of his layout. Don't offer any adverse criticisms; model rails are a proud breed, but if you see anything worthy of praise, praise it by all means. But even in the way of praise, use judgment; *he* knows what is good, and he'll think less of you if you praise something he is ashamed of. One of the reasons I prefer visitors who are seasoned modelers is that they know a good piece of workmanship when they see it, something I cannot say for the average nonrailroader.

Another thing that gripes model rails —I know it does me—is when you show your pike to some nonrailroader to have him, or her, say, as they almost invariably do: "I'd sure like to have my little boy see this layout!" Adult model railroaders do not build their pikes for the edification of "little boys," nor do they consider it a child's plaything, which such a comment implies, whether consciously or unconsciously.

This is not to say that model rails do not like to have visitors; most of them do. But it is only natural to enjoy appreciative visitors. Try to be one.

There are other customs peculiar to the hobby, some of which have a playful air. Many model rails wear brightly colored

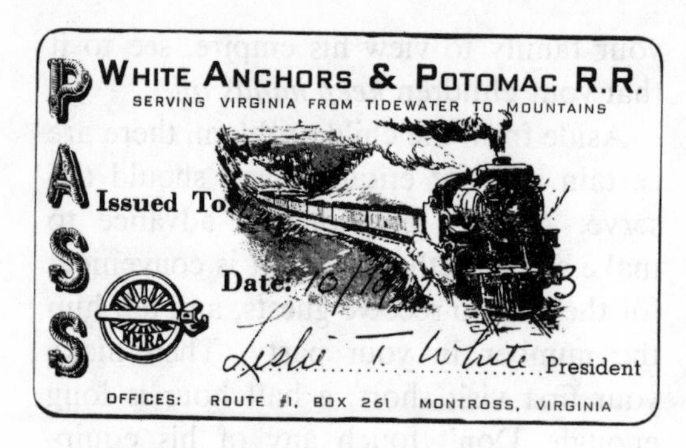

Fig. 14-1 Copy of My Pass

"railroad" shirts to the conventions, made up of emblems from different prototype railroads; sometimes their wives wear gay skirts or dresses with a railroading motif. Those cloth engineer's caps are common. The first time you wear such an outfit you may feel like a bit of a fool, as I did, but it's all part of the fun and gaiety and a harmless diversion.

Another amusing and interesting custom is the exchange of "passes." Sometimes these are replicas of the passes on real railroads, more often they are humorous, with such restrictions as "bearers of this free pass must not shoot out the car lights with revolvers after six o'clock," and similar nonsense.

Figure 14-1 is a copy of my own pass. I have several dozen such passes sent me by other model rails, and they make a fascinating and colorful collection.

Some model rails have timetables printed up of their train schedules; others have stationery with the name of their private empire emblazoned across the head. It's all part of the general camaraderie of the hobby.

One of the regions has as a slogan, "Never model-railroad alone!"—a take off on the old temperance slogan, "Never drink alone." But it has a built-in merit despite the humor. Invite a friend in to operate with you; maybe you'll win a convert to the hobby, and even if you don't, it will be more fun for you. Many skilled craftsmen do not have space for a layout of their own, and would be glad to work with you on your pike for the fun of it.

The problem of teen-agers is a touchy subject. Most clubs bar anyone under twenty-one because they do not believe teen-agers are serious enough. Other clubs take some teen-agers over sixteen for a probationary period to see if they are emotionally mature enough to behave properly. In some ways, this seems unfair to teen-agers for, while all too many are given to clowning, doing sloppy work, or running equipment too fast, many are as serious about the hobby as adults. Of late a number of teen-age clubs have started around the country and some of these ban adults—which somewhat evens the score. But the teen-age modeler of today will be the adult modeler of the future, and if he isn't helped off to a good start now, the hobby will suffer. It is a lucky family which has a model railroading partnership between a teen-age son and his father.

My son hasn't yet reached his teens but we've worked together so closely over the years that he knows almost as much about our pike as I do. It is the one big thing we have in common. As my wife phrases it, "that alone justifies the pike if nothing else does."

CHAPTER 15

In Summation

If all the information and data about scale model railroading and real railroading could be encompassed between the covers of one book, there would be no need for model or real railroad magazines. But both model railroading and the prototype are a vast subject and are constantly changing and growing. For instance, as this book is being written, the development of a new transistor control is going ahead by leaps and bounds and may well supersede the conventional controls now in popular use. The most I can hope to do is bring you up to date—from here on, it's up to you to keep abreast.

Also, in a book divided into technical chapters there is little chance to delve into the fascinating world of railroadiana, and a marvelous story that is. Railroads grew up the "hard way," developing customs and traditions in their own peculiar fashion. One such story that captivated me is why the conductor, rather than the engineer, is boss of a train. It seems something like making a ship's purser boss of a ship, instead of the captain. But the conductor *is* boss, and that issue was settled in he-man fashion between two stubborn men back in 1842.

It happened this way: Back in those heroic old days when hard-shelled martinets of the James J. Hill and Cornelius Vanderbilt stripe were fighting tooth and claw to see who bossed the railroads, nobody was quite sure who bossed a single train. Most enginemen assumed they did, and acted accordingly; and perhaps they would still be in charge if one of their breed, an engineer named Abe Hammil of the Erie Railroad, had shown as much guts as he did gall.

Hammil was a bullhead who wouldn't take orders from "no mere ticket taker" and decided he would stop his train only when *he* thought it necessary. But in that year he got a new conductor by the name of Ebenezer Ayres, who was a man of original ideas and had a mind of his own. As there was at that time no standard means for a conductor to signal his engineer, Ayres rigged up a system of his own—a long rope that ran over the top of the train from the caboose to the engine cab, with a chunk of wood on the front end to attract the attention of the engine crew.

At the beginning of their original run, Ayres explained his gadget to Hammil. "When you see that chunk of wood bobble, it means I want you to stop," he said.

Hammil made no comment but, once the train was moving, he cut off the wood and when Ayres yanked on his end, all he got was slack. Ayres said nothing during the outward run but when the train turned around for the return trip he again fastened the wood to the rope. Abe Hammil cut it a second time.

Ayres determined it was time to settle the issue in the good old-fashioned way. So when the train reached its destination, he peeled off his coat, rolled up his sleeves, and walked to the head end where he invited Hammil to step out of the cab. And that's where Abe Hammil let down future generations of engineers. He refused to come down. Ayres, however, wanted the issue settled, so he went up into the cab after Hammil and knocked him out of the cab. Once on the ground, the battle was engaged, and a right bloody fracas it was. When Hammil was too battered to get up, he weakly promised to obey Ayres' signals in the future.

From that day to this, the tradition remains unchallenged; the conductor is boss of the train.

In reading literature about old-time railroading, you'll frequently come across the term "jerkwater lines," all too often used disparagingly. But in all truth, the phrase is more descriptive than deprecatory. In the early days of railroading, when short lines were bobbing up between towns all over the nation, facilities were in short supply. When an engine crew discovered their water supply running low and knew there was not a water tank within miles, they did the only thing left for them; they stopped on a bridge over a river or a stream, heaved a leather bucket from the tender into the stream, and jerked the water aboard by the bucketful. Slow and laborious as it was, it was a literal case of life or death—and so the term was born. As railroad facilities improved and water tanks along the routes were commonplace, a line that had to haul its water out of a stream was referred to disparagingly as a "jerkwater line."

In various chapters of this book I have referred to soldering, but could find no logical place to develop the subject. You need it in trackwork, in electrical work, and in structures and in locomotive building, so let's have a look at it now in this collection of afterthoughts.

To be frank with you, soldering was for a long time a veritable headache to me. Having no one to demonstrate it to me, I had to learn it out of books and, as is too often the case when learning something from a book, we overlook some of the essentials in our anxiety to complete a job. My two basic troubles were: proper cleaning of the parts to be soldered and the wrong choice of iron. When I mastered these two elements, the rest was comparatively simple.

Let me stress the cleanliness of the work. Solder will not adhere to a dirty or greasy surface. All parts to be soldered *must* be either scraped, filed, sanded, or cleaned with a liquid cleaner before attempting to solder. I made up several different-sized scrapers from old files, which I ground to a sharp scraping edge for various jobs. These altered the whole picture for me.

I had to buy about half a dozen different irons before I found one that suited my purpose. Basically, soldering is the transference of heat from the iron to the metal being soldered. You read a lot about 25-watt irons and the like, and some experts who know their craft can use them. But for the beginner, I recommend a 250-watt iron with a thermostat to eliminate overheating. This size of iron gives you good, quick heat where you need it and helps you avoid "cold joints" that come loose in a few days.

Another sore point: Remember that your iron must be clean and well tinned. Any soldering iron will oxidize after use and periodically must be recleaned and retinned.

To clean an iron, take an old file and file away all old solder and oxidization until the copper appears bright and clean. Then heat the iron and apply a little rosin-core solder to the tip. (Never use acid-core solder in model railroading!) Next rub the point of the iron on a bar of sal ammoniac and apply a little more solder. Wipe with a piece of cloth and your iron should be properly tinned and clean.

Now, as I reiterated several times in this book, the ideas expressed herein are not necessarily the only methods, or even the best; they are the methods that I have gained by experience and have proven satisfactory to me. The NMRA Data Sheets have a whole lot on the art of soldering which you would be well advised to study.

Next to cleanliness of material and the proper iron, the important thing is the choice of solder and flux. Solder is an alloy of tin and lead, and the so-called "common solder" is a poor conductor of electricity. For model railroad work a solder with a higher tin than lead content is advisable. I prefer 40/60 solder, that is, an alloy of 60 per cent tin to 40 per cent lead. This makes for easy flowing and yet is not too high in tin content to make a good solid joint.

It is essential to have a good mechanical joint before soldering; do not depend on solder alone to carry the load. For electrical connections, I twist my wires together firmly, then use a rosin-core solder, which has its own built-in flux.

Flux is used to dissolve oxides on the metal to be soldered and to keep the pores of the metal open. There are two general types of flux; corrosive and noncorrosive. Corrosive fluxes, such as acid-core solder and the like, should never be used on electrical connections, and very sparingly on anything else.

I use resin-core solder, which contains its own resin flux in a core of the solder, for electrical work; for other work, I prefer two fluxes, "Nokorode" and "Sal-met." They do an excellent job and have, over the years I have been using them, shown no evidence of corrosion.

There are times when you need more heat than an iron can give you, such as when soldering a steam dome to a locomotive. Then you must use either an alcohol or a propane torch and resort to what is known as "sweat soldering." The customary way of doing this is to "tin" one surface. You accomplish this by putting a little flux on the bottom of the steam dome and applying a thin coat of solder to it. When cool, apply flux to the other part—in this case the loco boiler where the dome is to go—then clamp both surfaces together to hold them in place during the operation. Get your torch going and apply heat to the two parts until the solder oozes out at the edges. Then you have it made.

In attaching feeder wires to track, I use the same general plan, except I use an iron instead of a torch. I tin the end of the wire to be attached, scrape the track clean with a small scraper reserved for that particular job, and daub on a little flux with a toothpick. Then I hold the wire in place with a wooden skewer or pointed stick and apply a very hot iron to the top of the rail. If your iron is powerful enough and properly heated, a light touch is all that is needed to give you a firm joint. I read a lot about burning the plastic ties, but so far haven't had any such difficulty. You don't need to hold the hot iron to the track long enough to burn your ties. And don't use too much solder; it's not necessary and you will have a messy-looking connection.

To summarize: Soldering is not difficult if you get the work clean, use a good well-tinned iron, the proper flux, and the right amount of heat.

An allied hobby which has become practically an adjunct to model railroading is photography. It is not only good fun for your own amusement but profitable as well, for the model railroading magazines are a ready market for *good* model pictures. While not too difficult to learn, the photographing of models is exacting and presents special problems. Chief of these is depth of focus.

Admittedly a camera is only as good as the man behind it; a real expert can perform miracles with even the cheapest camera, but for the amateur, the better the equipment, the better the picture. The average camera simply does not have the depth of focus necessary for good miniature photography.

Roughly speaking, depth of focus merely means how sharp objects will be in front of and behind the object you have focused upon. For example, suppose you focus on an object 10 feet away—will objects at 8 and at 15 feet be clear cut and in focus?

In a somewhat checkered career, I was once a professional photographer and operated a portrait and commercial studio on the West Coast. However, when I tackled miniature photography, I found that my previous experience had been of little help except that it gave me an understanding of the problem. Now you all probably know that as you decrease the aperture of your lens opening, you increase the depth of focus proportionately, yet on some cameras even this is not sufficient. Then, too, your camera must permit you to get very close to your subject for miniature work.

The pictures in this book credited to Linn Westcott are almost perfect examples of good miniature photography. I do not recall the name of the camera he used, but it was a small—about 2¼" x 2¼"—reflex, and he had a bewildering array of lamps; the railroad room looked like a Hollywood studio with wires running in all directions. For myself, I used a bank of three floodlights and a 35 mm camera—a type of equipment very popular with model rails.

One big advantage of miniature photography is that your subject doesn't move. You can therefore stop down your lens as fine as you like, or take long-time exposures, using only your ordinary pike lighting. Study the model railroading magazines to see samples of good miniature photography and try to figure out how they did it. You can do the same with practice.

In railroading literature you will often find reference, usually used jocularly, to the famous railroad Rule G. This rule stemmed from the early days of railroading, when saloonkeepers set up shop at every whistle-stop along the tracks. In those stormy days, it was the custom of the engine crew and the caboose gang to pause for liquid refreshments to bolster them on to their destination. So Rule G came into being. Here it is:

Rule G: "The use of intoxicants by employes while on duty is prohibited. Their use, or the frequenting of places where they are sold, is sufficient cause for dismissal."

So watch your train crew's behavior.

LATE FLASH! As this book goes to press, we have learned that the Kurtz-Kraft Company has just brought out some flexible track in HOn3, which will be a great boon to narrow-gauge fans. Also, three manufacturers have come on the market with new transistor power controls for more realistic operation. As they haven't got down to my neck of the woods yet, I have not seen them, but *Model Railroader Magazine* gave them a very favorable review. But don't plunge into this blindly until you have had some experience with conventional control.

GLOSSARY OF MODEL RAILROAD TERMS AND WORDS

This dictionary of terms and words is not meant to be all inclusive, but rather is an attempt to set down those terms which are used in model railroading whose definition differs from that given in dictionaries.

TERMS OFTEN CONFUSED

Block—a length of track isolated by gaps or insulated breaks from all adjoining track. A block may be further subdivided into subblocks.

and

Section—a length of track of defined limits over which the direction of travel is controlled by one direction controller: i.e., a section consists of all the blocks in which the direction of travel is changed at the same time by the direction controller.

Scale—the reduction of prototype proportions as used in model railroading.

and

Gauge—the distance between the rails in trackwork, or a tool for making measurements, or such an indicator as a steam gauge. It does not refer to a reduction of the prototype and thus there is no such thing as an HO gauge man. Correctly stated there is an HO scale man.

Turnout—the separation of one set of rails into two or more tracks.

and

Switch—an electrical control device for closing or opening circuits, or the movable portion of the turnout; the movable rails and points.

Classification Lights—appear only on an engine to indicate the class of train.

and

Marker Lights—appear only on the last car of a train to indicate the direction of travel of the train.

Equalized Trucks—have side frames loosely fastened to the truck bolster allowing equal downward pressure on all wheels regardless of changes in track elevation. They may or may not be sprung.

and

Sprung Trucks—have the side frames separated from the bolster by springs providing a cushioning effect. They may or may not be equalized.

Spur—any stub-ended track leaving the main line with a single turnout.
and
Siding—a track auxiliary to the main track for meeting or passing of trains and connected to the main line at both ends by turnouts.

Meet—two trains traveling in opposite direction meet at a siding. One takes a siding while the other proceeds on the main line.
and
Pass—two trains traveling in the same direction; one takes the siding while the other passes by on the main line.

Staining the Scenery—the art of coloring the final scenic plaster by applying and blending several thin transparent washes usually made of artist's oils and turpentine.
and
Painting the Scenery—the art of coloring the final scenic plaster base by brushing or spraying full-strength coats of either water base or oil base paints of various colors.

Model Railroad or Pike—model railroad or pike is the total model railroad including scenery, benchwork, wiring, trackage, structures, and equipment.
and
Layout—layout is the plan or design of the track arrangement. It does not properly refer to the model railroad itself.
and
Setup—setup is an improper noun for a model railroad, unless it consists of no more than a train set put together in a nonpermanent location.

Crossing—a place where two or more tracks intersect with interchange between the tracks being impossible.
and
Crossover—a place where two or more turnouts connect parallel tracks.

Carrier Control—carrier current control uses higher frequency current superimposed on the rails to control the starting, stopping, changing direction and/or speed of an engine.
and
Electronic Control—electronic control is any type of control circuit using electronic circuits that use semiconductors, electronic tubes, or components.
and
High-frequency Control—HF—high-frequency (HF) control uses high-frequency current (usually in the radio spectrum) superimposed on the rails to control the starting, stopping, changing direction and/or speed of an engine.
and
Radio Control—RF—radio frequency (RF) control uses radio waves passing through the air to control the starting, stopping, changing direction and/or speed of an engine.

BENCHWORK

Ballast Board—a board with beveled edges, which is laid above the subroadbed to represent the ballast of a real railroad right-of-way. Ballast boards are often omitted in yard areas.

Bracket—a member used to support the railroad from a wall, eliminating the need for legs under the benchwork.

Cleat—a horizontal support often used between two or more risers. Used where roadbed is too wide for a single riser or to obtain a stronger joint on a single riser.

Cookie-cutter Construction—a flat-top panel which is cut along the sides of the trackwork so that it may be raised or lowered to different levels from the panel elevation.

Duck Under—a place under the benchwork where it is possible to pass from one operating space to another.

Framework—the entire track and scenery support of a model railroad. Used interchangeably with Benchwork.

Grade—the rise and fall of the trackwork as it progresses through the scenery.

Grid—the horizontal framework that forms the foundation for supporting the track and scenery in the grid method of benchwork construction. The grid is made with a front and back board, called stringers which are joined by cross members called grid joists.

Grid Construction—bench construction using stringers and cross pieces to form a grid work upon which the track base is laid. It is not covered with plywood or wall board except in yard areas. The advantage of this method of construction is that the track can change from one level to another easily and the scenery can be partly above or below the track level.

Grid Panel—a rectangular section of grid built as a unit. Several grid panels may be combined to support the entire railroad.

Grid, Lowered—part of a grid which is constructed at a lower level than the rest of the railroad to allow modeling a valley, gorge, or other scenic feature.

Grid, Raised—part of the grid which is raised to the track level or above. Used to make simpler the construction of yard or terminal, for placing trackwork on embankments, or constructing mountainous terrain.

Hanger—a wire or wood strut, or sheet metal brace used to hang the railroad from the ceiling, or suspend a portion of the railroad from some other supporting member.

Joists—see Stringers.

Layout—the plan or design of a model railroad and preferably not used to mean the physical model railroad.

Lift Out—a small opening in the benchwork for standing while making repairs. Also see Scenery section.

Lintel—see Riser and Lintel Construction.

Open Benchwork—see preferred usage, Grid Construction.

Operating Space—openings or aisles where the model railroad is operated and maintained.

Platform—any wide board which forms the roadbed for a yard, or foundation for a group of buildings.

Ribbon Roadbed—any roadbed cut out of sheet wood or plywood, curves and all as compared to segmented planks of lintel construction.

Riser and Lintel Construction—a method of building subroadbed which makes use of short planks or "lintels" which reach from one riser to another forming the base upon which the roadbed is laid.

Risers—vertical supports used to hold the roadbed or scenery at some level above the grid.

Roadbed—the horizontal boards which support the ballast and track. Roadbed is sometimes called Ballast Board.

Runner Construction—a method of supporting the roadbed. Two wooden runners are fastened edge up to each side of the risers. Runners are usually laminated from several thicknesses of stock and bent around curves. The advantage is that the roadbed is supported at all points, even on curves between risers.

Stringers—the longitudinal members that make up a grid. Refers to the longer members as opposed to the shorter members which are called joists.

Subroadbed—the horizontal members of the benchwork upon which the roadbed, ties, and track are laid. The subroadbed is sometimes called the roadway.

Supports—any member added above the grid or tabletop to support the track or scenery.

Tabletop Construction—in this method, the entire track and scenery are laid upon a flat platform or table.

CONTROL

Control terms are closely linked with Electrical terms and this listing is provided solely to furnish a convenient place to locate the many methods used in controlling model railroad operation.

Absolute Block—a block in which but one train is allowed at any time.

Acceleration Control—a method by which a train slowly accelerates or slows down in speed automatically by means of an electrical or mechanical device introduced between the throttle and the block wiring.

Automatic Control—the control of the train automatically by some predetermined electrical or mechanical method.

Automatic Train Control—ATC—a method by which trains are started and stopped automatically when certain conditions exist which affect the movement of the trains. See Electrical section—Protection Circuit.

Auto-stat Control—a form of section control in which control is automatically switched from one local control panel to another in sequential order as a train moves from one section to another.

Block—a length of track of defined limits used by trains under the protection of automatic train control, block signals, or manual train control. Also see Section, Track.

Block Control—each controlled block has its own on-off selector switch on the control panel, so any block can be cut in or out, but there is only one throttle for these blocks.

Block System—a series of consecutive blocks.

Cab—an engineer's control facilities.

Cab Control—a method of control wherein facilities are provided (usually for two or more enginemen) so a train can be controlled within the limits of track connected to each cab. Note: Other cabs may or may not be locked out by the first to obtain control of a block.

Cab Control System—each road engineer can operate a train over the entire railroad except for certain limitations.

Carrier Control—CC—the starting, stopping, changing direction, and/or speed of trains by superimposing higher frequency current on the rails. Also see High-frequency Control (HF) and Radio Control (RF).

Centralized Traffic Control—CTC—a method of establishing the routing from facilities located at one point. In model railroading, operating power may or may not be regulated from the CTC board.

Control—the controlling of the starting, stopping, changing direction and the speed of an engine. Note: Different methods of control can be used separately or together; e.g. Electronic Control may be set up in Cabs (cab control), with Protection provided by Automatic Train Control.

Automatic Control Automatic Train Control—ATC Cab Control	} See alphabetic listing

Carrier Control—CC
Centralized Traffic Control—CTC
Dispatcher Control
Electronic Control
High-frequency Control—HF
Manual Train Control
Plain Control
Progressive Cab Control—PCC
Radio Control—RF
Route Control
Section Control
Tower Control

} See alphabetic listing

Current of Traffic—the movement of trains on a main track, in one direction, specified by the rules.

Dispatcher Control—where all trains are under the control of a dispatcher by means of signals or other communication.

Division—that portion of a railway assigned to supervision of a Superintendent.

Double Track—two or more main tracks, upon one or more of which the current of traffic is in a specified direction and upon the other(s) in the opposite direction.

Electronic Control—the generic term for any control circuit using electronic circuits that use semiconductors, electronic tubes, or components. See Carrier, High-frequency, and Radio Control.

Engine—a machine propelled by any form of energy and used in train or yard service. Note: The word engine also applies to a Motor Car or Multiple Unit Car–MU when used in these definitions.

Engineer Control—See Cab Control System.

Extra Train—a train not authorized by a timetable schedule. It must be designated as:

Extra—for any extra, except work-train extra.
Work Extra—for work-train extra.

Floating Block—See Electrical section.

High-frequency Control—HF—a method whereby high-frequency current (usually in the radio spectrum) is transmitted through the rails to control the engine or other electrical devices. Also see Carrier and Radio Control.

Initial Station—any station at which a scheduled or extra train originates.

Interchange Block—See Electrical section.

Interlocking—See Signal section.

Main Track—a track extending through yards and between stations, upon which trains are operated by timetable or train order, or the use of which is controlled by block signals. Used interchangeably with Main Line.

Manual Block System—a block system in which the signals and/or propulsion power are controlled manually.

Manual Train Control—a method of train control which is all manual as contrasted to automatic train control.

Motor Car—a car propelled by any form of energy and used in train or yard service.

Multiple Unit Car–MU Car—a self-propelled car arranged to run as a train with other similar cars, with or without trailer cars, so that all propelling power can be controlled from one point.

Permissive Block—a block in which two or more trains are permitted at the same time when traveling in the same direction.

Plain Control—consists of speed and direction control without division of the railroad into sections or control blocks.

Progressive Cab Control–PCC—a form of control using blocks with automatic switching of the propulsion power to the blocks by the train as it moves along the track.

Radio Control–RF—the starting, stopping, changing direction, and/or speed of trains using radio waves passing through the air to the train. Also see Carrier Control.

Regular Train—a train authorized by timetable schedule.

Route Control—an electrical or mechanical method whereby a predetermined route can be set up before the train leaves a terminal. It affects only the blocks or turnouts as the train requires them.

Schedule—that part of a timetable which prescribes class, direction, number, and movement for a regular train.

Section, Track—a length of track of defined limits over which the direction of travel is controlled by one direction controller: i.e., a section consists of all the blocks in which the direction of travel is changed at the same time by the direction-control lever.

Section, Train—one of two or more trains running on the same schedule, displaying signals or for which signals are displayed.

Section Control—the model railroad is divided into sections of one or more blocks each. Each section has its own throttle and block selector switches, operated by the engineer. It may include signal indications and route control. He can move from one control panel to another with the train or pass the train to the adjoining section operator.

Single Track—a main track upon which trains are operated in both directions.

Speed

Limited —Not exceeding . . . . mph*
Medium —Not exceeding . . . . mph*
Slow —Not exceeding . . . . mph*
Restricted—Not to exceed slow speed nor exceeding that which will enable a train to stop short of a train ahead, an obstruction, switch points not properly aligned, or a broken rail.

Station—a place where a train enters or leaves the main track, or from which fixed signals are operated, or a place designated on the timetable by name where trains stop for traffic.

Block Station
Initial Station
Terminal Station
} See alphabetic listing

Subdivision—a part of a division so designated on the timetable.

Superior Train—a train having precedence over another train.

Terminal Station—any station at which a scheduled or extra train terminates.

Timetable—the authority for the movement of regular trains subject to the rules. It contains the classified schedule of trains with special instructions relating thereto.

Tower Control—the complete control over the movement of trains within a specified area of the railroad. The engineman controls the speed of the train in accordance with the aspects of the signal indications over the route set by the tower.

Track—the rails on which the train moves.

Double Track
Main Track
} See alphabetic listing

Train—an engine, or more than one engine coupled, with or without cars, displaying markers.

Extra Train
Regular Train
Section, Train
Superior Train
} See alphabetic listing

Train Signals—flags or lanterns displayed at the front (classification) and rear (markers) of a train.

Yard—a system of tracks within defined limits provided for making up trains, storing cars, and other purposes, over which movements not authorized by

* Values for limited, medium, and slow speeds are not specified by the AAR, are not adopted by several prototype roads, and where adopted are not uniform. Generally determined by terrain, curvature, traffic density, etc.

timetable or by train order may be made, subject to prescribed signals and rules, or special instructions.

CONSTRUCTION, MODEL

Assembled Model—an operating model without painting or lettering which may or may not be sold with couplers attached.

Cross-kit Model—a term often used in contests to denote a model built with the superstructure from one or more kits over a mechanism or frame from another kit.

Custom-assembled—a kit assembled or modified to an individual order. When the model is sold as custom-assembled the name of the builder must be given.

Custom-built—a model built to individual order and specification. When the model is sold as custom-built the name of the builder must be given.

Detailed Kit—a kit built with added or altered parts in addition to those supplied in the kit.

Free Lance—designates the use of an original design in the construction of a model as opposed to following a definite prototype.

Kit-built—a model constructed from stock and components sold with drawings and instructions as a serially produced commercial product.

Modified Kit—originally a kit, redesigned by the builder during the assembly so that when completed it differs from other kit-built models.

Parts-built Model—a model principally built up using assorted commercial parts as opposed to assembling a kit.

Professional Builder—one who builds models principally for sale.

Professional-built—a model built by a professional builder. When the model is sold as professional-built the name of the builder must be given.

Prototype—refers to following railroad or other real-life design.

Ready-to-run—RTR—a model completely finished and operating; lettered and with couplers attached at the time of purchase.

Scale, Exact—a model constructed to a precise scale reduction of all exterior surfaces including wheels, usually follow ing a specific prototype. Very seldom built.

Scale, Fine—a series of. Standards closer to exact scale than NMRA Standards. Used in Great Britain for O scale and in the United States by small groups of modelers in various scales, particularly S scale and various Narrow-gauge scales.

Scale, Hi-Rail—the preferred term for toy trains in which liberties have been taken with NMRA Standards such as flanges, wheel tread, rail, etc. Should not be confused with Ready-to-run.

Scale, NMRA—a model built using NMRA Standards where applicable.

Scratch-built—a completely builder-constructed model without the use of any commercial parts except:

1. Motor
2. Gears
3. Drivers & wheels
4. Couplers
5. Light bulbs
6. Trucks
7. Bell
8. Marker & Classification lights
9. Valve gear
10. Car brake fittings
11. Wood & metal shapes

Any and all exceptions from the above list must be given. Where items on the list have been scratch-built they should be so designated.

Superdetail—a model with considerably more detail of excellent quality than usually expected. The super shall refer more to the quality of the detail than to the quantity.

Super Scratch-built—a model fabricated from stock materials; metal, wood, plastic, paper, etc. All commercially cast, assembled, or fabricated parts must be listed.

Tin Plate—a term used to denote old toy trains using tin-plate track. Usually had large oversize flanges and very seldom to scale. Also see Scale, Hi-Rail.

DESIGN, LAYOUT

Design, Layout—the plan or design of the track arrangement. Does not refer to the completed model railroad itself.

Dogbone Railroad—tracks laid in the shape of a dumbbell.

Fan Railroad—has a main line which goes to several destinations via different routes which can be point to point out and back and/or loop.

Folded Dogbone Railroad—a dogbone type of plan in which the parts of the track are folded back until they overlap each other.

Out and Back Railroad—has one principal terminal. The main line departs from the yard and returns by a different route, entering the yard at the point of departure.

Point to Point Railroad—has the main line going from one terminal to another and trains must return via the same track. Terminals usually have facilities for turning the train.

Waterwings Railroad—See Dogbone Railroad.

DESIGN, MODEL RAILROAD

Around the Room Railroad—built against all walls of a room.

Canyon Railroad—a variation of the Walk-in Railroad where some or all the scenery extends to the floor making the aisles into simulated canyons.

Design, Model Railroad—the configuration of the benchwork and scenery.

Island Railroad—a railroad which is accessible from all sides.

Period Railroad—depicts a particular era in time, whether early or modern. Nothing designed after the period being acceptable nor should much earlier equipment be used unless reasonably accounted for.

Shelf Railroad—built against one or more walls of a room and normally protruding less than an arm's length from the wall.

Table Railroad—a variation of the Island Railroad, small enough so all parts can be reached when standing at the outer edges, there being no internal or walk-in spaces.

Walk-in Railroad—one in which the aisles protrude into the body of the railroad and from which operations can be conducted. Usually all trackage can be reached from the aisles.

DESIGN, TRACKAGE

Base Level—a reference point, generally the main yards, from which other track rises and descends.

Contour Lines—lines drawn on the model railroad plan to show the elevations of the terrain.

Curved Turnout—a turnout in which both branches curve toward the same side.

Datum Level—the level of the lowest trackage on the railroad or any other point, such as the top of framework, selected as the reference point for elevation measurements.

Degree of Curvature—sharpness of a curve measured by the number of degrees of turn in a unit distance, usually degrees per 100 scale feet.

Degree of Curve—total angle through which a curve turns.

Dual-gauge Track—three or four rails on the same ties for the accommodation of rolling stock of two different track gauges, usually narrow and standard. Also see Electrical section—Third-rail Power Distribution.

Elevated Rail—the outer rail on a curve of superelevated track.

Elevated Track—generally, track running above the level of streets. In model railroading, may refer to any track at higher levels.

Elevation—the height of track, terrain, and other features above a selected datum level. Track elevation is assumed to the top of the rail unless otherwise stated.

Fish Plate—see Rail Joiner.

Form Lines—sketched or broken lines to indicate shapes of hills, etc. Also see Contour Lines.

Gauntlet Track—two tracks laid on the same ties in an interlaced manner. Used to bypass locomotives at weighing scales, to extend the length of a turnout so a switch stand can be in a more convenient place, or to narrow the right-of-way for double track to pass through a tunnel, etc.

Guard Rail—metal or wood rail laid parallel to running rails to prevent wheels from running off the side of a bridge or into the walls of a tunnel if there is a derailment.

Level—the general elevation of a track, assumed to the top of the rail.

Loop—a length of track which turns back, passing over or under itself, used to gain elevation.

Loop, Reversing—a length of track which loops back, connecting with itself in the reverse direction so that a train is turned end for end. Also called a balloon.

Rail Code—the height of a rail measured in units of 1/1000 of an inch.

Rail Joiner—any attachment used to line up the ends of rails where they meet. Insulated joiners are used where electrical conductivity is to be broken.

Siding—a track, auxiliary to the main track for meeting or passing of trains and connected to the main track at both ends by turnouts.

Spiral—a transition curve with a uniform change of curvature.

Spur—any stub-ended track leaving the main line with a single turnout.

Superelevation—the raising of the outer rail above the inner rail in a curve to counteract the tendency of a train to overturn outward when running on the curve.

Switch—an electrical control device. See Electrical section.

Transition Curve—any curve used to ease the entrance and exit to a sharper curve.

Turnout—the device which separates one set of rails into two or more tracks.

Wing Rails—the short guard rails integral with the frog at the turnout or crossing.

Wye Turnout—a turnout in which the two branch tracks curve in opposite directions.

ELECTRICAL

Block—a length of track isolated by gaps or insulated breaks from all adjoining track. A block may be further divided into subblocks.

Block, Floating—sometimes called an Interchange Block. A subblock electrically connected to one or another adjoining block depending upon the alignment of the track turnouts.

Block, Interchange—see Block, Floating.

Block, Transfer—a block that can be electrically connected to one or another control panel.

Cab—the electrical equipment provided for one operator to control one train. The facilities might include the throttle, reverse lever, traffic-direction controller, cab signals block selecting equipment, etc.

Cab Control System—the methods that are employed in the control system to connect each cab to the track so a train can be controlled by: toggle switch, push-button switch, rotary switch, stepping switch, relay progression, or plug and cord.

CAPY Circuit—a kind of relay progression using diodes in a cab control system. Also see Detection Circuits.

Cascade—a word used for circuits in which one device operates the next in sequence.

Checkout Signal System—see Detection Circuits.

Common-rail System—that type of track wiring in which only one running rail is gapped and separated into blocks. Also see Independent Rail System.

Contacts—two metal surfaces that are mechanically brought together to close an electrical circuit (normally open), or separated to open an electrical circuit (normally closed).

Contacts, Switch Machine Transfer or Cutoff—the electrical contacts mounted on a switch machine to open the circuit to the coil being energized after the machine has been operated. Used on two-coil machine to prevent the operating coil from burning out.

Contacts, Track—contacts operated by the movement of an engine or car past a certain point on the track. See Detection, Checkout.

Control Rail—the running rail that is separated into blocks for control purposes.

Controller—a general term that should be preceded or followed by a word describing its function, i.e., Speed Controller.

Controller, Engine-direction—switch mounted on the engine, used to set the direction of the engine, forward or backward. Can be a relay in the engine.

Controller, Engine-reverse—a switch mounted in the cab, which determines whether an engine shall move forward or in reverse with respect to the established direction of traffic. Also see Controller, Traffic Direction.

Controller, Speed—see Throttle.

Controller, Traffic-direction—a reversing switch used only to determine the general direction of traffic on part or all of the railroad. It may be designated as a main-line, loop, or other district controller. Called Direction Controller when there is only one control board and one switch serves as the Engine- and Traffic-direction Controller.

Controller Unit, Engine—a unit containing the throttle, engine-reverse controller, and traffic-direction controller. May be in a separate housing or a part of a cab.

Detection Circuit—that circuit which, when completed, provides current flow to operate a relay or other device or equipment. Its prime use is to detect something in a block or section. The following are types of circuits used to detect an engine or car on a length of track:

CC—same as the Coolidge circuit except the detection relay power circuit or the propulsion power circuit is opened to release the lock up of the detection relay.

Checkout—a circuit in which a mechanically operated contact closes the detection relay circuit and the relay locks. Another mechanically operated contact opens the detection relay lock-up circuit to release the detection relay.

Coolidge—a circuit using a separate power source for the detection relay. The relay contacts connect the propulsion power and lock up the detection relay when the detection circuit is initially completed. The lock-up circuit is opened at regular intervals mechanically or otherwise to release those detection relays where the detection circuit is open.

MRE—a modification of the NMRA circuit, using two diodes to automatically align the traffic direction on the track with that set by the engine-reverse controller.

NMRA—a circuit using a diode to block the flow of current in the detection relay lock-up circuit but permitting propulsion current to flow when it is required.

Series Relay—a circuit in which the propulsion current flows through the detection relay coil. This current flow makes enough magnetism to operate the relay.

Detection Rail—is the same as the control rail in two rail. In third-rail power distribution it is the running rail to which the detection circuit is connected. Also known as the Signal Rail.

Electronic Control—a method of control using electronic circuits and components. See Control section.

Electronic Lighting—see Lighting, Radio-frequency.

Feeder—a heavy wire between two electrical terminals. Used for a common buss conductor and where heavy currents will have to be conducted.

Frog—the movable portion of a turnout.

Frog, Bridged or Jumpered—an insulated frog in a crossing or turnout with wired or other connections so electrical continuity is maintained along each rail.

Frog, Insulated—a frog in a crossing or turnout in which insulation is provided so that wheels may cross in either direction without causing short circuits.

Frog, Solid—a metallic frog in a turnout which is connected at all times to the four rails which immediately approach it. Gaps are usually provided near the frog to isolate the frog from the remainder of the track.

Frog Rail—a rail electrically connected to the frog of a turnout.

Grounded Brush—the brush of a motor which is connected to the frame of the motor.

Grounded Frame—the frame of an engine which is connected to the wheels on the right side of the engine.

Grounded Truck—the truck frame that is not insulated from the frame of the engine or car.

Grounded Wheels—the wheels which are not insulated from the grounded truck frame.

High-frequency or HF Lighting—see Lighting, Radio-frequency.

Independent Rail System—that type of track wiring in which both rails are gapped and separated into blocks for control purposes.

Indication Circuit—all wiring associated with the changing of signal aspects. See Signal section.

Insulated Points—points in a turnout which are insulated from each other as contrasted to being connected by a metal tie bar or other means.

Interchange Block—see Block, Floating.

Jumper—a wire used to connect two electrical terminals or nearby rails. Normally of short length and lighter gauge than a feeder wire.

Lever—a type of switch handle.

Lighting, Alternating Current—a method of lighting trains by line frequency when no motive power is supplied.

Lighting, Battery—small dry or wet cells placed in a car to provide current for the car lamps.

Lighting, Constant—a method of lighting trains independent of the propulsion power.

Lighting, High-frequency or HF—see Lighting, Radio-frequency or RF.

Lighting, Radio-frequency or RF—a method of lighting cars and engines regardless of the motive power by superimposing a radio-frequency current on the rails. The frequency is usually above 100 kilocycles, which is considered low radio frequency.

MRE Circuit—a modification of the NMRA circuit. See Detection Circuits.

Multiple Power Supply—a system in which power for each train comes from a separate power source. If desired the system can be of the common-rail type.

NMRA Circuit—a detection circuit using diodes. See Detection Circuits.

Pickup—any wheel, truck, shoe, wiper, trolley, or other device on an engine or car which is used to conduct current to the motor or to lamps.

Power, Propulsion—the power that turns the electric motor of an engine.

Power, Pulse—any electric current that is interrupted regularly in order to produce smoother operation of a motor at low speeds. A pulsating direct current.

Power Pack—a device that converts alternating current to direct current at a different voltage.

Power Rail—see Control Rail.

Propulsion Circuit—that circuit which, when completed, provides current flow to operate the electric motor of an engine. It may or may not contain all or parts of cab control, detection, dispatch, etc., circuits. It is the entire circuit from the Propulsion Power Supply to the rail.

Protection Circuit—that portion of the Propulsion Circuit which fulfills the function of Automatic Train Control by starting and stopping an engine automatically when certain conditions exist which affect the movements of the train.

Protection, Overload—a device such as a fuse, circuit breaker, or lamp used to prevent damage by excessive current flow.

Ramp—see Mechanical section.

Rheostat—see Throttle.

Section, Track—see Control section.

Section, Turning—that track associated with return loops and wyes, wired so that the polarity is not affected when adjoining sections are reversed.

Selector—any switching device for turning power on and off to several circuits, independently or in sequence. Usually by toggle switch, rotary switch, push-button switches, rotary relay, rotary stepping relay, etc.

Series Relay Circuit—a detection circuit using a series relay. See Detection Circuits.

Signal Circuit—that circuit which, when completed, operates a relay or other electrical device to change the aspect indication of a signal. It may or may not include the propulsion, protection and other control circuits. If protection is included, it should be called Signal and ATC circuit.

Signal Indication, Approach Lighted—a fixed signal in which the aspect lamp is lighted only when the approaching track is occupied.

Signal Indication, Normally Lighted—a fixed signal in which the aspect lamp is always lighted to show the condition of the block whether the approaching track is occupied or not.

Signal Rail—see Detection Rail.

Single Power Supply—a system in which several trains are powered from the same power source. Several batteries or power packs may be used.

Stud Contact Power Distribution—a form of inside third rail using a series of studs along the center line of the track. See Third-Rail Power Distribution.

Switch Machine—any motor, coil device, relay, rotary relay, or pneumatic device used to move the points of a turnout.

Third-Rail Power Distribution—a separate third rail mounted either in the center or on one side of the running rails to conduct propulsion power. Also called Three Rail. In two-rail power distribution in multiple gauge operation, the mixed gauge portions are sometimes called Three Rail, more properly called Dual Gauge.

Throttle—a device used to vary current flowing to a motor. Types include rheostat, variable transformer, etc.

Toggle—refers to a manually operated electric switch. Specific description should be given if other than toggle lever type is used.

Track Circuit—see Detection Circuits.

Track Contact—see Contact, Track.

Turning Section—see Section, Turning.

Twin Power Supply—a system in which all trains going in one direction are powered from one power source and all other trains are powered from a second power source. Usually used in common-rail systems.

Twin-T Circuit—a detection circuit using transistors. See Detection Circuits.

Two-Rail Power Distribution—a method whereby the propulsion power is conducted to the engines and the cars through the two running rails as contrasted to Third-Rail Power Distribution.

MECHANICAL

Coupler, Automatic—a coupler which is always ready to couple under any condition. Can be uncoupled by means of ramps or manual assist.

Coupler, Dummy—a model coupler, copying the Janney design in outline, but having no working knuckle, and must be coupled and uncoupled by hand, usually by raising one coupler out of the other.

Coupler, Prototype—see Coupler, Working Knuckle.

Coupler, Truck Mounted—a coupler mounted on the truck bolster so as to pivot with the truck.

Coupler, Working Knuckle—a coupler based upon the Janney design with working parts. It has a closed position and the knuckle must be opened to couple upon contact.

Coupler Ramp—a device used to uncouple automatic or working knuckle couplers. It may be either permanent or portable.

Coupler Ramp, Fixed—a device, without external control, which, when located below slack couplers will cause them to part when the slack is taken out.

Coupler Ramp, Magnetic—a device using magnetic rather than mechanical means to uncouple. It can be electromagnetic or per-magnetic.

Coupler Ramp, Working—a ramp operated by mechanical or electrical means which uncouples cars as they are pulled over it.

OPERATION

Card Operation—the movement of cars and making up of trains according to instructions obtained from previously prepared cards. This may or may not be in conjunction with a timetable or sequence operation.

Fast Clock—a speeded-up clock which does away with the necessity of using seconds in timetable operations and computations. Usually a proportion such as 4 to 1, 6 to 1, or 12 to 1 is used.

Movement of Trains

Operating Trains—the movement of trains according to a schedule or other method following prototype practice.

Playing Trains—the making of games and competitions out of the running of trains. For example, switching contests based upon the number of moves or elapsed time.

Running Trains—the movement of trains according to one's fancy without regard to prototype practice.

Operating Personnel

Agent—one who reports trains to the dispatcher and performs duties similar to the agent of a real railroad.

Brakeman—one who operates turnouts without the aid of a tower, couples and uncouples cars, and is a member of a train crew.

Conductor—one who usually is in charge of a train, but does not operate it. Used in way-freight and switching work.

Dispatcher—one who dispatches train movements, but does not operate trains.

Engineer—one whose specific job is to control the movement of one engine, any other duties being incidental.

Operator—the individual at a section control panel, who controls the movement of all trains through the section. The duties of engineer and towerman may be combined.

Pilot—a person assigned to a train when the engineman or conductor, or both, are not fully acquainted with the physical characteristics or running rules of the road, or portion of the road, over which the train is to be moved.

Towerman or Leverman—one who operates turnouts and signal indications from a tower. Other duties being incidental.

Train Crew—the operating personnel of a train; engineer, fireman, brakeman, and conductor.

Yard Master—the man in charge of a yard.

Scale Mile—a mile scaled down in the same proportion as the model to the prototype. In HO scale, 1 mile is approximately 61 feet.

Scale Time—the time registered by a fast clock.

SMILE—a proportioned-down mile from a scale mile in the same ratio as the fast clock to an actual clock. In HO using a 12 to 1 clock, this would be approximately 5 actual feet. Used in making up timetables.

Timetable Operation—the operation of trains according to a timetable. Usually a fast clock is used.

Train Order Operation

Verbal—the movement of cars and making up of trains according to oral instructions.

Written—the movement of cars and making up of trains to individually written instructions.

SCENERY

Abutment—the concrete, masonry, or (rarely) timber walls that support the ends of a bridge, trestle, or tunnel portal.

Backdrop—a photo, painting, or relief model painting on a wall or partition continuing the background scene to or above the horizon line.

Background—the area between the foreground and the backdrop.

Cardboard Strip–Paper–Texture-paint Scenery Method—a method of constructing scenery by spreading texture paint over a subbase made of cardboard strips covered with paper strips soaked in texture paint.

Color Terms

Chroma—the relative brilliance or saturation of a color. Example: when red is diluted with white the chroma or saturation is weakened, forming pink. Intense colors have high chroma while grays have low chroma.

Hue—the shade of a color. Refers to the mixture of the primary colors to make different colors. Example: red plus yellow makes orange.

Value—the darkness or lightness of a color in relation to a gray scale. Example: as color appears dark or light in a black and white photograph. A high value is a light color.

Cut—the removal of the uphill side of a hill to provide a right-of-way, where a trench is dug in a hill to allow a track or road to pass through, or the trench at the approach to a tunnel.

Detail—that part of the scenic effect not actually contained in the final plaster coat. Example: trees, fences, grass, shrubs, etc.

Diorama—a system of reducing the scale in the background near the backdrop to create the illusion of distance. It should only be used beyond the furthest visible track.

Fill—earthwork dumped to build up low areas above the surrounding ground level. Usually used in the approaches to bridges and culverts.

Flats—buildings or landscape built in bas-relief, or a painted cutout usually mounted between the background and the backdrop.

Foreground—the scenery in front of and directly surrounding the principal trackage.

Landscape—the general effect of terrain, vegetation, structure, and background.

Lift Out—a section of portable scenery which either lifts out, slides into place, or swings into position on hinges. Usually constructed separately from the basic permanent scenery, but blends in with the surrounding landscape. Used to fill in access holes when not in use and scenic spots on a model railroad which are too cramped to permit the use of tools. Also called a Hatch.

Painting the Scenery—the art of coloring the final scenic plaster base by brushing or spraying full strength coats of either water-base or oil-base paints of various colors.

Paper Laminate—layers of paper and glue used to build scenery base.

Papier-mâché—soaked paper material such as newspapers whch is worked into a pulpy mass and applied to the scenic subbase in the same manner as plaster and texture paint. Often an adhesive is added to provide strength.

Pier, Bridge—a support between spans of a bridge.

Plaster—the various materials normally used in covering the scenery base and providing the effect of terrain in the model scene. These materials can include casting plaster, building plaster, or concrete. Note: Plaster of Paris which is extremely fast setting is usually not used in model work because of its short working life.

Pop-up—an access opening, usually not visible from normal viewing points.

Right-of-Way—the area including and adjoining the track. It includes the grounds around stations, bridges, signals, and other railroad-owned structures.

Scenery Base—screen wire, chicken wire, or cardboard strips covered with paper, burlap, sacking, or any other material on which the terrain is placed.

Scenery Support—the bracing material, usually wood, which holds the scenery base in place.

Scenicking—the making of scenery including terrain, structures, and natural growth such as trees and shrubs.

Scenic Surface—see Terrain.

Staining the Scenery—the art of coloring the terrain by applying and blending several different colored thin transparent washes made of artist's oils and turpentine or water colors.

Structures—all buildings; also fixtures built along the railroad right-of-way including fences, telephone poles, and other man-made items.

Terrain—the part of the scenic work including soil, hills, streams, rocks, roads, trails, etc. Usually made of plaster or texture paint over the scenery base.

Terrain Detailing—the art of carving or molding rock work and outcroppings or other features of the terrain.

Texture Paint—a plasterlike powder which when mixed with water drys in several hours to a strong hard surface. Does not require as much thickness as does plaster nor does it set as quickly as plaster of Paris. Sold by most paint stores or lumber yards.

Vegetation—all scenery representing such growing things of nature as grass, shrubs, and trees.

SIGNALS

Absolute Signal—See Control section.

Approach Signal—a fixed signal used in connection with one or more signals to govern the approach thereto.

Aspect—the appearance of a signal from a point where the indication is visible. Also see Indication.

Automatic Block Signal—a block signal, the aspects of which are changed automatically by electric, pneumatic, or other means actuated by a train or certain conditions affecting the use of the block.

Block Signal—a fixed signal in which the indications are given by the color of a light only.

Color Position Light Signal—a fixed signal in which the indications are given by color and the position of two or more lights.

Communicating Signal—a signal between train and engine crews, usually audible and air-operated.

Distant Interlocking Signal—see Approach Signal.

Distant Signal—see Approach Signal.

Dwarf Signal—a small fixed signal.

Fixed Signal—a signal of fixed location indicating a condition affecting the movement of a train. The expression fixed signal covers such signals as slow boards, stop boards, car-limit signs, and turnout, train order, block, interlocking, semaphore, color light, color position light, position light, disc, ball, or other means for indicating "stop," "caution," or "proceed."

Flag Signal—see Manual Signal.

Hand Signal—see Manual Signal.

Home Signal—a fixed signal at the entrance of a route or block to govern trains or engines entering or using that route or block.

Indication—the information conveyed by the aspect of a visual signal.

Interlocking—an arrangement of signals and signal appliances (usually including operating power in model railroading) so interconnected that their movements must succeed each other in proper sequence and for which interlocking rules are in effect. Routing may be set up automatically or manually.

Interlocking Signal—one of the fixed signals of an interlocking.

Lamp Signal—see Manual Signal.

Manual Signal—a signal given manually. Applies to Flag, Hand, and Lamp signals.

Back—move object in circle.
Proceed—move object vertically.
Stop—move object sideways. Also any object moved violently by anyone on or near the track.

Permissive Signal—see Control section.

Position Light Signal—a fixed signal in which the indications are given by the position of two or more lights.

Semaphore Signal—a fixed signal in which the day indications are given by the position of a semaphore arm.

Signal—an indication of a condition affecting the movement of a train.

Signal Circuits—see Electrical section.

Signal, In Advance of—the territory beyond a signal as seen from an approaching train.

Signal, In the Rear of—the territory between an approaching train and a signal.

Signal Color—the aspect of a color light signal or the corresponding aspect of any other visual signal. When so used, green indicates proceed; yellow indicates proceed with caution; and red indicates stop. Other common uses are: blue indicates track pan, water pickup, or other uses prescribed by the rules; purple indicates stop (frequently used in dwarf signals and siding derails instead of red); lunar white indicates yard turnout (inside) or track pan.

Train Signals—flags or lanterns displayed at the front and rear of a train.

INDEX

H

I

L

M

N

O

P

R

S